Carrying out Investigations in Psychology: Methods and Statistics

Jeremy J. Foster and Ian Parker

BPS BOOKS

THE BRITISH PSYCHOLOGICAL SOCIETY

First published in 1995 by BPS Books (The British Psychological Society),
St Andrew's House, 48 Princess Road East, Leicester LE1 7DR, UK.

A catalogue record for this book is available from the British Library.

ISBN 1 85433 170 1

Printed and bound in Great Britain by
Biddles Ltd, Guildford and King's Lynn

Whilst every effort has been made to ensure the accuracy of the contents of this publication, the publishers and authors expressly disclaim responsibility in law for negligence or any other cause of action whatsoever.

Contents

Contents

Contents

Preface

Students of psychology spend a large proportion of their course time on practical psychology. This part of the curriculum involves learning about the methodological principles underlying empirical work, absorbing the skills of carrying it out, reporting it, and analysing the data it yields. In addition, there is acquiring the ability to select the most appropriate methods and techniques for investigating a particular issue.

All of these topics are dealt with in this book, but it is worth explaining why students are required to devote their time to these matters. Teachers of psychology have debated the value of studying the discipline, partly because of the need to convince funding authorities that it counts as a science (and therefore deserves more financial support than it would otherwise obtain), partly because of the need to justify the existence of a subject which is hugely popular (in terms of numbers of students recruited annually) but where the direct employment prospects are comparatively small.

In justifying the subject, one can distinguish between the *knowledge* and the *skills* that are acquired. In the psychological literature this is the distinction between declarative knowledge and procedural knowledge. Declarative knowledge is the more prominent, and is encapsulated in the numerous textbooks on the subject. But it can be argued that procedural knowledge is the more important – once you have the skills (including bibliographic skills) for finding out, you can use these to fill in any gaps in the existing corpus of knowledge. Suppose for example you were asked whether it is better to label different areas of a carpark by using letters, colours or symbols; if you could not find any research on this problem, and therefore a ready-made answer, you can find the answer for yourself so long as you have the skills needed to do the research.

Skills are learned by practice and feedback (a psychological truth known long before psychology), and comparatively little by simply watching skilled performers: how many people improve their golf or tennis by watching matches? So the justification for imposing a practical course on students is that it provides the opportunity to develop the skills which psychologists are expected to have, and these skills are acquired only by trying them out and receiving feedback on performance.

In psychology, the term 'methods' has two distinct meanings. One meaning refers to the overall design of an investigation, 'the basic plan or strategy of the research and the logic behind it (Oppenheim, 1992, p. 6). In this sense, which is how we use the term 'methods' in this book, it is usual to distinguish between experiments, correlational studies, surveys, observational studies, field studies, and case studies.

The other use of 'methods' distinguishes between interviews, questionnaires, attitude scales, performance tests and the other ways in which psychologists obtain indices of human behaviour and thought. We shall follow the precedent of referring to these as 'techniques'. It is confusing that some of the techniques are also the names of methods; you can use the technique of observation, recording the number of times people behave in a certain way, and use this technique within an experiment, a correlational study or any of the other methods.

As teachers of psychology, we appreciate the need for students to learn the range of methods and techniques that psychologists have used to further their discipline. The variety of methods and techniques is not always made clear in the texts for students, which tend to emphasize the classic laboratory experiment, paying less attention to the innovative methods which are often required when one is dealing with more real-life environments than that contained within the walls of a psychology department.

Over the last two decades, there has been an attempt to re-evaluate the methods used by psychologists. This movement has been a response to dissatisfaction with the achievements of psychology, and two approaches can be distinguished. One continues to accept the use of the traditional methods within the discipline. Being disappointed in the limited value of what these have revealed, it emphasizes the need to ensure that they are used in a way that makes the results relevant to life outside the laboratory, known as 'ecological validity'.

The second approach adopts a more radical position: it argues that the shortcomings of the traditional methods will not be overcome by trying to build in ecological validity, and that psychology needs to adopt different, qualitative methods. It is much less concerned with measurement and the use of statistics than the traditional approach, and its supporters argue that intensive analysis and single case studies might actually be more like natural science than traditional laboratory experimentalists believed. The more radical proponents argue that the attempt to model psychology on any version of the natural sciences was a fundamental error.

The two approaches differ in the research methods they prefer, the techniques most commonly used, and the way the data are treated once they have been obtained. The argument about their relative value has been developing over the last 10 years, largely prompted by disillusion among a group of social psychologists. Although traditional, academic psychology initially ignored the calls for reform coming from the radicals, the appearance of articles by them in the *British Journal of Psychology* (Henwood and Pidgeon, 1992) demonstrates that the radicals' arguments are gaining the attention of mainstream psychologists.

The distinction between the quantitative and qualitative approaches has a longer history than may be realized by the contemporary student. It can be seen in the contrast between early-century behaviourism and humanistic psychology (Wann, 1964), in the distinction between idiographic and nomothetic studies of personality (Allport, 1962), and even in the way that psychoanalysis has been assigned to the outer fringe by academic psychology.

We represent these two alternative strands. Jeremy Foster has had over 20 years' experience teaching students the traditional methods of psychology, particularly the value of the experimental method, and remains hopeful that the 'scientific' method is the way that psychology will make progress. Ian Parker is one of the main UK proponents of the 'new', qualitative approaches to the discipline, and believes that psychology needs a radical re-orientation if it is to make any progress to achieving its more benign aims or if its more dubious aims are to be challenged. In this book we do not try to hide this difference in our stances, nor do we try to offer some type of compromise position which embraces them both. Indeed, we doubt that such a position is achievable. What we have tried to do is provide a guide which will help the student appreciate the range of methods open to psychologists and their advantages and drawbacks, decide which are appropriate for any particular topic they wish to study, provide useful advice on how to apply them, and report their outcome.

Copyright acknowledgements

We would like to thank the Biometrika Trustees, the Institute of Mathematical Statistics and the American Statistical Association for permission to reproduce the Wilcoxon Statistical Test, Page's L Test and the Mann–Whitney Statistical Test.

Chapter 1

Introduction to quantitative and qualitative approaches to psychology

1.0 The nature of scientific enquiry

Psychology claims to be a science, the science of mind and behaviour. But what is 'science'? Why are some subjects, such as physics and chemistry, classed as sciences but others not? Can there be a science of history? Is archaeology a science? Psychology's claim has been based on the fact that Anglo-American psychology has tried to use the 'scientific method', interpreting this phrase in a very narrow sense as meaning the experimental method. But European psychology has typically used a range of methods, some of which might not be called 'scientific': Gestalt psychology and humanistic psychology, for example, were important Continental movements not wedded to the empiricist methods which dominated British and American psychology between 1920 and 1950. Just what 'scientific method' means is controversial, and some areas of psychology, such as parapsychology, are often denied the status of 'science' (see Box 1.2). First we shall summarize the traditional view of science, then consider some of the problems it generates.

1.1 The traditional view

According to the traditional view, science has a number of attributes.

1.1.1 Empiricism

Scientific study involves 'any activity that systematically attempts to gather evidence through observation and procedures that can be repeated and verified by others... It is this demand for publicly observable evidence that hallmarks the objective nature of the empirical approach' (Neale and Liebert, 1986, p. 7). Empiricism means gathering evidence by observing the phenomenon under study.

1.1.2 Measurement

Measurement of a phenomenon is one of the indices of the traditional scientific approach. Once an effect can be measured, you can measure changes in its

1

SAQ 1.1

Here are six definitions. Which ones are operational definitions?

1 Short-term memory: a storage system with a duration of about 12 seconds and a capacity of 7 ± 2 items.
2 Achieving orientation: organized study methods and competitiveness.
3 Achieving orientation: the total score on items 4, 7, 9 and 14 of the ASS scale.
4 Conservatism: a constellation of attitudes including pro-religiosity, pro-control/punitiveness and anti-liberality.
5 Conservatism: the respondent's score on the Wilson and Patterson questionnaire.
6 Conservatism: the respondent's score on the F Scale.

---

magnitude and try to relate these to changes in the various factors influencing it. This then leads (it is assumed) to increased understanding of the phenomenon and the possibility of controlling its magnitude. The emphasis on measurement leads to the use of statistics, which many students are surprised to find is a large component of a course in psychology.

1.1.3 Operational definitions

In psychology many of the constructs, such as memory, personality, and motive, cannot be observed directly: only their effects can be seen. You can measure only how much people seem to have remembered, and you have to use this as an indication of their memory. An operational definition means that you specify the empirical observations you will use to measure some entity such as memory. Test your understanding of this with SAQ 1.1.

1.1.4 Falsifiability

A major aspect of the scientific approach adopted by psychology is Popper's (1972) doctrine of falsifiability. In simple terms, this asserts that a scientific statement is one that is open to disproof. Statements such as 'There is a God', 'Eating people is wrong', 'Warhol was a great artist' are not open to disproof, and according to Popper's account these are not scientific statements. But a statement such as 'people have more accidents after drinking alcohol' can be tested against the data to see whether it is false.

Some of the most heated arguments in psychology have concerned the issue of whether or not particular statements or theories are scientific, in this sense of being disprovable. For example, Eysenck and Wilson (1973) argued that Freud's concept of reaction formation, in which a mental process may be expressed in a form diametrically opposed to its underlying reality, meant his theory of the motivation underlying behaviour became incapable of disproof and therefore not a scientific statement. The argument has gained new vigour because of the debate over whether the qualitative approach to psychology is scientific in this sense of yielding disprovable statements.

1.1.5 Replicability

A further feature of the scientific approach is the emphasis on the ability to repeat investigations so that their outcome can be confirmed. If an effect cannot be replicated, it is not accepted as a scientific phenomenon that needs serious attention. The inability to repeat experiments claiming to demonstrate telepathy, for example, is one of the reasons why many psychologists do not accept that it is a phenomenon worth investigating.

1.1.6 Impartiality

Traditional science claims to be impartial in two senses. First, investigators test their theories and predictions by comparing them with the data generated by investigations, and revising them if the data do not correspond to the predictions. Second, the data are gathered impartially: you do not, for example, select only the data that fit your prediction. This claim of impartiality has been challenged. Reason and Rowan (1981a), among others, have argued that it is illusory. On the one hand, scientists do not rely exclusively on the data to decide whether a theory needs revision (Kuhn, 1970), and, on the other, the way data are collected and interpreted is influenced by the investigators' expectations and interests (Latour and Woolgar, 1979). We shall return to these arguments later.

The traditional view of science in psychology is that it is a cycle of observation and theorizing, as illustrated in Fig 1.1. Scientists begin with observations, which may be previous researchers' findings. At first there may be a number of different and apparently contradictory phenomena, but eventually these are collated and organized into a summary statement, such as 'People are better at remembering pictures than they are at remembering words'.

The scientist then tries to devise a theory which will explain why the phenomenon occurs. For example, you might explain people's superior ability to remember pictures by arguing that when they try to remember a picture they store it in their memory in two ways, as a visual image and as a verbal description, whereas they store a word in only one way, as a record of how it sounds. So if asked to remember a certain picture you might store both an image of a particular male face with moustache and flamboyant clothes, and also store a verbal label: 'The Laughing Cavalier'.

From the theory, the scientist deduces specific hypotheses, predictions about what will happen if a particular new set of events is made to occur. For example, the theory about superior memory for pictures might suggest that pictures which readily suggest a label will be remembered better than those which do not. These predictions are then tested: the researcher investigates to see whether they are

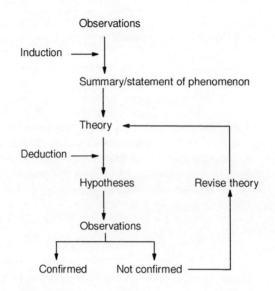

Fɪɢ. 1.1. *The idealized model of science*

supported when the situation is brought about. In this example, you might perform a study of memory for pictures and words, using some pictures that have familiar labels and others that do not. Your prediction might be that people will remember the first type of pictures better than the others.

If the prediction is fulfilled, then, according to this view of how science operates, this supports (but does *not* prove) the theory. If the hypothesis was not supported, this is taken as disproving the theory, and the theory is then modified or abandoned, and the cycle repeated.

This model of impartial reliance on the outcome of empirical studies is just that: an idealized model. Real-life scientists exhibit more human failings than the model acknowledges. In many ways, scientific debate can be seen as a contest, with the original researcher proposing a theory and stating it publicly, inviting other people to accept it, test it, attack it.

Researchers have a personal involvement in the success of their theories, and are unwilling to discard them as soon as a study failing to support them is reported. So when a study attacking the original proposal appears, they are likely to try to defend their theory by counter-attacking, criticizing the nature of the attack upon it.

The counter-attack usually tries to demonstrate that the opposing work was inadequate in some way. Counter-attacks may make one or both of the following points. (1) The attacker misunderstood the original theory, and deduced an inappropriate hypothesis to be tested. Therefore the attacking study is in fact irrelevant to evaluating the original theory. (2) The attack does test an appropriate deduction from the original theory, but the hypothesis was not tested properly, so

Box 1.1 Example of attack and counter-attack in scientific debate

A recent example showing how scientific debate can be seen as attack and counter-attack is provided by Annett's work on handedness (why people are left-handed or right-handed), the attack on it by McManus *et al.* (1993) and Annett's (1993) counter-attack.

Annett was interested in why some people are left- or right-handed, and whether being left- or right-handed produces other differences. The details need not concern you, but she argued that handedness is the result of a special type of genetic process and that people who are strongly right-handed perform less well on some types of task. She carried out a number of studies in which people were divided into groups according to how strongly they were left- or right-handed, and their ability at various tasks was assessed.

McManus *et al.* criticize Annett's theory and the research underlying it on a number of grounds. They claim that the theory was wrong from the outset, because 'We believe that Annett has misunderstood some of the fundamental principles of population genetics' (p. 518). They criticize the way Annett's research was conducted, arguing that the way groups were formed was flawed: 'The selection criteria for Annett's groups do not constitute clearly distinct groups in terms of phenotype' (p. 520). Also, they claim the analysis of the scores was faulty: 'The method of data analysis of Annett cannot therefore fully demonstrate heterozygote advantage' (p. 524). They challenge the stability of the results used to support Annett's theory: 'The second purpose of this report is therefore to examine the replicability of Annett's findings' (p. 518); after reporting their own investigation, they conclude: 'This study has found no empirical evidence to support Annett's contention' (p. 529). So McManus *et al.* are saying that the theory is wrong, as it is based on a misunderstanding, and that the research allegedly supporting it is flawed.

Annett (1993) counter-attacks, defending her theory and research against these criticisms. She says that McManus *et al.* (MSB) are in their turn wrong when stating her theory: 'MSB say that .... This is quite untrue and suggests a misunderstanding of the development of RS [i.e. Annett's] theory' (p. 539). Her theory does not include the misunderstanding which McManus *et al.* alleged: '... the idea ... does not rest on a misconception about gene and genotype proportions' (p. 540).

Annett criticizes McManus *et al.*'s research as flawed. She states that 'MSB's proposal to test the RS model using three subgroups of 24 subjects ... is extraordinary' (p. 542). Annett claims their research is faulty because (1) it used small groups of very able people so that any effect would probably not be detected, (2) the groups were selected on the basis of a separate, inappropriate test, and (3) 'left-handers ... were omitted' (p. 543).

SAQ 1.2
From the summary given in Box 1.1, can you identify the main lines of Annett's counter-attack to McManus *et al.*'s criticism of her work?

---

the results can be discounted. The reasons why the hypothesis was not tested properly can include using inappropriate types of participants, having flaws in the procedure, applying the wrong type of statistical analyses, misunderstanding the results. Box 1.1 summarizes an example of attack and counter-attack. Read Box 1.1, and then try to answer the question posed in SAQ 1.2.

1.2 The logic of the experiment

The characteristics of the scientific approach outlined above do not mean that only one type of investigation is scientific. But since the experiment has been the preferred form of scientific study in psychology for those adopting this traditional view, it is worth summarizing the logic underlying it.

The basic idea underlying the experimental method is simple. You bring about a change in some aspect of the situation, the independent variable, and observe its effects on the person's behaviour, the dependent variable. If everything else has been kept constant, you can argue that any alterations in the dependent variable were caused by the change in the independent variable. Box 3.1 in Chapter 3 is an example of this form of argument.

Suppose you are considering some aspect of human behaviour, such as people's ability to remember a set of items. You can measure performance in a number of ways, the most obvious one being to present people with the items to remember, then ask them to recall the items and count how many they report. The measure of performance is the dependent variable. You want to know how performance on the dependent variable is affected when there is a change in some feature of the situation, such as giving people practice in the special technique intended to improve their ability to remember. The feature that you change (technique for remembering, in this example) forms the independent variable. In an experiment, you bring about a change in the independent variable and measure the dependent variable, with the aim of seeing how changing the independent variable influences performance on the dependent variable.

So the aim is to understand the relationships between *variables* and more particularly to understand the causes of changes in dependent variables. The logic of the experimental method was considered by John Stuart Mill in his *System of Logic*, which was published in the middle of the nineteenth century. Mill distinguished a number of methods, the main one being the joint method of agreement and difference. Essentially this says that one variable (A) causes another (B) if it can be shown (1) that whenever A occurs, B follows, and (2) whenever A does not occur, neither does B. Another of Mill's methods, the method of concomitant variation, asserts that two variables are connected by some link of causation if they vary together, if one increases or decreases as the other does. This is the basis for the correlational method of investigation.

Mill's methods have been the subject of considerable debate, and do not actually establish that one variable causes another. But they do allow you to eliminate variables that are *not* involved in causing the phenomenon. If you find that varying the retention interval never has any effect on how much people remember, you could conclude that it is not causing changes in memory performance.

This traditional use of the laboratory experiment is seen by many psychologists as the most powerful weapon in their armoury. Traditional American social psychologists' faith in experiments is shown in this quotation: 'In our judgment, the controlled experiment *still* remains the single most powerful tool for enabling investigators to disentangle just what causes what, and is the standard against which other research methods continue to be measured' (Aronson *et al.*, 1990, p. xvii, original italics). Similarly, the British psychologists Teasdale and Barnard (1993, p. 99) write: 'The power of experimental paradigms...is that they provide a wealth of detailed information against which to test and develop the adequacy of theoretical models'.

One aspect of testing a model involves the concept of disproof. But it is important to appreciate that failing to disprove something does not mean that it is proved. This is worth emphasizing.

1.3 Disproving and not proving

The doctrine of falsifiability states that a scientific statement can be disproved. Suppose we make some prediction, such as 'Increasing the retention interval leads to poorer performance on the memory test', and carry out a study to obtain relevant data. If the data fail to meet the prediction, we may conclude that the theory which yielded the prediction has been disproved. But if the data do come out as predicted, it is *not* proper to conclude that the theory has been proved.

Many students are initially confused by this: they argue that if failure to meet the prediction is disproof, then surely confirming the prediction is proof. This is a fallacy. An example may help to make this clear. Suppose I propose a theory that people come to like things they experience regularly. From this theory, I deduce the hypothesis that people unfamiliar with computers will come to have a positive attitude to computers after they have used them regularly. I test this by having two groups of people: one has a computer course every week for a year and the other does not. At the end of the year, I measure how much they like computers. You will probably agree that if the computer users do not like computers at the end of the year, my theory was wrong. But if they do end up liking computers, this does not prove that the theory was correct: the positive attitude to computers could have been caused by something else, such as the friendly behaviour of the person who taught the computer course. The theory that people like what they are exposed to could be wrong, even if the prediction were fulfilled; it is not hard to think of things such as accounts of cruelty or torture which people will probably not come to like even if they are exposed to them often.

So when you find the prediction or hypothesis is confirmed, this does not prove the theory is true. It does 'fail to disprove' the theory, but this is not the same as proving it!

1.4 Criticisms of the traditional view

Although psychological research has traditionally relied on the experiment as the preferred method of investigation, there are many topics that cannot be studied using experiments because it is ethically unacceptable or practically impossible. For example, it is sometimes claimed that children who are abused are more likely to become child abusers themselves when they are parents. It would be unacceptable to run an experiment in which some children and not others were abused, just to see how they reacted later in life. (Since there are so many other factors influencing people's behaviour between the time when they are children and the time they become parents, such an experiment could not be conclusive anyway.)

It can be argued that the use of the experimental method is not what defines a science: for centuries, astronomers did not perform experiments and yet astronomy was thought of as a science. Conversely, parapsychology does use experiments but many psychologists do not consider it a science. Some of the issues underlying parapsychology are explained in Box 1.2.

Even in those parts of psychology where the experiment has been the dominant method of investigation, critics have argued that it has not produced the results that had been hoped for. Commentators such as Joynson (1973), Neisser (1976), Claxton (1980) expressed doubts about the progress made by psychology using experimental methods.

There were two main reactions to these views. One was to accept the need to retain the use of the experimental method but to emphasize the need to ensure experiments had ecological validity: abstruse laboratory studies on memory should be replaced by investigations that looked at memory of ordinary people in ordinary situations (Cohen, 1989; Middleton and Edwards, 1992). The other, more radical reaction was to argue that since the experimental method had made so little progress, and distorted the very processes with which psychology should be concerned, it should be abandoned and other methods, qualitative methods, used instead.

1.5 Qualitative approaches

Critics of the traditional, quantitative approach, such as the contributors to Reason and Rowan (1981b), believe that in the attempt to measure phenomena it

Box 1.2 Is parapsychology a science?

Parapsychology covers the study of paranormal experiences, such as 'mind reading' (telepathy), psychokinesis (the ability to move objects by non-physical means), clairvoyance, precognition, hauntings, and poltergeists. Many people (probably the majority of people alive) believe in at least some of these phenomena, but parapsychology is seen by most psychologists as very unrespectable.

The academic study of parapsychology has been active for over a century, but the attempt to put it on a properly 'scientific' basis dates from the 1930s and the work of J. B. Rhine in America. This attempt involved using the experimental method: Rhine conducted numerous experiments in which he tried to demonstrate that people could communicate telepathically. The basic idea was that one person (the sender) looked at each of a set of cards as they were turned over, and another person (the receiver) tried to 'read the mind' of the sender and wrote down the order in which the cards had been turned over. The receiver's score could be measured and compared with what would be expected if they had merely guessed. If the receiver performed better than would be expected by guesswork and there had been no physical communication between sender and receiver, this was taken as evidence of telepathy.

Why, if the experimental method was used, is the whole field still seen by most academic psychologists as unscientific? Surveys of parapsychological research tend to fall into two clearly identifiable camps. There are those by believers (e.g. Beloff, 1993) and those by nonbelievers (e.g. Hansel, 1966), and it does seem to us as though the arguments are closer to religious controversy than to impartial scientific argument. The nonbelievers typically argue that parapsychological phenomena must be illusory because they conflict with the laws of science, because many examples have been shown to be based on fraud, and because successful results are nonreplicable: they occur only with star performing participants, the 'stars' seem to lose their ability with repeated testing, and the phenomena cannot be demonstrated on demand.

You might expect that the question 'Is parapsychology a science?' could be answered with a simple 'yes' or 'no'. But this is not the case: proponents claim it is a science, opponents deny it that status. This demonstrates that defining 'science' (and the scientific method) is not straightforward: the controversy over what is science has been a notable feature of psychology over the last 20 years, and has led to the debates about the value of the qualitative methods which are described in this book. The whole issue has been lively: as Eysenck and Keane (1990, p. 3) noted: 'Nearly all the fundamental tenets of the traditional view of science have been savaged by 20th-century philosophers of science'.

Box 1.3 Attack, counter-attack and rhetoric in science

Attack and counter-attack in science is often more than a simple matter of logical, reasoned debate. Some of the most dramatic changes in scientific thinking have been brought about by persuasion and trickery. Mendel fiddled his results on the inheritance of characteristics in the sweet pea, for example, but we now have much evidence to show that his hunch was right, and his experiments are still valuable. There are occasional transformations in scientific thinking that change our whole world view. The famous case of Galileo is described by the historian of science Thomas Kuhn (1970), who sees science as moving through phases of 'normal science', 'crises' and 'revolutions' and then to 'new paradigms'. Galileo changed our way of seeing when a 'crisis' in the science of astronomy was brought about by the increase in inexplicable observations. The observations did not fit with normal science in the 'old paradigm' that held that the Sun rotated around the Earth. The crisis was resolved when a new paradigm emerged which held that the Earth rotated around the Sun, and so a new period of normal science was inaugurated.

Galileo did not have an easy job persuading people, especially in the Vatican, that the Earth moved. Feyerabend (1975) points out that Galileo had to convince sceptics that what you could see through telescopes was worth taking account of. Some of the new observations did not fit accepted theory, and these anomalies had to be explained away. Galileo also wrote in the more popular Italian rather than conventional scientific Latin to win over people outside astronomy. Feyerabend (1975, p. 154) concludes from this that reasonable argument is not sufficient to bring about scientific change: 'It will have to be brought about by irrational means such as propaganda, emotion, ad hoc hypotheses, and appeals to prejudice of all kinds.'

There is a lot of irrationality in debates over method in psychology. Even when historians of science are brought into the argument, the arguments do not become impartially 'scientific'. Kuhn's ideas, for example, were used in the early 1970s to attack quantitative psychology, and the attack was, again, clever rhetoric. Harré and Secord (1972) argued that a scientific crisis had beset social psychology and that we needed a revolution in our ways of thinking about people, moving away from the laboratory experiment to a qualitative 'new paradigm'. This was a good way of persuading psychologists that they could be good scientists and leave 'old' psychology behind. Harré and Secord (1972) did not point out, because it would have damaged their argument, that Kuhn's work was on the natural sciences, not social sciences. People who now follow in the wake of Harré and Secord's 'paradigm revolution', such as those who gather accounts and do discourse analysis, see psychology as a social, or human science, and argue that the discipline should be a science of rhetoric rather than behaviour (e.g. Billig, 1987).

misrepresents and distorts the phenomena it is studying. In addition, the quantitative approach is seen as irrelevant to many areas of the discipline, such as counselling or clinical work, where one is trying to understand why an individual acts in particular ways. Consequently, psychology needs to adopt a new methodology which avoids these mistakes, and this new methodology is qualitative, not quantitative. Some of these writers would argue that attack and counter-attack in science is a matter of rhetorical skill, not reasoning based on the observation of facts (Box 1.3).

The movement proclaiming this view was largely based in those areas of the discipline where the experimental method seemed particularly inappropriate (such as personality, counselling and clinical psychology), or where it seemed to have been misused by applying morally questionable practices (e.g. social psychology). The qualitative movement questioned the very basis of the conventional scientific approach. For example, there had always been a concern with the ecological validity of psychological research: were the findings true outside the laboratory? But the radical critics from the qualitative school rejected the idea that one could hope to establish 'truth'. For example, Reason (1981, p. 242–3) argued that psychologists should: 'move away from the idea that there is *one* truth, that there is some simple continuum between 'error' and 'truth'... we need to consider not only "is it right?", but also "is it useful?"'. The concept of validity, according to this view, has to be redefined: 'validity in new paradigm research lies in the skills and sensitivities of the researcher... Validity is more personal and interpersonal, rather than methodological...' (p. 244). So, the new-paradigm, qualitative researchers have fundamental disagreements with the traditionalists about what science is, and what psychologists should be doing.

1.6 Conclusion

There are distinct contrasts between the quantitative and qualitative approaches to psychology. The traditional view's emphasis on objectivity, impartiality and replicability is redefined by qualitative researchers, who argue that the value of research depends on its acceptability and meaningfulness to those who have acted as participants. Taking a traditional line, one might reject the qualitative methods because they are not scientific in the sense of accepting the fundamental assumptions of what science is, and allow prejudice and personal opinion to masquerade as knowledge. Alternatively, one might believe that the rigid pro-science doctrines derived from the behaviourist movement are inappropriate for gaining understanding of the significant features of people's minds and behaviour. These are extreme views, rejecting one approach entirely. It is becoming more common for investigators to acknowledge that both approaches have their strengths and weaknesses, that for many topics most progress can be made by using both the traditional and the new methods. For example, Entwistle and his colleagues have investigated the ways in which students learn; initially this research used quantitative methods (e.g. Entwistle *et al.*, 1971) but more recently a qualitative approach has been adopted (Entwistle and Marton, 1994).

Which approach you adopt is for you to decide; it is impossible to say that one is 'right' or 'acceptable' and the other is not. One should use whichever methods are appropriate to advance the study of the subject one is examining. You are likely to find that the different approaches complement each other, that both can be valuable. Qualitative methods may apply to topics where the quantitative ones seem to have little relevance, or you might use the different approaches at different stages of an investigation. The work on student learning mentioned in the previous paragraph has moved from quantitative to qualitative methods. In other cases, you might use qualitative methods to give you an initial experience of the topic and suggest hypotheses which you then investigate with quantitative procedures. You should try to be open to the promise and the limitations of all the alternatives.

Ethical issues

Before starting to carry out a study, at the very beginning of the planning stage, every investigator needs to consider the ethical implications of what is being planned. Ethical issues have gained increasing prominence in recent years, partly because some of the classic lines of investigation raise serious questions to which the investigators may not have paid sufficient attention. One topic concerns the use of animals in psychological research, especially where physical damage or surgery are involved. Another involves the evaluation of clinical or educational innovations where a full experimental comparison will involve a treatment being given to some and withheld from others, who may then suffer harm. A third is subjecting people to experimental conditions which may cause psychological or physical damage, as in Milgram's experiments on conformity in which people were instructed to inflict pain on other people (Milgram, 1963, 1974).

You may be tempted to believe that ethical principles are of little relevance to students. Such a view is quite wrong. It is necessary to instil an appreciation of the ethics of research from the beginning of a student's training, so that it becomes as normal a part of planning research as deciding on the research design or the nature of the statistical analysis to apply. Students are frequently so enthusiastic about their research ideas that they are blind to the ethical implications: and this is of course true of researchers long past their undergraduate days!

The issue of ethics in psychological research has prompted The British Psychological Society (BPS) to produce a statement on 'Ethical Principles for Conducting Research with Human Participants'. The most recent version appeared in *The Psychologist* for January 1993. We summarize it here, but all researchers should make themselves familiar with the original. There are no national or international mechanisms to enforce the principles, but most teaching institutions and research bodies have an ethics committee to monitor the way research is conducted. When no such committee is available, there is an even stronger responsibility on research workers to ensure their work is in accordance with the principles. Before gathering any data, you should go through the ethics checklist at the end of this chapter.

The BPS statement begins by stating that investigators must consider the ethical implications and psychological consequences for the participants in a piece of research. The investigation should be seen from their standpoint, and foreseeable threats to psychological wellbeing, health, values or dignity should be eliminated.

Box 2.1 An example of a 'declaration of informed consent' form (based on Sternberg, 1993, p. 42)

I give my informed consent to participate in this study of .... I consent to publication of study results so long as the information is anonymous and disguised so that no identification can be made. I further understand that although a record will be kept of my having participated in the study, all data collected from my participation will be identified by number only.

1 I have been informed that my participation in this study will involve me in ....

2 I have been informed that the general aim of the study is to ....

3 I have been informed that there are no known expected discomforts or risks involved in my participation in this study, and have been asked about any medical conditions which might create a risk for me when I participate.

4 I have been informed that there are no 'disguised' procedures in this study.

5 I have been informed that the investigator will explain after the study sessions the precise aims, and will answer any questions regarding the procedures of this study.

6 I have been informed that I am free to withdraw from the study at any time without penalty of any kind.

Concerns about any aspect of the study may be referred to ....

Signed:

.... Investigator

.... Participant

.... Date

Where the participants are of a different cultural or social background, age, or sex from the investigator, the best judge of whether a study may cause offence is a member of the participant population.

Investigators have a primary responsibility to protect participants from physical and mental harm during the investigation: the risk of harm should be no greater than in ordinary life. Participants must be asked about any pre-existing factors that might create a risk (such as medical conditions) and must be informed of how they can contact the investigator after the research in case of stress or harm.

Protecting participants also encompasses invasion of privacy: if the research involves behaviour participants may regard as personal or private, they must be protected from stress. Observational studies must respect the privacy and wellbeing of the individuals studied. If those observed have not been asked for their consent, observational research is only acceptable where those observed would expect to be observed by strangers. In all studies, information obtained about a participant is confidential unless agreed otherwise in advance.

All participants should be informed of any objectives of the study that might reasonably be expected to influence their willingness to participate. It is now generally recognized that participants should give informed consent before they take part in a study. This should involve a formal stage in which, after they have been informed of the nature of the research, they are invited to sign a consent form. An example of such a form, based on Sternberg (1993, p. 42), is shown in Box 2.1. Details appropriate to the particular study would have to be added to the form.

Research with children requires their consent and that of their parents. If real consent cannot be obtained from people with an impairment, the investigator should obtain approval from someone well placed to appreciate the participant's reaction, such as a member of the family and from independent advisors. Investigators must ensure participants are aware of their right to withdraw from the study even after the data have been collected.

Withholding information or misleading participants is unacceptable if they are likely to object or show unease once debriefed. Intentional deception should be avoided whenever possible, and done only with the approval of independent advisors. When deception is necessary, participants must be given sufficient information as early as possible.

Debriefing, explaining what the study was really about, is essential. When the data have been collected, it is the investigator's duty to inform the participants so they understand the nature of the research. Verbal debriefing may not be sufficient: investigators must ensure participants receive debriefing in the form of active intervention before they leave the research setting. In addition, they should discuss with participants their experience in order to monitor unforeseen negative effects. (Although obtaining subjective reports is an aspect of quantitative research which seems to have become less common, the participants' comments on the research can frequently help to illuminate what happened.)

All psychologists have the responsibility to see that the ethical principles are being observed both in their own work and in that of fellow investigators.

Ethics checklist

Before gathering any data, you should go through this set of questions. If any of the answers raise ethical issues, we have suggested the steps you should take.

1   Are the participants likely to suffer any threats to their wellbeing, health, values or dignity?
If the answer is 'yes', you need to consider altering the procedure.
If the answer is 'no', go to question 2(a).

2(a)   Are the participants from a different cultural or social background, or of different age or sex from the investigators?
If the answer is 'yes', go to question 2(b).
If the answer is 'no', go to question 3.

2(b) Have members of these groups been asked whether the procedure is likely to threaten participants' wellbeing?

If the answer is 'yes', go to question 3.

If the answer is 'no', you should ask members of the participants' group about possible threats; only if no objections are raised should you proceed.

3   Have potential participants been informed of the aim of the study?

If the answer is 'yes', go to question 4.

If the answer is 'no', you should add to your procedure a stage where participants are told about the aim of the investigation. If you believe this would undermine the study, you should seek approval from your ethics committee before starting the study.

4   Are any of the participants unable to give informed consent for themselves?
    (For example, they may be too young, unable to understand, or mentally ill.)

If the answer is 'no', go to question 5.

If the answer is 'yes', you must write out the steps you have taken to obtain agreement from any participants unable to give informed consent for themselves. These should be considered by your ethics committee before starting the study.

5   Does the study involve withholding information about the experiences the participants will have?

If the answer is 'no', go to question 6.

If the answer is 'yes', you should add to your procedure a stage where participants are told about the procedure of the investigation. If you believe this would undermine the study, you should seek approval from your ethics committee before starting the study.

6(a) Does the study involve giving misleading information about the experiences the participants will have?

If the answer is 'no', go to question 7.

If the answer is 'yes', go to question 6(b).

6(b) Has the approval of independent advisors been obtained?

If the answer is 'yes', go to question 7.

If the answer is 'no', you must obtain approval from independent advisors before starting the study.

7   Are the debriefing arrangements full and properly timed?

If the answer is 'yes', go to question 8.

If the answer is 'no', you should add at an appropriate point in your procedure a debriefing stage where participants are told about the aim, design and procedure of the investigation, and where they can contact one of the research team later should that be necessary. If you believe this would undermine the study, you should seek approval from your ethics committee before starting the study.

8   Have participants been informed of their right to withdraw from the study at any time, including after the data have been collected?
If the answer is 'yes', go to question 9.
If the answer is 'no', you must ensure this information is given to all participants before any data are collected.

9   Have anonymity and confidentiality arrangements been made?
If the answer is 'yes', go to question 10.
If the answer is 'no', you must warn participants before any data are collected that the results will not be confidential.

10 Have participants been asked about medical conditions or any other features that might create a risk for them when they undergo the study?
If the answer is 'yes', go to question 11.
If the answer is 'no', you must add to your procedure, before any data are collected, a stage where participants are asked about such conditions. Any participants who report medical conditions or other features that increase the risk to them when they undergo the experiences of the study should be invited to withdraw and should not be used.

11 Does the procedure include assuring participants that personal questions need not be answered?
If the answer is 'yes', go to question 12.
If the answer is 'no', you must revise the procedure so that the briefing of participants includes such an assurance.

12 Does the study involve any invasion of privacy?
If the answer is 'yes', you should revise the procedure so there is no invasion of privacy. If you believe this would undermine the study, you should seek guidance and approval from your ethics committee before starting the study.

Quantitative approaches:
the experiment

3.0 Introduction

Psychologists use a range of different methods, and this book introduces most of them. Any method can yield both quantitative and qualitative data, so you should not think of quantitative and qualitative methods, but of quantitative and qualitative approaches which share the same methods but use them with rather different aims. The most striking difference between the approaches is in the data that are obtained and how they are dealt with, rather than the methods used to obtain them.

The methods often differ in the amount of control that the investigator exerts over the situation. The extent to which the participants' behaviour is an accurate indication of how they behave when they are not being observed, referred to as 'ecological validity', cannot be guaranteed with either quantitative or qualitative approaches. Quantitative approaches do try to control ecological validity, however, through careful planning, observation and measurement.

It is usual to begin an exposition of research methods in psychology with the experimental method, as it has been the most widely used. We shall follow this convention here.

The laboratory experiment has usually been regarded as the strongest technique of investigation. This is because it was thought that it allowed the investigator to establish what caused behaviour. Faith in the laboratory experiment has been shaken as a result of criticisms made by such workers as Orne (1962), Rosenthal (1966) and Sears (1986). Some of the criticisms are described later, but briefly they were that experiments do not establish the 'causes' of behaviour, because it is affected by many other factors, and that laboratory experiments are so artificial that the findings are not true outside the laboratory. This second criticism does not apply to some of the methods, such as field experiments or natural observation, where the observer investigates a 'real-life' happening. But these have their own problems: the researchers must be present when the event occurs, and ensure they observe and record significant events and antecedent conditions.

3.1 Variables and levels

3.1.1 Dependent and independent variables

In an experiment, the experimenter arranges for there to be a change in some aspect of the situation. This is the independent variable. The participants' performance on a task is measured, and this measure is referred to as the dependent variable. If the experiment has been designed and carried out properly, it is assumed that any changes in the dependent variable are the result of the changes in the independent variable. Box 3.1 summarizes an experiment on the use of a technique for helping people remember the names of faces. Here the independent variable is whether or not the participants were trained in the mnemonic technique, and the dependent variable is the score on the test of name/face recall. The investigators argued that the changes in the dependent variable (the scores on the recall test) were brought about by the independent variable (training in the mnemonic technique).

The independent variable is sometimes referred to as a 'factor'. You will also come across the word in the phrase 'factor analysis', which refers to mathematical procedures for analysing the correlations between scores on psychological tests.

The distinction between dependent and independent variables is not restricted to experiments: whenever you are trying to link some phenomenon with pre-existing conditions, it is helpful to think of them as dependent and independent variables. Correlational studies involve measuring at least two attributes of each respondent: for example, you might measure people's academic achievement and their attitude to studying. If you use the score on one attribute to predict the score on the other, the predicted score is the dependent variable and the predictor is the independent one.

3.1.2 Levels of independent variables

The difference between variables and levels of a variable is a common source of confusion, but it is essential to appreciate it since it is fundamental to statistical analysis and to understanding the design of any study.

Assume you are planning an experiment to compare the performance of people at remembering people's names or occupations. You prepare a set of faces and label each one with either a name or an occupation. You present the participants with each of the faces and its label. You then measure performance by presenting the faces without the labels, and find out how many names or occupations can be remembered. The type of label (name or occupation) is the independent variable, and the amount remembered is the dependent variable. The only variable that has been manipulated is the type of label, and as there are two types this variable has two levels. This would be a single-factor, two-level experiment. In Box 3.2, an experiment by Stanhope and Cohen (1993), which is similar to the one we have just described, is summarized. Note that they had three types of label for the faces, so there were three levels of one independent variable.

Box 3.1 Example of an experiment on memory for faces

Morris *et al.* (1978) investigated whether a special way of learning names for faces really worked. Two sets (A and B) of 13 faces were assembled, and a name was given to each face. Two groups of 20 undergraduates were formed. All members of each group were tested on their ability to remember the names of one set of faces. They were shown each face with its name and then shown the faces again and asked to recall the name. Half of each group were shown the faces in set A and the other half were shown set B.

One of the groups of participants was then given an explanation of how imagery can be used to improve memory for names of faces, and practised using the imagery technique. The other group spent a similar amount of time doing a spelling task instead. Both groups were tested again on their ability to learn names of faces, using the set of faces that they had not seen before.

The group without training scored 4.9 on the first test and 5.4 on the second, whereas the respective scores for the group who received training were 5.7 and 10.2.

The untrained group did not improve significantly, but the trained group did. Morris *et al.* concluded: 'The mnemonic technique considerably improved recall of the names to the photographs.... The lack of a significant improvement in the performance of the control (untrained) group demonstrates that the better performance of the mnemonic group on the second tests was not simply the result of practice at the task' (p. 336).

You may be interested in whether distinctive, unusual names or jobs are remembered better: if someone is called Felix or has the job of an ostler, will the name or job be remembered better than for someone called John or who is a clerk? To investigate this, you might design a more complex study in which you use unusual names or common names and unusual jobs or common jobs, so you have four conditions. Here you have two independent variables: label type (names, jobs) and distinctiveness (unusual, common). Each has two levels, so the experiment would be described as a 2 × 2 (two by two) design. The number of digits in the expression indicates how many independent variables there are (here there are two), and the value of each digit indicates the number of levels there are for the relevant variable. Of course 2 × 2 = 4, which shows the total number of different conditions there are.

Stanhope and Cohen, in the experiment described in Box 3.2, did in fact vary distinctiveness (high or low) as well as label type (name, occupation or name plus occupation), giving six conditions: low distinctive name; high distinctive name; low distinctive occupation; high distinctive occupation; low distinctive

Box 3.2 Example of an experiment where one variable has three levels

Stanhope and Cohen (1993, experiment 1) studied people's ability to remember names. They presented respondents with sets of faces paired with a label showing a name, an occupation, or both a name and an occupation. Each participant took part in all three conditions. Respondents were tested by being presented with each of the faces and asked to recall its name, its occupation, or both, depending on which had been given at the first presentation. So this was an experiment which manipulated one independent variable: the type of label. As there were three types (name, occupation, both), this was a single-factor, three-level experiment.

Stanhope and Cohen report the percentage of names and occupations recalled correctly in each condition, and these data are given in Table 3.1. When they were asked to recall both names and occupations, participants did less well than when they were asked to recall just names or just occupations. Stanhope and Cohen argue that 'information about occupation interferes with memory for the name' (p. 59).

TABLE 3.1 *Percentage correct recall from Stanhope and Cohen (1993) Experiment 1*

	Face plus name	*Face plus occupation*	*Face plus name and occupation*
Names	53.25	–	23.25
Occupations	–	70.75	60.75

name plus occupation; and high distinctive name plus occupation. So they had a 2 × 3 design. There are two independent variables (distinctiveness, label type), so the expression contains two digits. One variable has two levels (high or low distinctiveness), so is represented by the number 2. The other variable has three levels (name, occupation, name plus occupation) so is represented by a 3. Hence we get the expression 2 × 3. (The order in which the variables are shown is unimportant, so you could also call it a 3 × 2 experiment.) Check your understanding of this using SAQ 3.1.

3.1.3 Between-subjects and within-subjects variables

When different respondents feature in two or more conditions of an investigation, you have a between-subjects, or independent-groups, design. In Box 3.1, for

---

SAQ 3.1

1 An experimenter compared people's reaction time to visual and to auditory stimuli when a warning signal was given 0.1, 0.5, 1.0 or 1.5 seconds in advance of the main stimulus. How would this experiment be represented?

2 A researcher compared people's ability to recognize faces. She used male and female participants, showing them faces of children, adults and elderly people, and also had male and female faces in each age grouping. How many independent variables are there? How would this experiment be represented?

---

example, different participants were used in the 'without training' and 'with training' conditions, so this was a between-subjects design and the with/without training variable was a between-subjects variable. If the same respondents are used in the different conditions, you have a within-subjects, or repeated-measures, design. The Stanhope and Cohen study described in Box 3.2 was a within-subjects design, as all participants took part in each of the three conditions. They varied the type of label paired with the faces that respondents saw, so this variable of label type was a within-subjects variable.

It is, of course, possible to combine within- and between-subjects variables in a single study, giving a mixed design. For example, Flin *et al.* (1992) compared the accuracy of children and adults at remembering a staged 'real-life' incident. There were three age groups (six-year-olds, nine-year-olds and adult), and this was a between-subjects variable. Each participant was interviewed twice, one day after the incident and again five months later. So the length of delay (one day or five months) was a within-subjects variable, and the experiment was a mixed 3 × 2 design.

3.2 Extraneous variables and dealing with them

3.2.1 Confounding variables

Extraneous variables are all the variables other than the independent variable which can affect people's behaviour on the dependent variable. As we explained in Chapter 1, the logic underlying the experimental method is that changes in the independent variable cause any change in the dependent variable. This argument depends on ensuring that the only thing that distinguishes between the conditions is the levels of the independent variable: the difficulty with experiments in psychology is that one can never be certain that it *is* only the levels of the independent variable that distinguish between the conditions! For example, in the experiment described in Box 3.1, different people were used in the two conditions: those who had the training in using the memory technique were not the same people as those who were given the task of remembering the names without the training. So it is possible that the difference in performance on the dependent variable (score on the memory task) was due to other (extraneous) factors. The group given the training may have included people who had a better memory anyway. Part of the art of designing experiments consists of arranging matters so that it is reasonable to assume that only the independent variable has a consistent effect on the dependent variable, that any extraneous factors do not prejudice the comparison of the two conditions. Extraneous variables cannot be eliminated, but you must arrange that they do not favour one group of participants over another and therefore undermine the experiment.

If groups of respondents have some consistent difference in addition to the levels of the independent variable, the effect of the independent variable is said to be confounded with the effect of the extraneous variable. For example, imagine we were studying whether people's ability to remember an incident was affected by the kind of interview they had afterwards: a 'cued recall' interview or an 'enhanced' interview (Flin *et al.*, 1992). The simplest procedure would be to have two groups of people, one receiving the cued recall interview and the other the enhanced one. If the only difference between the conditions is the type of interview, any differences in the ability to remember the information (the dependent variable) are interpreted as being *caused* by the different levels of the independent variable.

Suppose we have formed two groups of respondents, one to be given the cued interview and the other the enhanced interview. If one group of respondents was 80% men and 20% women while the other group was 80% women and 20% men, then the sex composition would be confounded with the levels of the independent variable. Confounding means the experimental outcome is ambiguous, because the conditions differed on some factor in addition to the levels of the independent variable. Suppose we found the first group scored higher on a memory test than the second one. We could not say whether this was because group A had one type of interview and group B the other, or whether it was because group A had a majority of men in it whereas group B had a majority of women. We would not be justified in arguing that the differences in the dependent variable were due to the differences in the independent variable, and the experiment would be useless for identifying causative links. (There might be some useful findings, but the main aim of carrying out the study would be ruined.) So it is vital to ensure an experiment does not involve confounding variables.

The importance of *confounding* variables lies in their ability to wreck the logical argument upon which an experiment is based, that the independent variable caused any changes in the dependent variable. Confounding variables must be avoided! But *extraneous* variables cannot be avoided: it is the task of the researcher to ensure that they do not become confounding variables. How can this be done?

Note that extraneous variables are not necessarily confounding. SAQ 3.2 tests your ability to distinguish between them.

Having participants press keys to indicate different responses can introduce a confounding variable because people react faster with their preferred hand: right-handed people can press a key faster with their right-hand than with their left and

---

SAQ 3.2 Distinguishing confounding and extraneous variables

In an experiment, participants were shown faces on a computer screen and had to indicate as quickly as they could whether each face was familiar or not. The respondents had to press the A key if the face was familiar, and the L key if was not. A student, reporting this experiment, commented on the fact that respondents were sometimes confused about which key to press, and this did not allow a fair comparison to be made between the time to respond to familiar and unfamiliar faces. Is this confusion a confounding variable?

---

vice versa. So if you had right-handed participants, and always used the right-hand key to indicate 'yes' and the left-hand key to indicate 'no', there is a problem. The 'yes' responses will be faster than 'no' responses partly because the right-hand response is faster anyway.

To prevent this confounding, you have a number of options. You can keep the keys the same but ensure half the respondents in each group are left-handed and half are right-handed. Then half the respondents would be using their preferred hand and the other half would be using their non-preferred hand to indicate 'yes'. This is difficult to arrange, and is open to objection since less than half the population is left-handed. So the usual procedure is to split the group into two halves. For one half the right-hand key indicates 'yes' and the left-hand key indicates 'no'; for the other half the keys are reversed, and the right-hand key represents 'no'. This form of counterbalancing was used in an experiment reported by Ellis *et al.* (1993).

It has been known for experimenters to try to deal with the problem by switching the keys half way through the experiment for each respondent: this introduces great confusion for the participants, and is definitely not recommended!

Another possibility is to ask the respondents always to respond with their preferred hand. To do this, you ask them to put the forefinger of their preferred hand on a particular point midway between the two response keys before the stimulus is presented. For example, you might arrange it so that the respondent starts the experimental trial by pressing the B key on the keyboard, and responds by pressing the A or L keys. But the reaction time will then include the time taken to move the finger from the starting key to the response key, and it is still possible that people can move their finger from key B to key L faster than from key B to key A. So it is sensible to keep to the counterbalancing used by Ellis *et al.*

3.2.2 Controlling extraneous variables

Extraneous variables can be divided into three types: participant, investigator and situational. Participant variables are such things as sex, handedness, amount of previous training on the task: long-term characteristics of the people being studied which may affect their performance. Investigator variables arise if different people are collecting the data from different respondents, as often happens in group projects; if some of the team are male and others female, then sex of investigator is a relevant extraneous variable which has to be dealt with. Situational variables refer to any aspect of the task, physical environment, or temporary features of the respondents (such as hunger) which might influence performance. When designing any study, it is important to ensure that extraneous variables of any category do not undermine the comparison between the levels of the independent variable. There are four main ways of dealing with extraneous variables.

Keeping them constant
The first involves keeping them constant for all participants. If everyone experiences the same level of any extraneous variable, then it cannot cause differences in their performance under the various experimental conditions. So you should use the same instructions for everyone, ensure that no one has any additional information which would give them an advantage in doing whatever task they are being presented with, ensure everyone has the same amount of practice at the task, and keep the physical conditions equivalent for everyone.

Balancing
Another procedure is to balance the extraneous variable so that it affects each group equally. If you were carrying out a group project and had two people collecting data from two groups of participants, it would be wrong to have one investigator collecting data from one group and the other investigator studying the other group. If you did, investigator would be confounded with participant group. To avoid this confounding, each investigator should collect data from half the participants of each group. By balancing investigators across the two groups in this way, any effects of using one investigator rather than the other will affect each of the groups to a similar extent.

Balancing can be used for situational variables too. Suppose you are running an experiment testing two groups of 10 people at 15-minute intervals, with some people tested in the morning and others in the afternoon; you would need to ensure that if four of one group were tested in the morning, four of the other group were also tested in the morning.

When you have a between-groups experiment, the order in which the researcher tests the groups can be important: on later sessions, the experimenter may become more competent or more bored. Suppose you have two groups, A and B, with ten members in each. If you test all group A and then all group B, you may be better at running the experiment (or totally exhausted and bored with it) before you ever get to the group B subjects. So you should organize the testing so that any effects of this kind are balanced out. For example, you might divide each of the groups into equal-sized subgroups. The first subgroup of group A could be tested first, then the two subgroups of group B and lastly the second subgroup of group

A. This is a form of ABBA ordering, designed to ensure that any effects of experimenter skill or fatigue affect the two groups equally.

Balancing is especially important if you are using a within-subjects design, where the same people are tested under a number of different conditions. It is vital to arrange the order in which participants carry out the various tasks so that practice or fatigue affects the various conditions to an equal extent. This is considered in more detail in section 3.4.3.

Randomizing

Not all variables can be kept constant for all the participants. Some respondents may do the task at a different time from others, the people doing one task may be different from those doing another, or it may be necessary to have different investigators collecting data: these and other aspects of the study mean that the conditions cannot be the same for everyone. The third approach to controlling variables is to ensure that unavoidable variations do not help or hinder one group or condition more than another. There are two procedures which do this. The first is randomizing. If you are using a between-subjects design, there will be numerous differences between the people in each group, and one way to prevent these having any consistent effect is to allocate people to the groups using a random procedure. (How to do this is explained in Box 3.4.) The assumption underlying random allocation is that any extraneous participant variables will be more or less equally represented in each group, and so will not act as confounding variables. Randomly allocating people to groups or conditions is the crucial factor that determines whether the study is a true experiment.

The control group

Keeping extraneous variables constant, randomizing and balancing are meant to prevent them becoming confounding variables but do not guarantee that extraneous variables have no effect on the respondents. The fourth way of dealing with them involves measuring their effects, using a control group of respondents. People in the control group are not given the independent variable, so their performance reflects only the influence of extraneous variables. You compare the results of the experimental group with those of the control group; as the experimental group had the independent variable and the extraneous variables while the control group had only the extraneous variables, any difference between them should be due to the effect of the independent variable. Check that you understand the aim of using a control group by doing SAQ 3.3.

SAQ 3.3
The experiment described in Box 3.1 used a control group. Why? What did the use of the control group allow Morris *et al.* to conclude?

3.3 The experimental hypothesis and the null hypothesis

In a typical experiment you have at least two groups of participants and predict that the groups will differ in their performance on the dependent variable. This prediction is the experimental hypothesis. The null hypothesis states that there will be no difference between the groups' scores on the dependent variable. If you simply predict that the two groups will differ, you have a non-directional hypothesis. But if you say which group will obtain the higher score, you have a directional hypothesis. In the experiment described in Box 3.1, the experimental hypothesis states that the group given training in the mnemonic technique will perform better on the second memory for names task than the untrained (control) group. As it says which group will gain the higher score, it is a directional hypothesis.

3.3.1 Why you should not perform a study designed to confirm the null hypothesis

Your experimental hypothesis should always be positive, predicting that there *will* be a difference. You should never carry out a study designed to confirm the null hypothesis. Why? Because a finding of no difference may have a number of reasons. You may have a confounding variable which has obliterated the effect of the independent variable. Extraneous variables may have made the experiment insensitive, so that any effects of the independent variable are obscured. The levels of the independent variable may have been insufficiently different, or the dependent variable measure might have been too coarse. It is always possible to do an experiment where the independent variable has no detectable effect, merely by using inadequate procedures. So an experiment which supports the null hypothesis is always ambiguous: it could be that the independent variable has no effect, or it could be that the way the experiment was performed failed to detect the effect that was there. Box 3.3 gives an example that you should *not* follow!

3.4 Experimental designs

A major aim when designing experiments is to ensure that the outcome is unambiguous, uncontaminated by confounding or extraneous variables. A crucial aspect is how participants are assigned to the various conditions, how subgroups are formed. This has yielded four major types of experiment: between-subjects, within-subjects, matched-subjects and mixed designs. Each has advantages and disadvantages.

In explaining the different experimental designs, we shall begin with the simple case where two groups are being compared. But all the designs can easily be extended to cover more than two groups. You may have more than one independent variable, and any one independent variable may have more than two levels. If you have three or more levels of one independent variable, you can detect any trends in the data. The graph shown in Fig. 3.4, for example, illustrates the effects

---

Box 3.3 A mistaken attempt to confirm the null hypothesis

Here are two problems, known as syllogisms. For each one, decide whether the conclusion is valid or not.

> All As are Bs
> No Bs are Cs
> Therefore no As are Cs.

> All mothers are female
> No females are boys
> Therefore no mothers are boys.

People's ability to reason with problems like these has been the subject of many investigations, and the field is surveyed by Evans *et al.* (1993). Stimulated by reading about this topic, a student set out to confirm the (null) hypothesis that there is no difference between people's ability to solve syllogisms when they are presented in an abstract form like the first one above or a concrete form.

The student created ten abstract and ten concrete syllogisms; five of each group had the logically valid conclusion and five had an invalid conclusion. Twenty respondents were given the concrete syllogisms and 15 were given the abstract ones. For each syllogism, they were asked to indicate whether the conclusion was valid or not. Two minutes was allowed to respond to the set of syllogisms, and the number of correct responses was recorded. The results showed that the average number of correct responses for both the abstract and concrete syllogisms was 0.48. The student concluded that there was no difference in the ability to solve abstract and concrete syllogisms, i.e. the null hypothesis was supported.

The problem here is that the task in either form was apparently too difficult. The results suggest a 'floor effect': hardly anyone could do any of the problems, so any possible effect of abstract/concrete form had no chance of being observed. The experiment did not allow a proper test of ability, and the student's conclusion is not justified.

---

of delay on a short-term memory task. Since a number of delay intervals were used, it gives a clearer picture of how delay interval affects memory than you would get if just two intervals had been compared.

3.4.1 Between-subjects (randomized groups) experiments

In this design different people are allocated to form groups and each group is exposed to its own level of the independent variable. (A control group may have zero level of the independent variable. Box 3.1 describes such an experiment, as some people were given training in memory for names while others were not.)

The assumption underlying this design is that the groups are more or less equal before the exposure to the independent variable occurs, so that any differences in the dependent variable can be ascribed to the independent variable and not to any pre-existing differences between the groups. This assumption is accepted if the pool of participants is allocated to the various groups by a random procedure (hence the term 'randomized groups'). With random allocation you assume that the groups created will be equivalent on any feature likely to influence performance on the dependent variable. For example, if you use a random method of dividing 40 people into four groups of 10, you assume that the four groups are equivalent in terms of the number of left-handers, the number of males and females, the mean intelligence level, etc. How to obtain random allocation is explained in Box 3.4.

Post-test only experiments

A post-test only experiment is one where you measure people's performance only after you have administered the independent variable. The two-group post-test only design is illustrated in Fig. 3.1. The groups have different levels of the independent variable, or there is one experimental group which has the independent variable treatment and a control group which does not. Any differences between the two groups on the dependent variable are taken as being caused by the differences in the independent variable. Stanhope and Cohen (1993, experiment 2) carried out an experiment using this design. They showed people's

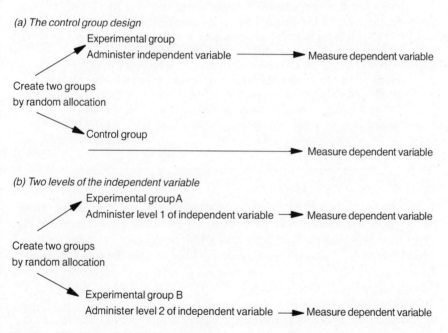

(a) The control group design

Experimental group
Administer independent variable ⟶ Measure dependent variable

Create two groups
by random allocation

Control group

⟶ Measure dependent variable

(b) Two levels of the independent variable

Experimental group A
Administer level 1 of independent variable ⟶ Measure dependent variable

Create two groups
by random allocation

Experimental group B
Administer level 2 of independent variable ⟶ Measure dependent variable

FIG. 3.1. *The simple two-group experiment*

Box 3.4 Forming randomized groups

Random allocation does not mean haphazard or uncontrolled allocation, which may well produce biases. Proper random allocation relies
on a random-number table, such as Table N1 on page 243. Each entry
in the table is a digit that was chosen at random from the ten possibilities, so you can start at any point and move in any direction (left,
right, up, down, diagonally) to obtain a list of numbers in a random
order. Since the original table was constructed by sampling with
replacement of those selected, digits recur and you might obtain a
sequence like this: 4 8 2 6 2 1 7 4 6 2 9 0 2 1.

Suppose you have 60 respondents, and need to form three groups
using random allocation. Begin by writing down the numbers 01 to 60.
Start at any point in Table N1, and read the numbers in pairs so that 4 8
is 48. If the number is greater than the total of participants you have (in
our example 60), ignore it and go to the next number (remember you
can move left or right, up or down) until you find a number that is in
the range you require (01–60). When you find the first one, allocate
that number to group A, cross out the number on the list you made (so
you keep track and do not allocate one person to two groups!), and go
to the next number in the table. If it is within the range 01 to 60 and
has not already been allocated, put that number into group B and cross
it off your list. Then read the third number from Table N1, and if it is
within the range and not already allocated, put it into group C and
cross it off the master list. Go on like this, putting the fourth number
into group A, the fifth into B, the sixth into C, etc., until all the numbers have been allocated. You will then have three groups of 20
numbers. When you have numbered each of the respondents from 1 to
60, your list will tell you which group each person is in.

If the number of participants does not divide equally into the
number of groups, you will have an odd person or two left over. Decide
whether they are to go into group A, B or C by entering Table N1 and
finding the first number that is in the range 1 to c, where c is the
number of groups you are creating. (In this example, $c = 3$.) If it is 1,
put the person in group A, if it is 2 put them in B, if it is 3 put them in
C.

faces accompanied either by a name or by an occupation; then they presented the
faces again and asked participants to recall the name or occupation. 'The
experiment was a between-subjects design with two conditions, name only and
occupation only ... subjects were randomly allocated [to the two conditions]'
(p. 60).

Pre-test post-test experiments
If you measure people's performance before and after you administer the
independent variable, so that you assess how much they change, you use the

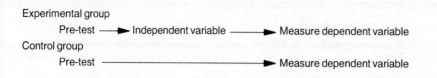

Fig. 3.2. *The two-group pre-test post-test experimental design*

two-group pre-test post-test design, illustrated in Fig. 3.2. The pre-test is used to provide a baseline of the group members' performance so that a 'gain' score can be obtained. (You expect the two groups to have similar scores on the pre-test, as the groups have been formed by random allocation.) An example of this design is Morris *et al.*'s experiment described in Box 3.1, where the first test gave a measure of people's ability to remember names before any training was given.

The drawback to this design is that when respondents take the pre-test, they become aware of the type of task they are being asked to do, and this may lead them to react differently. If this effect differed between the two groups, you would have a confounding variable. Even if the effect is the same for both groups, it may mean the experiment is leading people to act in an unnatural manner.

Solomon four-group pre-test post-test experiment
Giving a pre-test may influence people's behaviour. To see whether this is the case, you can use the Solomon four-group pre-test post-test design, illustrated in Fig. 3.3. This assesses the effects of the pre-test, as two of the groups have it and two do not, but is rarely used because there are two control groups who provide little information about the effects of the independent variable.

Concluding comments on randomized-groups experiments
Randomized-groups designs are frequently used, and avoid some of the problems that arise if you use matched-groups or within-subjects designs. But they are not always feasible: for example, they cannot be used if you want to investigate the

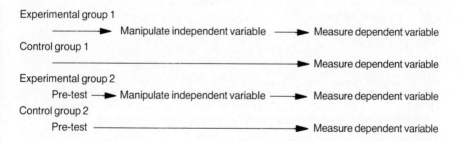

Fig. 3.3. *The Solomon four-group pre-test post-test experimental design (allows assessment of the effects of the pre-test)*

effects of individual-difference variables which you cannot manipulate, such as the person's sex or age. All randomized-group designs assume subgroups of respondents are formed by a random allocation procedure, and that consequently the subgroups will be more or less equal on any dimension you care to consider. When you have a limited number of participants, as is typical of most experiments, the groups may still differ: you may find that the sex composition varies, for example, with group A having 60% males and group B only 40%. There are a number of ways of dealing with this situation. First, you can ignore it and accept that that was the outcome. If the experiment were repeated with a fresh allocation of people to groups, then these differences would be unlikely to recur and any possible biases would be as likely to be reversed. Second, you may use a within-subjects design in which the same respondents are used in each of the experiment's conditions (see section 3.4.3). The third possibility is to use a matched-group design.

3.4.2 Matched-groups (randomized-blocks) experiments

By creating subgroups of participants that have been deliberately matched as closely as possible before they carry out the experiment, you can be certain they are equivalent on whichever attributes you used to match them. How to create matched groups is described in Box 3.5. But matched groups designs have disadvantages and so they are comparatively rarely used.

Disadvantages of the matched-groups experiment
First, there are the practical problems of testing the respondents and forming the groups before you can start carrying out the experiment proper; you are asking respondents to give you more time and effort, and asking them to return for the main experiment after the initial pre-testing. Many respondents may be unwilling to do this: losing people will wreck your neat design. You also have to decide which attributes you are going to use in your matching: there are any number of possibilities. The more attributes you decide to use, the more data you need in advance of carrying out the main study, and the harder it will be to match the groups on every dimension.

The second drawback is that by matching groups on one or two attributes, you may be creating inequality on other dimensions. If, for example, you create groups matched on reading ability, this may mean they are very different on extraversion.

A third problem is that by giving people a preliminary test, you are making them aware of the type of behaviour you are studying and this may mean that they react differently from the way they would if they had been left unaware.

3.4.3 Within-subjects (repeated-measures) experiment

This involves every respondent taking part in every one of the conditions or levels of the independent variable. The Stanhope and Cohen experiment described

Box 3.5 Creating matched groups

First, decide which variable(s) are to be used to match the groups of participants. Usually it is a variable or variables that you assume influences performance on the dependent variable.

Suppose that, like Bednall (1992) in the study described in Box 3.8, you were investigating the effect on visual scanning performance of presenting lists of names with empty lines between different surnames. You need two groups, an experimental group to scan material with the extra spacing and a control group to scan lists printed with normal spacing throughout. Scanning ability varies so much that you decide it is important to ensure the two groups have equivalent skills.

The first step is to assess the skill of all the participants, using an appropriate test. Then put them in rank order from the most skilled (having the highest score on the test) to the least, as in Table 3.2.

To create two groups, go down the list of rank-ordered names, drawing a line after every second name. (To create three groups, draw a line after every third name.) One member of each subset is allocated to each of the groups, using a random procedure. The first pair of participants have sequential numbers 1 and 2, so go to Table N1 and starting at any point read up, down, left or right until you come to either 1 or 2. If the first digit you come to is 1, then respondent 1 is allocated to group A and respondent 2 will be put into group B. If the first number is 2, respondent 2 goes into group A and respondent 1 into B. For the second pairing, read Table N1 for a 3 or 4; if the first one you come to is a 4, respondent 4 goes into group A and respondent 3 into group B. Repeat this procedure for every other pair. You will end up with groups of equal numbers, where the groups' mean scores on the matching variable are almost equal. The final column in Table 3.2 shows one possible allocation of respondents to two groups.

TABLE 3.2. *Example of creating matched groups*

Name	Score on initial test	Rank score	Sequential number	Group
Jane	34	1	1	A
Mary	32	2	2	B
Bridget	31	3.5	3	A
Alan	31	3.5	4	B
John	30	5	5	B
Peter	29	6	6	A

in Box 3.2 used this design, since all respondents participated in every one of the three conditions. The problem is that there may be transfer effects: when the respondents come to the second task, their performance may be better or worse simply because they have already done the first task. It is vital to try to prevent this biasing the experiment. You do this by controlling the order in which the tasks are given.

One way of dealing with order effects is to counterbalance the order in which the tasks are given. If there are two conditions, A and B, then half the people have the order A–B and the other half have the order B–A. With three conditions, A, B and C there are six orders: ABC, ACB, BAC, BCA, CAB, CBA, so you need six subgroups to ensure all orders are used equally often. With larger numbers of conditions, complete counterbalancing becomes impractical. You can get round this by using a separate random order of conditions for each participant and assume that any order effects will then average out. Table N2 (p. 243) can help you decide on the orders of conditions for each participant, as each panel shows the numbers 0 to 9 in a random order.

Counterbalancing or randomizing order is effective only if the magnitude of transfer effects is constant. Imagine you are giving people two tasks, A and B. If task A is much more exhausting than B, people will be very tired when they do task B second, and perform badly. But if they do B first, they will not be tired when they do it, and so they will perform much better at this task simply because it comes first. As task B is not exhausting, their performance on the second task (task A) will be as good as it would have been if they had not done another task first. So the comparison of performance on the two tasks will be undermined, with fatigue operating more strongly when task B comes second than when task A comes second. This has led some authorities to argue that within-subjects designs should not be used (Poulton, 1982).

Within-subjects designs cannot be used for studying some topics, such as comparing two methods of teaching a skill. Once a participant has learned the skill using one method, they cannot 'unlearn' it and be taught it again with the second method.

Another problem is that when using a within-subjects design you have to match the tasks and materials across the conditions. Read Box 3.2 again, where Stanhope and Cohen's within-subjects experiment is described. They presented sets of faces paired with names, occupations, or both. Every participant had every condition, seeing different sets of faces for each one. For simplicity, suppose they had just three sets of faces, A, B and C, and we shall refer to the three conditions as 1, 2 and 3. They could have used set A faces paired with names (condition 1), set B with occupations (condition 2) and set C with names and occupations (condition 3). But this would have confounded the set of faces with the conditions. If set A faces had some feature that made them easier to remember than the other sets, then the condition using this set would have had an unfair advantage. It is necessary to avoid this possibility, and ensure that every set is used in every condition. Some people must see set A faces in condition 1 (paired with names), some must see set A in condition 2 (paired with occupations) and others must see set A in condition 3 (paired with names and occupations together). This rotation of face set around conditions has to be done for all the sets, so you get a structure like this, with 6 subgroups of participants:

set A condition 1; set B condition 2; set C condition 3
set A condition 1; set B condition 3; set C condition 2
set A condition 2; set B condition 1; set C condition 3
set A condition 2; set B condition 3; set C condition 1
set A condition 3; set B condition 1; set C condition 2
set A condition 3; set B condition 2; set C condition 1

Stanhope and Cohen used this arrangement, but you can see that it does make life complicated. Remember that the order of conditions still has to be organized, so that order effects do not bias the outcome.

A further problem is that within-subjects designs can be very misleading. The example described in Box 3.6 illustrates the point that what is true when the same people are tested repeatedly may not be true when people are tested only once.

Within-subjects designs do have the benefit of eliminating the difference between participants as a possible source of error, so they are frequently used. But they do need to be designed with care.

Box 3.6 The Petersons' experiment on trace decay forgetting in short-term memory

Peterson and Peterson (1959) gave participants trigrams (sequences of three letters) to remember. As soon as the trigram had been shown, the respondent was asked to count backward in threes for a period from 3 to 18 seconds and then recall the trigram. Textbooks (e.g. Gross, 1992) often summarize the outcome in a graph such as Fig. 3.4. The graph indicates that after nine seconds people could recall only about 30% of the trigrams. You may think this is rather surprising: given three letters to remember, you would expect to be able to remember them quite well for a mere nine seconds, whatever you were doing during those nine seconds! You would be right. The graph summarizes the results when people are tested repeatedly, so that they confuse the items presented on the current trial with the items they had on earlier trials. If people are tested only once, there is little forgetting: 'performance is at virtually 100 percent at all delays on trial 1' (Baddeley, 1976, p. 125).

The usual way the Peterson findings are summarized is misleading because it fails to make clear that the forgetting does not occur on the first trial. It summarizes the results from many trials on each person, a repeated-measures experiment. If a between-subjects design is used the findings look rather different: the amount of forgetting is much less and the curve is level after a five-second delay.

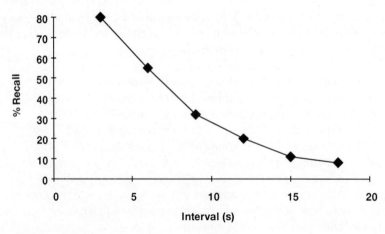

FIG. 3.4. *Results of Peterson and Peterson (1959)*

3.4.4 Mixed-design experiments

A mixed design is where there are at least two independent variables, and so is one kind of factorial experiment as described in the next section. A mixed design has at least one within-subjects variable and one between-subjects variable. An example is described in Box 3.7.

The between-subjects variable may involve classifying people into categories, such as age groups, sexes or levels of ability, and using a within-subjects design in each category (as in the experiment described in Box 3.7). When people are divided into categories, you are not manipulating that variable: people either are or are not female, aged between 20 and 30, etc. As this variable is not manipulated, you are not justified in arguing that it *causes* the changes in the dependent variable.

3.4.5 Factorial experiments

Factorial designs are where you have two (or more) independent variables. They can involve a mixed design as described in the previous section, a randomized-groups design, matched groups or even repeated measures. The advantage of factorial experiments is that you can see whether the independent variables interact: is the effect of the first variable influenced by the level of the second one?

The meaning of 'interaction'

The concept of interaction is best explained using an example. Box 3.8 describes an experiment by Bednall (1992) in which she compared the effects of two independent variables on the speed with which people could find names in lists on a computer screen. As Fig. 3.5 illustrates, one variable was spacing, which had two levels: in the spaced condition surnames were not repeated, in the

---

Box 3.7 Example of a mixed design experiment

Ellis *et al.* (1993, experiment 2) investigated the effects of a priming task on people's ability to recognize faces as familiar: can you decide more quickly that a face is familiar if you have seen a picture of that face a few minutes beforehand? Two age groups, children and adults, were used, so age was a between-subjects variable. Each person was shown the faces of 12 people they knew, and asked to say whether the person was male or female. After a five-minute gap, they were shown 24 faces and had to decide as quickly as possible whether each of these was familiar or not.

Of the 24 test faces, six had been used in the earlier gender-decision task and so had been primed, six were familiar faces which had not been used in that task (unprimed), and 12 were unfamiliar. So the familiar faces were of two types: primed or not. (There were further variations in the experiment which we shall not describe here.) The primed/unprimed variable was a within-subjects factor, as every respondent was shown both primed and unprimed faces. Since there was a within-subjects variable and a between-subjects variable, this was a mixed design.

---

nonspaced condition they were. The other variable was blanking, which also had two levels: in the blank condition an empty line was placed between surnames, in the no-blank condition this was omitted. The results in seconds are shown in Table 3.3.

You can see that there was little difference between the blank/no blank conditions when the spaced condition was used (2.743 v. 2.778 seconds). But in the nonspaced condition, the difference between the blank and no blank conditions was much greater (2.844 v. 3.085 seconds). So the effect of one variable, blanking, depended on the level of the other, spacing. This is what is meant by interaction. In this example, the effects of blanking interacted with the effects of spacing: 'The blank line effect depends on whether or not the screens are spaced' (Bednall, 1992, p. 380). The effects of an interaction are shown if the data are plotted on a graph, as in Fig. 3.6. You can see that the lines are not parallel, and this means the variables interacted. (It is not necessary that the lines should cross, just that

TABLE 3.3. *Response times (seconds) to each screen format*

	Spaced	Nonspaced	Overall
Blank line	2.743	2.844	2.794
No blank line	2.778	3.085	2.932
Overall	2.761	2.965	

Data from Bednall (1992).

Condition 1: spaced/blank line

BEECHAM	B_____62
	D...............57
	F_____90

BORLAND	E.................61
	H_____41
	J..................50

Condition 2: spaced/no blank line

BEECHAM	B_____62
	D...............57
	F_____90
BORLAND	E.................61
	H_____41
	J..................50

Condition 3: nonspaced/blank line

BEECHAM	B_____62
BEECHAM	D...............57
BEECHAM	F_____90

BORLAND	E.................61
BORLAND	H_____41
BORLAND	J..................50

Condition 4: nonspaced/no blank line

BEECHAM	B_____62
BEECHAM	D...............57
BEECHAM	F_____90
BORLAND	E.................61
BORLAND	H_____41
BORLAND	J...............50

FIG. 3.5. *Examples of the screen layouts used by Bednall (1992)*

they should not be parallel.) If the lines had been parallel, this would have meant that the two variables did not interact. An example of a graph which has parallel lines and therefore demonstrates that two variables do not interact is given in Fig. 6.1 in Chapter 6. Check you understanding of the concept of interaction by doing SAQ 3.4.

Looking at graphs such as Fig. 3.6 to see whether the lines are parallel or not gives you an 'eyeball' impression of whether the variables interacted or not. But you should not rely on this visual impression; the statistical procedure of analysis of variance is used to determine whether there is a 'real' interaction. Sometimes

SAQ 3.4

Bruce *et al.* (1994) followed up the research of Stanhope and Cohen described in Box 3.2. They presented their participants with 12 faces, each paired with a name and an occupation. The name or occupation was unique, or shared between two faces, or shared between four faces. One independent variable was the label: name or occupation. The second independent variable was sharing: whether the label was unique or shared. Participants saw the faces paired with the name and occupation, and then were shown the faces individually and tried to recall the appropriate name and occupation. This was repeated for six recall trials, and the total number of labels recalled correctly was recorded.

1 The results from Bruce *et al.*'s experiment 1 are shown in Table 3.4. From an 'eyeball' inspection, do these data suggest that the variables interacted?

2 In a second experiment, Bruce *et al.* (1994) used meaningful labels, such as 'porter', which are known as both names and occupations. The procedure was the same as in the first experiment, and the results are shown in Table 3.5. From an 'eye-ball' inspection, do these data suggest that the variables interacted?

TABLE 3.4. *Results from Bruce* et al. *(1994) experiment 1: mean number of labels recalled correctly*

	Unique	*Shared by two*	*Shared by four*
Names	6.5	9.4	13.0
Occupations	6.6	8.8	13.6

TABLE 3.5 *Results from Bruce* et al. *(1994) experiment 2: mean number of labels recalled correctly*

	Unique	*Shared by two*	*Shared by four*
Names	12.7	14.1	17.4
Occupations	16.1	15.3	16.9

the graph may suggest there is an interaction which is not in fact statistically reliable, and on other occasions you may find that an interaction is statistically reliable even when the lines do not seem to diverge very much. If you are investigating a possible interaction between variables, you will need to use the analysis of variance to see whether it is statistically significant.

Design of factorial experiments

If you have two variables, each with two levels, you will need four groups of participants, as shown in Fig. 3.7. The number of groups increases rapidly as you

---

Box 3.8 Example of a factorial experiment with interaction

Bednall (1992) studied the way that the layout of the computer screen affected the speed with which telephone directory enquiry operators could find target information. In one experiment (experiment 3), the four screen layouts shown in Fig. 3.5 were compared. Two independent variables were manipulated. 'Spacing' had two levels: in the spaced condition, the same surnames were not repeated, whereas in the nonspaced condition they were (compare conditions 1 and 3). 'Blanking' also had two levels: in the blank line condition, an empty line separated different surnames but in the no blank line condition there were no empty lines (compare conditions 1 and 2). All four possible combinations of these two levels of each variable were used, giving a 2 × 2 factorial experiment. On each trial, participants were shown a target name which they then had to find on the screen; they had to type in the number corresponding to the target name and the time taken to respond was measured. The average time in seconds to make a response under each screen format is shown in Table 3.3.

---

add more variables or levels. Factorial experiments are appealing, but be warned that as you add more variables and more levels of the variables they become very complicated to analyse and understand. Students often suggest studies in which they have three or more variables, with two or three levels of each. Avoid using more than three variables, and embark on such a study only when you have had plenty of experience and know how to apply the statistical analysis required. If you insist on studying more than three variables, consider a series of separate studies rather than a single all-embracing one.

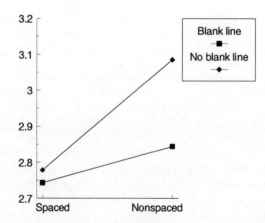

FIG. 3.6. *Graph of the data from Table 3.3. The fact that the lines are not parallel shows the interaction of the two independent variables*

Experimental group 1
Independent variableA level 1 + independent variable B level 1 →Measure dependent variable
Experimental group 2
Independent variableA level 2 + independent variable B level 1 ·Measure dependent variable
Experimental group 3
Independent variableA level 1 + independent variable B level 2 →Measure dependent variable
Experimental group 4
Independent variableA level 2 + independent variable B level 2 →Measure dependent variable

FIG. 3.7. *Factorial experiment (two independent variables)*

3.4.6 Single-case experiments

In some areas of research you have only one case to investigate. The 'case' may be a single individual, or a single group such as a school class. The main feature of this type of study is that you obtain a series of measures on the same person or persons over a period of time. (You can, of course, repeat the study on a number of cases, but the method is still 'single case', because you analyse the results from each case separately and do not merge them by calculating the average of all the participants.) Box 3.9 describes a single-case investigation of a form of therapy; it is single-case, even though four individuals were studied.

In many single-case experiments, the manipulation of the independent variable involves presenting some treatment intended to alter the person's behaviour, as in the study described in Box 3.9. The aim is to demonstrate that the treatment brings about the change in behaviour. The simplest design, as in the Box 3.9 study, is to measure the behaviour before the treatment (condition A) and then give the treatment and measure the behaviour again (condition B). This design is not really acceptable for demonstrating that any change in behaviour was caused by the treatment, because the change may have occurred even if the treatment had not been given.

The design known as A–B–A is better. Here the behaviour is measured before the treatment, after the treatment, and then when the treatment has been removed. If behaviour returns to its original level when the treatment is removed, you have firmer grounds for arguing that the treatment caused the change in behaviour. You can extend the sequence to A–B–A–B ... to confirm the treatment has a consistent effect which is absent when the treatment is absent.

You can only use this A–B–A design if the behaviour can be expected to return to its initial level once the treatment is removed. It would not be sensible in a study of learning or attitude change, since the person's knowledge or attitude cannot be expected to return to its original level. The example described in Box 3.9 could not use it because the therapy is expected to produce a permanent alteration, not one that will disappear after a period of time.

Box 3.9 Example of a single-case experiment
Note that the study described here was carried out by trained experts.
Only a brief summary of their procedures is given here, and you must
not attempt to copy them.

Chadwick *et al.* (1994) investigated the effects of cognitive therapy on
four people who were suffering from delusions. One patient, HJ, is
described as 'a 56-year-old woman with a history of schizophrenia
dating back over 20 years. The delusion was that an unknown man was
persecuting her and was intent on killing her. The main source of the
evidence for the delusions was persistent auditory hallucinations' (p. 37).

Cognitive therapy involves two procedures, verbal challenge and
empirical testing. Verbal challenge is 'disputing the reliability and
validity of a belief; the belief is considered alongside an established
data set (the 'facts') to determine whether it corresponds with 'reality'
or distorts it. If the belief is found wanting, the person is encouraged to
generate alternative interpretations that tally better with the facts'
(pp. 35–36). Empirical testing is 'planning and performing an activity
that validates or invalidates a belief or part of a belief' (p. 36).

Chadwick *et al.* subjected HJ's delusions to reality testing and then
to verbal challenge. Initially there was a preliminary interview and then
baseline measures of her conviction that the delusion was true were
taken over five weeks. A reality test, devised in collaboration with HJ,
was then given. It consisted of her periodically wearing ear-muffs to
see if she could still hear the voices. She had agreed that if she could
still hear them, she would be more certain that they were internal
voices. Verbal challenge meant that the therapist challenged the
evidence for the beliefs, drew attention to the irrational and inconsistent aspects, suggested the beliefs were a response to a specific
experience and assessed the delusion and the therapist's alternative.

The level of HJ's conviction that the voices were real was 100%
throughout baseline and reality testing but declined during the verbal
challenge phase. In the final two weeks of verbal challenge it was 0%.
When measured again after one, three and six months it remained no
higher than 30%. Independent evidence of her improvement was also
obtained. Staff at her day hospital reported her coping better with her
problems.

Chadwick *et al.* studied four people and 'verbal challenge and
reality testing precipitated a major reduction in belief conviction in
three of the four participants' (p. 46).

Chadwick *et al.* comment on the value of the single-subject method
they used. Delusions are personal to the individual and best studied
individually. The data showed that 'changes in the main dependent
measure, belief conviction, was specifically due to the intervention'
(p. 48). They could track changes over time for each person and see the
differences between the four individuals in their reactions to the
therapy. As they used other measures as well as the one described here,
they could look at how the different measures interacted over time.

3.5 Quasi-experiments

If you are planning research outside the laboratory, you may find that it is impossible to control the extraneous variables in the ways described in section 3.2.2. For example, it may be impossible to allocate participants to the different groups on a random-allocation basis. When faced with this problem, you have to run a quasi-experiment. You design the study so it is as similar as possible to one of the experimental designs described above, but without the crucial feature of equivalent groups at the outset. There are a number of quasi-experiment designs, some of which can give provisional support to the argument that changes in the dependent variable are caused by the independent variable.

3.5.1 Acceptable quasi-experiment designs

The *pre-test post-test with non-equivalent groups design* resembles the design shown in Fig. 3.2 except that the two groups are not created through random allocation of respondents and so cannot be assumed to be equivalent. Both are given a pre-test, one is given the independent variable, and both groups are then given the post-test. If the two groups are more or less the same on the pre-test but differ on the post-test, you cannot be sure that it was the independent variable that caused the difference, but it is a reasonable assumption which can perhaps be tested more strictly with a 'proper' experiment later.

The *interrupted time series* design has one group of respondents assessed on a number of occasions before the independent variable is given, and then again afterwards. It demonstrates whether the performance after the independent variable is given shows a different trend from that exhibited beforehand.

The *regression discontinuity* design includes a number of participants, each measured on a pre-test. Those who score above a certain level are given the independent variable, while the others are not: the design resembles a conventional two-groups experiment, except that the groups are created not by random assignment but by score on the pre-test. All participants are given the post-test, and the researcher sees whether those given the treatment differ from those not given it.

3.5.2 Quasi-experiment designs to avoid

In the *one-group post-test* design, respondents are given the independent variable and their performance on the dependent variable is then measured. Performance on the dependent variable may have been caused by many factors apart from the independent variable, so this design is of little value for showing whether the independent variable causes changes in the dependent variable.

The *two-group post-test design only with non-equivalent groups* has two groups. One group is given one level of the independent variable and the other receives another level. It resembles the post-test only design described in section 3.4.1, but since the two groups are not formed by random allocation, they are not equivalent at the outset. Any difference between their performance on the dependent variable might be due to pre-existing differences between the groups.

The *one-group pre-test post-test* design involves testing a group of respondents, giving them the independent variable, testing them again and comparing the scores on the two tests. Any change in performance between the two tests cannot be attributed to the independent variable as it might have occurred anyway. Robson (1993) comments that this design can be useful for seeing whether a change does occur between the two test sessions, but not for revealing whether any such change was caused by the independent variable.

3.6 The validity of the experiment

3.6.1 Internal validity

When you carry out an experiment you want to argue that changes in the dependent variable were caused by the independent variable. To justify this argument, the experiment has to be 'internally valid', meaning that no other factors could have brought about the differences in the dependent variable.

There are many things that can reduce the internal validity of an experiment. Dealing with extraneous variables and avoiding confounding are crucial, but do not guarantee the experiment is valid. In a within-subjects (repeated-measures) design, some extraneous event may occur between the test sessions which alters behaviour, people may become more practised at the task, or the mere passage of time may mean they are more mature and competent towards the end of the experiment.

Between-subjects designs have their own problems. People in the experimental group may tell their friends what has been happening, so the control group may get to know what the independent variable is. They might then want the same treatment, decide to try harder than they would have done, or complain that they are not being treated equally. Groups of participants may differ in the number who turn up for later testing sessions.

Part of the skill in designing, running and interpreting experiments lies in avoiding these problems, controlling for them, or being aware of their possible effect on the conclusions you can draw.

3.6.2 Ecological validity

This refers to the extent to which the findings of a study apply in the real world. One of the criticisms of laboratory experiments is that they are so artificial that the phenomena observed do not occur outside the laboratory, and so have little interest except to academic researchers. There are three ways of dealing with this criticism. First, you can stop using the experiment and rely on other methods instead. Second, you can carry out further work to see whether the results of experiments apply in other contexts. For example, there have been countless studies of memory in the laboratory, but in recent years people have deliberately sought to discover whether the conclusions from the laboratory research are also found (replicated) in the real world (e.g. Cohen, 1989). Third, you can argue that the benefits of the laboratory experiment outweigh its drawbacks, and assume the results can be applied in the real world unless it is shown that they do not.

The fundamental issue of ecological validity is whether the results can be generalized to other environments, other times and to other people (population validity). In this book we are deliberately referring to British and European research more frequently than American work, partly because there is always a doubt about how far American findings are true of Europeans. The doubts are stronger when you ask if the results apply to people outside the dominant culture of Europe or America. Much American work uses as respondents young, well educated, middle-class males who are motivated to take part by the bribe of 'course credit'. This tendency to use a particular type of person in the research but then draw conclusions about people in general has been the subject of strong criticism (Sears, 1986). If the participants are volunteers, one must ask whether what is true of them is also true of people who did not volunteer (Rosenthal, 1965). In recent years, the women's movement has emphasized the fact that research has often used male respondents, and queried the extent to which the results apply to females (Gilligan, 1982).

These questions apply not only to laboratory research, and indeed are even more relevant to some other forms of investigation. Surveys particularly are really only snapshots of those people who took part at that time and in that place. It is not usually assumed that the results will apply years later or in a different culture.

Experiments are prone to other sources of contamination. 'Experimenter expectation effects' refers to the fact that the researchers may be committed to producing a certain outcome, and may inadvertently bias the way the experiment is performed (Rosenthal, 1966). There is always, of course, the possibility of overt fraud – massaging the data so that they fit the hypothesis. The assumption of the scientific study is that researchers never do this.

Another problem is the social demands put upon the respondents taking part in an experiment: the 'demand characteristics' (Orne, 1962). Participants are not blank, inanimate entities: they try to make sense of the situation, to decide what the study is about. They may then react by trying to help the experimenter obtain the results which they believe are the intended ones. The participants' interpretation of the aim of the study may be wrong, so their attempt to be 'helpful' can be the opposite! Alternatively, they may decide to provide data which are contrary to what they believe the experimenter wants. There has been considerable debate about the ways the researcher should deal with this problem. At one time, it was thought that keeping respondents ignorant of the study's purpose was sufficient, but this simply means that the researcher allows the participants to develop their own, probably inaccurate, interpretations of its aim. Many studies deliberately misled the participants about the aim of the study. This is now seen

SAQ 3.5

1 Wogalter *et al.* (1987) studied the effects of warnings on behaviour. One experiment involved participants using chemical laboratory equipment which was shown with some instructions which included a warning that the chemicals could produce skin irritation. (In fact the chemicals were harmless.) There were two different kinds of warning, one headed 'WARNING' and the other headed 'Note'. Different participants had the two types, and their accuracy at the task and the time they took to put on gloves were recorded. Was the study a true experiment or a quasi-experiment?

2 Another study reported by Wogalter *et al.* (1987) involved them observing how many people drank from a water fountain, then putting a warning notice ('Water Contaminated – Do not Drink') on it and seeing how many people drank, and then putting another warning notice which included a symbol as well as the verbal message and recording how many people drank. Was the study a true experiment or a quasi-experiment?

3 The study by Bednall (1992), described in Box 3.8, compared the four screen layouts shown in Fig. 3.5. There were two independent variables: 'spacing' and 'blanking'. Both were within-subjects factors, so all participants did all four conditions. Was the study a true experiment or a quasi-experiment?

as being unethical: respondents should give informed consent before they participate in a study, and informed consent implies they are properly instructed in its aims.

There is another aspect of population validity which causes confusion. Many students worry that an experiment has little value if the participants are not a representative sample of the population. But this shows a misunderstanding of the issue. In an experiment you study the effects of manipulating the independent variable. The assumption is that the variations in the level of the independent variable apply to other people *unless* there are grounds for thinking that they do not. If you are using 'ordinary' people and find some effect, you assume the same effect would be found on any other 'ordinary' people. Although one might ask whether the results found with students apply to people in general, even students are usually assumed to be 'ordinary' people!

Although laboratory experiments have traditionally been seen as the strongest kind of research, because they allow you to establish causative links, it is not always practical to use them. Quasi-experiments are one alternative. Check that you can distinguish between experiments and quasi-experiments by doing SAQ 3.5. Sometimes even quasi-experiments may not be feasible. Consequently, psychologists use a number of other methods, which are described in the following chapters.

Chapter 4

Quantitative approaches:
beyond the experiment

4.0 Introduction

Non-experimental methods allow you to study behaviour in more natural settings than the psychology laboratory. But they give weaker grounds for drawing conclusions about causation. It is particularly important to remember that if two variables are correlated it is not necessarily the case that one causes changes in the other.

4.1 Correlational studies

A correlational study involves measuring two or more attributes of the respondents and discovering whether there is a relationship between them. A crucial feature is that the investigator does not manipulate an independent variable, so has less control than in an experiment or quasi-experiment. You may already be familiar with the correlation coefficient, a statistic which can vary between -1.00 and +1.00 and expresses the degree to which two sets of data are related. It is important to appreciate that a correlational study does not necessarily involve calculating correlation coefficients: the Fisher and Hood study described in Box 4.1 is a correlational study which did not use correlations but compared the scores of subgroups of participants. A correlational study is defined in terms of how the study is conducted, not the statistics used to analyse it.

In a cross-sectional study, you measure various attributes of the same participants at one time. In a longitudinal study, you measure a set of people at different times. Examples of both are described in Box 4.1.

Correlational studies use the logic of J. S. Mill's method of concomitant variation (described in Chapter 1): if two measures vary together, one of them may be causing the other. But it is not a firm argument for establishing causation. If two variables, x and y, are correlated, you cannot conclude that x causes y; it is possible that y causes x, or both may be related to some underlying variable. If you find a correlation between two variables, and wish to establish whether there is a causative link, then you should in principle try to carry out an experimental study.

Box 4.1 Examples of correlational studies

A cross-sectional study
As part of a study of stress among Californian dentists, DiMatteo *et al.*
(1993) collected scores from a sample of just over 100 respondents on
a questionnaire of dental stress. This assesses feelings of stress in
dentists' work environment and it was found that the results correlated
+0.54 with scores on a questionnaire of mental health functioning, the
RAND Mental Health Index, which was administered at the same time.

A cross-sectional study does not allow you to draw conclusions
about the causative link between the variables which are correlated. In
this example, you could not argue that mental health functioning
caused feelings of stress: it is just as likely that the stress caused the
level of mental health. It is much more likely that both stress and level
of mental health are influenced by other variables, such as the demands
made on the respondents, their age, physical wellbeing, etc.

A longitudinal study
Fisher and Hood (1987) were interested in the factors affecting
homesickness among students who go away to university. They gave
questionnaires to a set of students two months before and six weeks
after the start of the university term. At the second test period, the
students who did not live at home were subdivided according to
whether they reported feeling homesick or not. Compared with those
who were not suffering homesickness, those who were homesick had
scored higher on the questionnaire of psychological disturbance (the
Middlesex Hospital Questionnaire) two months before joining the
university.

Longitudinal studies like this also fail to establish causality between
the two variables which are found to be correlated. Since the homesickness occurred after the level of psychological disturbance had been
measured, you could argue that homesickness could not have caused
the psychological disturbance. But this does not mean that the psychological disturbance caused the homesickness: both might have been the
result of some underlying personality trait, for example.

If you are planning a study which will yield correlation coefficients, remember
that the size of the coefficient depends on the range of scores: if all the scores are
in a narrow range, it will be lower than you would get with a wide range. So,
think carefully about the people you will use, and try to avoid using people who
are all similar. A second point is that the correlation coefficients you are likely to
meet indicate how far two variables have a linear relationship. You should always
plot the data from a correlational study to see whether there is any indication of
a non-linear trend.

4.2 Surveys

Oppenheim (1992) draws a distinction between descriptive and analytic survey designs. A descriptive survey is designed to answer the question 'How many?' by providing a summary of the opinions, attitudes or behaviour of a population. The familiar example is the political opinion poll, in which a number of respondents (in Britain, about 1200 is typical) are asked for their opinions and the responses are then taken as indicative of the opinion of the whole population of voters. 'Population' means the wider set of people about whom you are hoping to draw a conclusion. If you wanted to discover the opinion of Danish housewives under 40 years of age, then people who fit this definition are the population. Surveys used in correlational studies, where the investigator looks at the relationships between the sets of data, are the analytic type. Remember that while correlational studies can reveal interesting relationships they cannot establish that one of the variables caused the variations in the other.

When you are planning a survey, you have to answer three main questions. Who will be asked? What will they be asked? How will they be asked: by questionnaire or interview?

4.2.1 Who will be asked? Sampling

It is rarely possible to ask everyone in whichever population you are studying, and even if you did ask everyone you would find some people unwilling to answer. So you have to use a sample of the population, and argue that what is true of them is true of the population as a whole. Whether this argument is valid depends on the size of the sample, and whether it is representative of the population – whether it mirrors the features of the population in all respects. If the population you are investigating has 20% of people between the ages of 20 and 40, then a representative sample will also have about 20% of this age group.

When planning a survey, you have to balance the need to have as representative a sample as you can get with the practical problems of the time and the costs involved in obtaining the responses. It is important to get a representative sample. If you want to find out something about all students in your college and obtained responses from 50% of them, this would be a large sample. But if your respondents were all men, and half the students in the college were women, the sample would not be representative: you would not be able to generalize from the sample to the whole student body.

Obtaining a representative sample
There are two main types of sampling, probability and nonprobability. In probability sampling, everyone in the population has an equal probability of being included in the sample. In *simple random* sampling, the names of those in the sample are selected from the population by a random procedure, so everyone has an equal chance of being included. To obtain a *systematic* sample, you start

with a list of the population names, and pick every 10th, 20th, 50th name, depending on the ratio of people to be included.

Stratified sampling involves dividing the population into strata, such as age groups, and then using simple random sampling within each of the strata. Usually you use proportionate samples, so that if the population has, say, 30% of people in one age group then you ensure the sample has this proportion too.

Cluster sampling can be used when the population naturally forms into groups or clusters. The population of a school, for example, is divided into classes. You can then create random samples within each cluster such as the school class.

Nonprobability samples are those where every member of the population does not have an equal chance of being included. The most common one is an *opportunity sample*, where you just use the people who are available. So you might sample the students at your college by asking everyone who happens to be in the coffee bar when you are looking for respondents. Samples like this are unlikely to be representative, and make it difficult to know how far the results are true of the whole population.

Quota samples are where you specify in advance the numbers of particular types of people. For example, you may decide that to have a sample that reflects the students in your college you want four males and five females who are studying psychology, six males and nine females who are studying biology, and so on. You then go out to find people who fit these specifications. Although this type of sampling is widely used in market research, it has the drawback that the respondents picked may not represent all the people who fit the specification.

Read SAQ 4.1 and decide what type of sampling was used in the study described.

How large should a sample be?
The desirable size of the sample depends on the variability of the population: the more variable it is, the larger the sample needs to be. Reaves (1992) gives a table showing the sample size needed for different sizes of population, assuming different levels of desired accuracy. An extract from her table is given in Table 4.1, which shows the sample size needed if you want to be 95% sure that the response frequency of the sample is within 5% of the population's response frequency. Notice that as a proportion of the population, the sample size decreases

---

SAQ 4.1 Example of sampling for surveys
Parker *et al.* (1992) carried out a survey on drivers' attitudes to driving violations. They interviewed drivers from four geographical areas chosen on the basis of population size, location in the north or south of England, and proximity to the motorway system. Respondents were from five age bands: 17–25, 26–35, 36–45, 46–55, and over 55. There were intended to be 400 men and 400 women, 160 respondents from each age group and 200 from each area. What type of sampling strategy had Parker *et al.* used?

TABLE 4.1. *Sample sizes needed for different population sizes*

Size of population	Size of sample
50	46
100	79
200	135
300	170
400	199
500	219
1000	279

From Reaves (1992)

rapidly: when the population grows from 100 to 1000, the sample size only grows from 79 to 279.

4.2.2 What will they be asked?

The questions you ask will obviously depend on the topic you are investigating. If you are finding out people's opinions or attitudes, you may use one of the standard ways of measuring them (see section 8.1). Alternatively, you may have to create your own questionnaire (see section 8.2).

Some surveys are intended to reveal information not about what people believe but about how they behave. Even if people try to give a truthful answer, they may be inaccurate, especially if you ask about socially undesirable activities such as smoking or drinking. One way of obtaining more accurate information is to ask them to keep a diary, but even then they may be tempted to 'fiddle' the data so that the records come closer to what is socially acceptable. If you want to know how people behave in a real situation, perhaps it is better not to ask them but to observe them. The observation method is described in section 4.3.

4.2.3 How will they be asked: interview or questionnaire?

Once you have identified the people you are going to ask and what you are going to ask them, you need to decide how: will you use a questionnaire or an interview? Questionnaires are easy to distribute and take you less time than carrying out a series of face-to-face interviews. On the other hand you will only get back a small fraction of the number you distribute, and are then left wondering whether the results of those who did reply are also true of those who did not. You also have no idea of how the respondents approached the task: they may have taken it as a joke, asked someone else to fill it in, or deliberately given misleading responses.

An interview allows you to confirm that the respondent understands what you are asking, and be on hand to make sure all questions are answered. But an interview is a time-consuming social situation, and the respondents' reactions will be influenced by the relationship they have with the person asking the questions. Because interviews take so much of the researcher's time, you can expect to interview a smaller number of people than could be given a written questionnaire, and it is more difficult to obtain a representative sample of respondents.

So questionnaires are suitable if you want to contact a large number of people, but only a minority are likely to respond. Interviews can be more informative, but reduce the number of people who will provide data. The aim and scope of your study and the resources available to you will have to guide you in deciding which format to use.

4.3 Observation

Box 4.2 describes how observation has been applied to the study of television advertisements. Observational studies let you record behaviour as it occurs, in typical behaviour situations, and can be used with participants who cannot tell you what they are doing, such as animals or young children. But it depends upon the observer being present at the right time and place, and remember that the contemporary attitude towards research ethics means that one must be wary about observing people who have not given their consent. One type of observational study which avoids both these problems uses a self-report technique: the participants observe themselves. Box 4.3 describes a study using the *experience sampling method* where people reported on their own experiences.

Observation may seem impartial, but there is usually so much activity that you have to decide what to observe and what to ignore. This can produce distortion and bias. You can see reports of journalists' observations every day in newspapers or on TV, but do these form an acceptable body of data for the scientist? Even 'fly-on-the-wall' TV programmes, in which people make a video recording of their behaviour over lengthy periods, are open to suspicion: how much material has been selected (and how much has been left out)? Anyone who has written up a report on an interview or edited a set of photographs knows how easy it is to slant the material by careful selection and deletion of the original content.

There are a number of issues underlying the use of the observational method. What is the aim of your observations? Who are you going to observe, where and when? Which behaviour are you going to observe? How are you going to record what you observe? How reliable are your observations: if someone else observes the same events, do their observations agree with yours? These issues are discussed in Chapter 9.

One problem with simple observation is that you might want to observe a particular situation and find that when you go out to make the observations the situation does not happen: you want to observe how people react to a beggar, and find there are no beggars! So you ensure the situation does occur by exerting some control: paying the beggar to be on his site, for example. You are then performing a field study.

Box 4.2 Example of an observational study using content analysis

Do advertisements reflect the changes in the role of women that have occurred over the last 20 years? Manstead and McCulloch (1981) coded the characteristics of the two most prominent adults in 170 advertisements on a number of dimensions, including: (1) mode of presentation – visual or auditory; (2) sex; (3) credibility basis – product user, authoritative source of information, neither; (4) role – dependent or autonomous; (5) location – home, occupational setting or other; (6) arguments presented in favour of products – scientific, non-scientific or none; (7) reward type – social approval or other; (8) product type – domestic, auto, sports, other.

Manstead and McCulloch report how many of the 177 male central figures and how many of the 92 female ones were associated with each level of the other dimensions. For example, with respect to mode of presentation, there were 58 men and 85 women shown visually. So of the 143 figures seen, 40.6% were men. But the voice-over figures, who were only heard, were men on 119 (94.4%) occasions: on only seven occasions were they women. Manstead and McCulloch concluded: 'Adult males and females appearing in the sample of British television commercials were portrayed in markedly different ways. Males were typically portrayed as having expertise and authority, as being object-ive and knowledgeable about reasons for buying particular products, as occupying roles which are autonomous, and as being concerned with the practical consequences of product purchase. Females, on the other hand, were typically shown as consumers of products, as being unknowledged about the reasons for buying particular products, as occupying roles defined primarily in relation to other persons, and as being concerned with the social consequences of product purchase' (p. 117).

4.4 Field studies

A field study avoids the artificiality of the laboratory experiment because it studies the behaviour of people in their natural environment, but is more controlled than simple observation, as the investigator brings about the situation to be studied. You might, for example, carry out a field study of helping behaviour by deliberately arranging for someone to ask bystanders for help in finding the toilets in a shopping centre. In a field study there is only one condition, and the investigator records how people react to it.

The field study has many of the benefits and the drawbacks of an observational study: it looks at 'real' behaviour, but how far can one generalize to people other than those who were actually observed? Would their reactions be repeated by people of different ages or sex, or who were from a different country? Are the

---

Box 4.3 A study using the experience sampling method

Clarke and Haworth (1994) investigated students' experience of 'flow', the feeling that 'accompanies performance in a situation where the challenges are matched by the person's skill' (p. 511), testing the prediction that 'flow' is the most enjoyable of nine alternative subject-ive states. They had 35 student volunteers, and used the experience sampling method, which they describe in these words: 'This method-ology involves subjects answering a short questionnaire when they receive a signal from a pre-programmed chiming watch' (p. 513). Clarke and Haworth note that the method 'does rely heavily on the ability of the subjects to accurately rate their feelings and describe the situation' (p. 513) but has the advantages that data can be collected in a real-life location, and it is less prone to problems of recall or distortion which arise when people are asked to recall events after they have happened.

The results indicated that the students spent almost half their time in a state where their skills were greater than those required by a situation providing low challenge, a state of boredom. The 'flow' condition was not the one that yielded the highest ratings of enjoyment; these were associated with a condition of 'control', where the person's skills were higher than those demanded by a moderate degree of challenge.

---

reactions of the participants affected by the feature that the researchers thought important? This last point can be made clearer if you use a field experiment, rather than just a field study.

4.5 Field experiments

In a field experiment, the researcher compares two or more conditions. Box 4.4 describes an example. The situation resembles a conventional experiment, but the groups of respondents are not formed by randomly allocating people to them. Since the study is conducted in the real world, ecological validity is increased, but there is less control of possible extraneous variables. Therefore you are on weaker ground when arguing that differences between the behaviour of the groups is caused by the variations in the independent variable.

4.6 Case studies

Case studies are similar to the single-case experiments described in Chapter 3, but do not involve giving and then withdrawing the 'treatment'. The researcher cannot control the independent variable but can only observe what has happened

Box 4.4 Example of a field experiment

Houston and Bull (1994) studied people's reactions to someone with a facial disfigurement. Four different types of facial appearance of one confederate person (an accomplice of the experimenter) were used, three involving disfigurements created by a make-up artist. The data consisted of how many people chose to sit in a railway carriage in the three seats to either side of the confederate. The results were that 'significantly fewer new persons chose to occupy seats near to the confederate when she had a port-wine stain' (p. 282). This was interpreted as indicating that 'facially disfigured people may not merely be imagining that they are avoided' (p. 283).

Note that this is an experiment, as the researchers manipulated the level of facial disfigurement (none, port-wine stain, scar, bruise). It is a field experiment as it was performed in the real-life setting of a commuter train.

Box 4.5 Example of a case study

During the 1960s there was a considerable amount of research into human memory, leading to the notion that there were two distinct memory systems: short-term memory (STM) and long-term memory (LTM). It was believed that information could enter long-term memory only by passing through short-term memory. So people could have a damaged long-term memory but an intact short-term memory. But if they had a damaged short-term memory, this would produce failures in long-term memory as well.

Shallice and Warrington (1970) describe a patient (KF) who had a very limited short-term memory. They report a number of experiments on KF. In one of these (experiment 2), three-letter words were read out at the rate of one per second, and KF was then asked to count upwards in ones, starting from one, as quickly as he could. After a certain time, which varied from 0 to 15 seconds, he was asked to recall the words that had been read out. There were 21 trials for each duration, the data from the first five trials being discarded. The average percentage correctly recalled was just over 50% with no counting interval, and then declined slightly, remaining level for the 5-, 10- and 15-second delays. This and other tests led to the conclusion that KF's short-term memory capacity was greatly reduced.

Further work had shown that KF had a normal long-term memory, leading Shallice and Warrington to argue that the results 'indicate that the frequently used flow diagrams in which information must enter STM before reaching LTM, may be inappropriate' (p. 270). So this case study of a brain-damaged patient suggested that the models of memory current at that time were inadequate.

after it has occurred. This creates problems because there is no control over extraneous variables, and there must be doubts about whether the results can be generalized to other people.

Case studies may be of a single individual, a set of individuals or a larger unit such as a school class, a company, a neighbourhood. They are particularly common in the field of neuropsychology, where individual patients suffering from brain damage or from psychological disability are investigated.

Box 4.5 summarizes a case study of an individual with a particular memory deficit which illustrates a point made by Neale and Liebert (1986): case studies can be valuable for disconfirming the implication of a theory. They are of little value for confirming a theory, however, since there are so many uncontrolled factors; the person may for example be faking, deliberately telling the researchers what they want to hear.

Robson (1993) observes that a case study may employ various methods of investigation, including questionnaires, interviews, observation, role playing, and documentary analysis. The investigator needs a clear understanding of the aim and a lack of bias: none of the approaches described in this chapter or anywhere in this book should be used to substantiate a preconceived position.

4.7 Concluding comments on quantitative approaches

Psychology is in a state of change, even 'crisis' (Parker, 1989). For some half-century the experiment was seen as the preferred form of investigation. Only gradually did mainstream academic psychology acknowledge its limitations, although in some areas of the discipline there were always thriving schools which never adopted the experiment with the ardour of those interested in what is now termed 'cognition' or 'cognitive science'. The historical position of the experiment in psychology means that it occupies a large proportion of the space in any discussion of methods in the discipline. But there have always been researchers using the other quantitative methods described in this chapter, and acquiring a familiarity with them has properly been part of any student's training. The trained psychologist should be able to make an informed decision about which of the methods of investigation is most appropriate for studying any of the topics that comes within the discipline. SAQ 4.2 invites you to consider how you could use different methods to investigate a real-life problem. Typically, when faced with real-life problems such as that featured in SAQ 4.2, the laboratory experiment is often not relevant, which is why you may need to turn to quasi-experiments or the other methods described here.

Underlying the methods described in this chapter is the assumption that the psychologist needs to measure the phenomena under investigation. But there is a growing school of thought which argues that this assumption is misplaced: in measuring something it has to be simplified, even distorted, to such an extent that the measurements you get are meaningless, with no sensible connection with what you were interested in. This school of thought, which is present in

---

SAQ 4.2

Every year a number of accidents involve drivers of lorries or buses trying to get under a bridge which is too low for their vehicle to pass. How would you investigate the psychology of this type of accident?

---

other social sciences as well as psychology, believes that knowledge and understanding will come through the use of the qualitative research methods, described in the next chapter.

Qualitative approaches

5.0 Introduction

Qualitative approaches in psychology offer insights into action and experience that can enrich our understanding of findings obtained through traditional research, as well as producing new material that experimental methods miss. Qualitative research is 'the interpretative study of a specified issue or problem in which the researcher is central to the sense that is made' (Banister *et al.*, 1994, p. 2). The best way to approach qualitative research in psychology is through a little history. In the late 1960s and early 1970s, psychology was hit by a 'paradigm crisis', in which the conventional, experimental way of looking at human behaviour (what was called the 'old paradigm') was challenged, and a new set of methods came to the fore. These new methods were at the time called the 'new paradigm', though in fact they were methods that had been around for many years in humanistic psychology and in neighbouring disciplines such as anthropology and sociology. Against experimental approaches, which new-paradigm writers saw as treating people as if they were objects, the rallying cry of the new, qualitative research movement was 'for scientific purposes treat people as if they were human beings' (Harré and Secord, 1972, p. 84). Many of the new-paradigm writers were not at all hostile to science, and saw the new paradigm as a better way to carry out investigations.

It is worth noting here that to use one of the range of qualitative methods for your investigation is not to take the easy option. Qualitative approaches can often be more time-consuming and confusing than running a simple experiment and checking a correlation. Qualitative research in a discipline like psychology needs to be as rigorous as quantitative study, and when we gather accounts, look at the role of language, and reflect on our own position in the research process, we need to bear in mind that this will need to be assessed by clear 'scientific' criteria. In this chapter, we will describe some of the assumptions that underpinned new-paradigm qualitative research, some examples from this ethnographic tradition, some changes in these assumptions since the 1970s, and recent reflexive arguments.

Qualitative research also highlights the importance of ethical considerations in psychological investigative work. When qualitative researchers focus on the personal meanings that run through or underlie an account, they are faced with a number of issues that need to be taken seriously. Informants in interviews, for example, may be revealing material that is emotionally charged, and the researcher has to be prepared for this. The particular danger here is that the research interview may then turn into something approaching a counselling interview. The researcher then needs to be able to keep the boundaries of the interview clear, but should, at the same time, respect the interviewee's need for support as a result of the situation the researcher has been responsible for. These issues are considered in feminist research (e.g. Finch, 1984), but we need to learn lessons from those reflections for all varieties of qualitative enquiry. We will return to the issue of ethics at the end of this chapter, and pick up the way in which a reflection upon the moral position of the researcher is important to all varieties of psychological investigation as we describe qualitative and quantitative methods through the rest of the book.

The different methodological procedures that can be used within a qualitative framework are described in Chapter 8, and interpretation of the data is discussed in Chapter 12. First, what might it mean to treat people as if they were human beings?

5.1 Actions and accounts

It will be helpful here to describe a distinction Harré and Secord (1972) made between 'movements', 'actions' and 'acts'. It would be possible to describe the way my arm was raised holding a piece of paper towards a class noticeboard as a collection of movements. Thus far, we have made little interpretation of the movement (though we have, of course, already used the words 'arm' and 'paper', which indicate that the observer has some prior understanding of what is going on). A strict behavioural experimental or observational study will restrict its description to a sequence of movements. If we imagine that we are observing these human movements as an ethologist would observe animal behaviour, we would want to go a little further, and say that I was pinning the paper on the noticeboard. To talk about it in these terms, as an action, is to attribute some intention to the activity (and then we could compare it with similar actions and ask when and why they might happen). This is the level of description that is adopted in most cognitive psychology experiments, where you talk about people reading random letter sequences, for example, or learning certain tasks.

There is a third level of description, however. Pinning a piece of paper on the board might simply be a compulsive activity that I have learnt, but it is more likely that it means something, is a social 'act' of some kind. In this case it could be the act of announcing examination results. This is where, if we do not already know the rules in this social world, we have to ask what the action means. To do that, we have to speak to people, and the parameters for the research will then necessarily be less certain than they would be for a controlled experimental or observational study. Part of the research process, which should be discussed in the report and which we describe in Chapter 14, will be a negotiation with the 'subjects' about their participation in the study and the sense they make of it.

Much of human psychology is displayed in talk, and the new paradigm was characterized by an attention to language, in particular to the different ways in which people accounted for what they did. The most radical of the paradigm 'crisis' writers wanted to understand how psychology dehumanized people (e.g. Armistead, 1974), but it quickly became clear to most new-paradigm researchers that the best way to rehumanize human psychology in the discipline was to treat what people said seriously. In one of the most important manifestos for the new paradigm, by Harré and Secord (1972), it was argued that the best way to get at real human psychology was to look at real talk. Most of what we do is, after all, conducted in one way or another through language, and it would be difficult to imagine a human activity that was not embedded in shared social meanings, if not in spoken language. Speech, writing and even nonverbal communication are all structured through shared social rules. We understand other people through employing those rules, and new-paradigm writers argued that we needed to focus on those rules to understand what psychology was like in this culture and in subcultures, in what were called 'social worlds'.

To say that human conduct is rule-governed is not to say that we deliberately and consciously follow a rule for every discrete piece of activity. The rules are

---

Box 5.1 The metaphor of 'life as drama'

The 'paradigm revolution' in social psychology introduced many psychologists to the work of social psychologists operating in the neighbouring discipline of sociology. In sociology this variety of social psychology, which focuses on individuals' interactions with one another, is called 'micro-sociology', and a key player has been the writer Erving Goffman. A powerful study by Goffman (1961) on life in an asylum illustrates how systematic work can be carried out on a single case within a qualitative framework. It also demonstrates how important metaphor is in science to illuminate our understanding of things we normally take for granted. The asylum Goffman described was an example of a 'total institution', in which the person's identity is stripped away and a new 'self' has to be created as a survival strategy in a hostile environment. Goffman employed a 'dramaturgical' metaphor in which people are seen as if they are actors playing to an audience, and as they work their way through the different scenes that make up their time in an institution or group of any kind, they are constructing 'moral careers'. Goffman defines a moral career as 'any social strand of any person's course through life' (p. 119).

Goffman was also part of the social world he studied, and so the book *Asylums* is also an example of participant observation. Only by participating, he argues, is it possible to understand how 'any group of persons – prisoners, primitives, pilots, or patients – develop a life of their own that becomes meaningful, reasonable, and normal once you get close to it' (Goffman, 1961, p. 7). Goffman was able to show how patients in an asylum survive by playing to the psychiatrists 'as if' they were mentally ill, and then turn back from that stage to their own 'backstage' life with their fellows to act out another reasonable life

— *Continued* — — — — — — — — — — — — — — — — — —

mainly tacit, that is, we do not routinely reflect upon them. The task of the researcher is to make the rules explicit, to describe clearly what rules are being followed. One person's account may be illuminating here, and we may want to explore, through an ethnographic or semi-structured interview, what sense an individual made of different actions and the way they were understood as acts of a particular type. Many of the new-paradigm writers, however, were concerned with gathering sets of accounts from a defined social world and building a picture of what was going on, as if they were collecting the bits of a jigsaw and piecing them together.

Because they were observing behaviour like animal ethologists, but asking for the particular sense that people gave to their behaviour, some of the new-paradigm writers used the term 'ethogenics' to describe their approach (Harré and Secord, 1972). Harré (1979) argued that when we follow social rules, we always play out certain roles. Ethogenics adopted a 'role-rule' model of the human being, and, it was claimed, provided a psychological theory to back up the work of the micro-sociologist Erving Goffman (1959). From Goffman, ethogenic

— *Continued* — — — — — — — — — — — — — — — — — — —

with a moral career structured by different rules. The power of the total institution is such that the inmate's moral career as 'patient' is the one that is legitimized by the hospital authorities, but the paradox is that what appears to be irrational 'mad' behaviour is scripted within the context of the only stage the doctors will allow.

There is also a lesson here for a researcher carrying out psychological investigations, for the people who have agreed to take part in your study are never as stupid or compliant as you think. This is not to say that quantitative methods necessarily lead psychologists to dehumanize people, but there is a tendency for the neutral observation and measurement of human experience to work in this way. There are psychologists who use quantitative approaches to challenge this tendency, and for empowerment, but they then, of course, have to turn around and look at what psychology itself is doing. This is where qualitative research makes an important contribution, for the debates over alternative, qualitative methods in psychology have directed our attention inwards, at the discipline, and have prompted psychologists to understand how the discipline works and where it comes from. This is a vital part of critical reflexive work.

In a laboratory experiment the subjects carefully study the situation and guess how to fulfil or sabotage what they think is the hypothesis, and in an interview study your interviewees will always have their own agenda. You present yourself to them as a competent researcher, and they present themselves to you as particular characters, characters with stories to delight or shock you. It is well to remember Goffman's metaphor of life as drama if you are ever tempted to think you are finding out what someone really thinks.

SAQ 5.1

If the 'new-paradigm' approaches in psychology wanted to be scientific like the other natural sciences, why was it not sufficient to call their approach 'ethology'?

---

new-paradigm research took the idea that the everyday world is like a stage, and that one can see people as though they are playing theatrical parts to impress real and imaginary audiences. Box 5.1 gives an account of life as drama. When I pin up a paper to award degree results, for example, I perform that action for an audience; to do it without anyone watching or otherwise knowing would be pointless and a bit bizarre. SAQ 5.1 invites you to consider why the term 'ethogenics' is appropriate for this approach.

5.2 Roles, rules and ethnographic study

The task of a psychologist carrying out qualitative research can be thought of as being much the same as that of an anthropologist. Instead of travelling to distant lands and trying to understand the different kinds of rituals and beliefs that 'other' people use, however, psychologists will be turning aspects of their own culture into something strange. Psychology focuses upon problems. Most research in psychology involves an attempt to understand something that does not seem quite right, to make sense of an issue that is causing distress or unhappiness of some kind. Sometimes that attempt to understand involves 'problematizing', making strange something that appears too self-evident, too coherent. Then we have to break down the phenomenon into its component parts to see what they do and where they come from. Traditional psychology often directs its attention outward, and onto individuals who are not, generally speaking, seen as psychologists. Sometimes it seems as if quantitative methods facilitate this way of conceptualizing individuals and their problems.

When Harré and Secord (1972) outlined their manifesto for a 'new paradigm' in social psychology, they struck a chord with many people who had been concerned about the consequences of psychologists trying to be 'neutral' all the time and failing to reflect upon the images of the human being that were emerging from psychology journals and textbooks (Shotter, 1975). Ethogenics, which was designed to be a scientific approach which would focus upon the sense that people made of their lives, and ask them openly about their accounts for what they did, was also intended, then, to be what Shotter (1975) called a 'moral science of action'.

One of the classic examples of ethogenic research was a study by Marsh *et al.* (1974) of the rules and roles that held together the social world of fans at Oxford United Football Club. This is described in Box 5.2. We can take this example to illustrate how the qualitative researcher moves from an external, observing position to an internal, participating one. After some initial observation and hypotheses about the nature of the social world, it is necessary to ask people what they mean

---

Box 5.2 Discovering the order of things

Marsh *et al.* (1974) started by videoing the 'home end' of the terraces, the part of the ground they wanted to focus on, and noticed that the same clusters of people seemed to appear on most Saturday afternoons. These clusters of people also seemed to stand in roughly the same parts of the terrace. Some of these fans wore the club regalia, while some, at the front and at the sides, did not. These first observations helped the researchers to frame some questions for interviews with the fans. The interviews were where the 'accounts' from this social world were gathered, and the researchers entered this world in much the same way as anthropologists doing an ethnographic study of another culture. Questions about the clustering of people on the terraces led to a systematic picture of the relationships on the terrace. The group at the front, for example, were younger 'novices' who spent much of the time looking, not at the game, but back at the older supporters. As years went by, some of these novices would appear with full club colours and scarves as fully fledged fans. Older men at the side were either 'hard' 'town boys' who had been core fans once upon a time but now looked with disdain on that group, or 'part-timers' who were viewed as not having a full commitment to the club.

Two aspects of the fan's world were highlighted by the stories they told of the rules about where they were allowed to stand, and who was allowed to lead the chants. The first concerned the 'moral careers' that structured this social world. One career involved moving from 'novice' to being a fan, and then graduating to the older 'town boy' position. The second aspect concerned the ritualized aggression. This appeared, at first sight, to be mindless and chaotic, but could be 'accounted' for as a series of displays to different audiences, mainly by a subgroup of 'hooligans' to the larger fan group. Together, these two aspects threw new light on the world of the fans. The trouble that did occur could not be solved by simply removing individual trouble-makers, for the issue was a structural one, and this structured world gave meaning to violence. As the title of Marsh *et al.*'s book makes clear, the task was to uncover 'the rules of disorder'.

---

by what they do, and to build up the picture for the report in a rigorous scientific manner. When you have read Box 5.2, try SAQ 5.2.

You should note that the researchers studying the rules of disorder among the football fans described in Box 5.2 are not collecting a sample of football terraces, and so they will be very cautious about extrapolating from Oxford United to other clubs. This is an intensive 'case study'. While it is not peculiar to qualitative research to focus on a single case, it is more likely to operate in this way. It is perfectly permissible, as long as no grand claims are made, on the basis of one case, for all others. We will look again at exactly what claims might be made in Chapter 14.

SAQ 5.2

If we were using the 'dramaturgical' metaphor to understand a situation, would we focus on 'movements', 'actions', or 'acts'?

5.3 Discourse analysis

The ethogenic study of rules and roles could be treated as the 'first wave' of the new-paradigm revolution and of the emergence of qualitative methods in psychology. If this first wave from the 1970s involved a turn to language, then the second wave, from the mid-1980s, involved a turn to discourse, and the way discourses produce contrasting images of the world. While the first wave looked at how a set of accounts held together one social world (such as that of the fans on the football terrace), the second wave looked at how different discourses pulled that social world in different directions.

There are two criticisms that can be made here about the ethogenic studies from a discourse analytic point of view. First, as Potter *et al.* (1984) pointed out in one of the precursors of discourse analysis in psychology, Marsh *et al.*'s (1974) version of what was going on in the social world of the fans was only one more account. The study only ever claimed to be presenting a provisional picture of the rules and roles at work, but it did not see its own story as one among many stories that could be told. Second, the ethogenic studies were looking for some underlying consistent reality, or structure, to explain how the accounts were held together. Perhaps this search for one coherent picture was a mistake, and psychology itself is inconsistent.

The discourse analytic criticisms of ethogenics can also be turned against much traditional psychology, and the ways in which researchers assume that their account both explains away other people's accounts and forms the only coherent account that could be given. Gilbert and Mulkay (1984) illustrated this point with examples of scientists' talk. They distinguished between two different 'interpretative repertoires' that scientists use to explain how they arrive at theories. On some occasions the 'empiricist' repertoire is used, in which there is an appeal to data that should be clear to any neutral observer, and on other occasions the 'contingent' repertoire is used, to talk about hunches, intuitions and speculations. The point here is not to catch people out, but to focus on the variability of language, the ways in which talk was constructed out of available repertoires, and the functions that were served by using different repertoires at different times. The term 'interpretative repertoires', which was taken up by Potter and Wetherell (1987) in their introduction to discourse analysis, was later replaced by some writers with the term 'discourses' (Parker, 1992), and here we will use these terms interchangeably. SAQ 5.3 gives you the chance to check your understanding of the distinction between contingent and empiricist repertoires.

SAQ 5.3

Briefly describe what you expect to happen in the next psychological study you plan to carry out. First write what you expect by referring only to previous scientific evidence and the objective procedures you will follow to test hypotheses. Then write a short paragraph which focuses on the hunches you have about the results and what you really hope will happen. Compare the two accounts. Which of the two would you expect to draw upon a 'contingent' interpretative repertoire, and which would draw upon an 'empiricist' interpretative repertoire?

The first basic rule of discourse analysis, then, is to look for contradiction in accounts. Rather than bring different themes together, a discourse analyst will be drawing apart the contrasting ways of talking about a topic, exploring ways in which those manners of speaking are constructed, and explaining how this variation between discourses makes one account seem more powerful than another. Discourse analysis can also be used to 'read' any text, including the texts of psychology itself. Squire (1990), for example, described how social psychology textbooks are structured around three different narratives: the detective narrative (in which researchers solve a puzzle by picking up the relevant evidence), the autobiographical narrative (in which researchers describe how events in their own lives led them to a particular theory), and the science fiction narrative (in which researchers permit themselves to speculate about different future forms of psychology). It should be said, *apropos* scientists' empiricist and contingent repertoires, that Potter and Wetherell's (1987) own stages in the analysis of discourse and Parker's (1992) analytic steps often appeal to intuition, as can be seen in Box 5.3.

5.4 Reflexive analysis

The role of 'intuition' in research raises a number of problems for traditional experimental psychologists who would argue that an objective account should proceed according to scientific rules of enquiry and that the researcher should be neutral with regard to the validation or falsification of results. Potter and Wetherell (1987) would respond by saying that it is arguable whether this objective rule-following is always apparent in science. Researchers in psychology using 'grounded theory', a sociological approach which involves the exhaustive coding of data until a 'theory' emerges, would say that it is a mistake to start with a theory and then try to test it (Henwood and Pidgeon, 1992). Instead, the activity of the researcher is central, and, as we said at the beginning of this chapter, qualitative approaches are characterized by the importance accorded to the role of the researcher. Qualitative research does not pretend that the researcher has no prior assumptions or stake in the research process. Rather, it takes seriously a

Box 5.3 Getting your teeth into discourse analysis

An example of discourse analysis is contained in the introductory qualitative methods text by Banister *et al.* (1994). It illustrates how even the most innocent piece of text can contain particular theories of what people must be like to be seen as normal and sensible in this culture. The text was the set of instructions from a toothpaste tube, which went as follows: 'Choose a children's brush that has a small head and add a pea-sized amount of Punch and Judy toothpaste. To teach your child to clean teeth, stand behind and place your hand under the child's chin to tilt head back and see mouth. Brush both sides of teeth as well as tops. Brush after breakfast and last thing at night. Supervise the brushing of your child's teeth until the age of eight. If your child is taking fluoride treatment, seek professional advice concerning daily intake. Contains 0.8% Sodium Monofluorophosphate.' The discourse analysis encompasses a series of methodological steps which starts with the identification of objects referred to in the text and arrives at discrete patterns of meaning that hold the text together (Parker, 1992).

Four discourses were identified: (1) 'rationalist' – in which the ability to follow procedures ('directions for use') requires choices of implement and judgement of amount ('small head' and 'pea-sized amount') and is predicated on recognition of appropriate authority in health care (following 'directions' and seeking 'professional advice'); (2) 'familial' – in which ownership ('your child') runs alongside supervision and continuous care (the assumption that the child is

— *Continued* —

point made by Harré (1979): the moral position of the researcher should not be concealed but made explicit. It is then easier for a reader to assess how that position may have influenced the data.

Reflecting on the 'position' of the researcher has also been one of the key concerns of feminists in psychology. This is partly due to the feminist movement's general concern with power imbalances, and partly because women have been a large majority of the students while men have been predominant in teaching and research. A psychologist does enjoy some measure of power in the formulation of research questions, and in an observational study, experiment, questionnaire or structured interview, the 'participant' has no power to challenge the assumptions that frame the study. There may also be issues that affect researchers themselves, and make the research particularly challenging or difficult. To look back upon these aspects of research as they touch the individual or the form of method chosen is to engage in what Wilkinson (1988) calls respectively 'personal' and 'functional' reflexivity. The feminist interest in

— *Continued* — — — — — — — — — — — — — — — — — — —

present each breakfast and 'last thing at night') and is framed
by the image of bad parenting (the figure of 'Punch and Judy');
(3) 'developmental–educational' – in which the teaching of the child
(parental activity) precedes supervision (the child's still tutored but
self-governed activity) and then reaches an identifiable stage as a
developmental milestone (the 'age of eight'); and (4) 'medical' – in
which the process of using the toothpaste is necessarily linked to
hygiene (brushing after meals), professional supervision ('fluoride
treatment') and the specification of ingestion and chemical
composition of substances ('daily intake', '0.8% Sodium
Monofluorophosphate').

The analysis, which already involves some reflection on the way the
perceptions of the reader play a part in bringing out some discourses
and neglecting others, has been taken further in an additional analysis,
which draws on psychoanalytic theory (Parker, 1995). Here the
Freudian notions of the Oedipus complex, the reality principle,
infantile helplessness and confusion, and resistance were used to
amplify the reading of the toothpaste text. Psychoanalysis has always
been a controversial theory in traditional quantitative psychology
because it allegedly cannot be tested, but it has recently become of
interest to researchers working with the interpretation of texts, particularly with some feminists who want to emphasize the role of reflexivity
in psychology (e.g. Hollway, 1989). Whether psychoanalytic theory is
a useful addition to qualitative approaches remains to be seen. Many
traditional psychologists are suspicious even of less speculative studies
in this new approach.

reflexivity has been particularly important because it has drawn attention to the
ways in which psychological investigation is always from a certain standpoint.
When women carry out research, they cannot forget their own experience and
pretend that it is not relevant.

Wilkinson (1988) described a third form of reflexivity: 'disciplinary' reflexivity
refers to the way in which we focus upon how the discipline of psychology offers
or blocks opportunities for different groups (and one of the ways of conceptualizing
this issue is described in Box 5.4). It has been argued, for example, that
experimental research which is concerned only with 'hard' facts supports a male
way of understanding the world, and that women are often alienated by the way
in which the discipline is organized (Burman, 1990). A consideration of these
issues brings us onto the ground of politics, and it may well seem, in retrospect,
that the paradigm crisis that opened this Pandora's box of different approaches to
language, discourse and reflexivity, was in part a political matter from the start
(Parker, 1989).

Box 5.4 Reflecting upon the discipline of psychology

It is interesting to take the document called 'The Future of the Psychological Sciences' produced in 1988 by The British Psychological Society and reflect on some of the ways it represents the task of psychologists. This document, which was produced by a committee of the Scientific Affairs Board of the BPS, and which gathered evidence from individuals and from a conference in Harrogate, which brought together psychologists from different areas, provides a rare case of sustained reflection by the discipline on itself. One of the striking things about the document is the way it reproduces an image of the discipline as a kind of gigantic individual, governed by the same sorts of anxieties and internal structures that we imagine to lie inside people's heads. Parker (1994) drew attention to three oppositions at work in the discourse of the document.

(1) *Rational functioning versus irresponsible action.* The document starts by noting that at every meeting of the Scientific Affairs Board there has, as they put it, 'been a discussion of some new threat to the psychological sciences' (p. 2). The Scientific Affairs Board characterizes itself as the rational core of the BPS charged with the function of assessing how serious these threats are, and looking to ways of countering them. The model of the BPS as guided by a rational mechanism is then augmented by an account of where the threats may come from. The document then goes on to say that the threats may not only come from outside, but that 'the psychological community could be its own worst enemy' (p. 3), and a particular problem is identified, which is that 'energies directed at conflict should be diverted to constructive endeavour' (p. 3).

— *Continued* — — — — — — — — — — — — — — — — — —

5.5 Conclusion

The theoretical background to the development of qualitative approaches is important, but we are more concerned in this book with the practicalities of the investigative process. At this point we can take stock of the debates since the late 1960s and summarize them as drawing attention to the role of language, the ways in which accounts can be studied to construct a picture of the world, the way different discourses paint different pictures, and to the importance of reflexivity in the account that researchers give of their work. We will discuss the ways in which these aspects of qualitative research should be included in the design and reporting of practicals and other projects later.

— — Continued —

(2) *Internal versus external activity.* One of the declared aims of the document is to bring about a situation where there might be constructive debate between different areas of psychology, but the way it does this is to separate what might go on inside the discipline from what happens when a psychologist moves outside. On the one hand, there is a concern to establish 'mechanisms which ensure mutual communication ... and opportunities for synthesis' (p. 7). On the other hand there is a worry that psychologists might treat discussions with those outside in the same way as they would with professional colleagues. The committee notes that some participants at the Harrogate conference 'insisted that psychologists had better learn to give unequivocal answers' (p. 24). The document then goes on to say that 'We believe that this is overly simple'. The clear implication is that perhaps a certain equivocation when dealing with outsiders is necessary.

(3) *Development versus immediacy.* The document is not only looking to the future, but also situating the discipline, again as if it were a person, on a developmental route from a state of infancy to adulthood. 'If psychology has come of age, there is surely no reason why it should not follow the good example of others?' (p. 80). It is, however, haunted by the possibility that perhaps it has not come of age, and we return to the worry about 'premature' demands that may be fuelled by unruly energies that should be channelled towards more reasonable goals. The committee points out that 'At present, the psychological sciences are in many ways fragmented' (p. 12), and part of the rationale for the document is to identify 'growth points for the future of the psychological sciences in Britain' (p. 1). There is, then, a third opposition, between developmental stages and premature demands for immediate gratification, and this is then mapped, in turn, onto another, wider, cultural, opposition, between the realms of emotion and creativity on the one hand, and rationality and the development of knowledge on the other.

Parker's (1994) analysis also notes the way in which psychoanalytic notions inform these three oppositions. The point to be emphasized here is that it is possible to direct our attention inwards, and to look at the assumptions that we make as a psychological community. This is one of the contributions of qualitative research when it takes the moral/ political role of scientific investigation seriously.

Chapter 6

Psychological techniques: measuring performance

6.0 General introduction to techniques

Faced with the huge number of studies described in the textbooks and journals, there may seem an overwhelming number of techniques that psychologists use to obtain data. Table 6.1 illustrates one way in which the techniques can be grouped. It distinguishes five major types of technique. Physiological measures are typically used to assess conditions such as arousal. Performance measures refer to those instances where you give participants a particular task and see how they perform. In many studies, researchers construct their own task to give to the participants and performance is usually assessed by measuring how long the task takes or how accurately it is done. In some areas of psychology there are well-established procedures for obtaining particular kinds of data: the psychophysical methods are an example. When these procedures are used, the particular stimuli vary from one investigation to another, but the way they are presented is consistent. In other cases the actual stimuli or items are also kept constant, and this is particularly true when you use standardized psychometric tests, described in Chapter 7.

The third major grouping is self-report measures, where the participants answer questions about themselves. There are various ways of asking people questions, and in Table 6.1 we have distinguished between attitude scales, which are 'single-issue' instruments, questionnaires, interviews, which involve face-to-face questioning, and a number of other, specialized procedures, such as the repertory grid technique and Q-sort. This group is described in Chapter 8.

The fourth grouping, covered in Chapter 9, includes those situations where one observes and records people's real-life behaviour. We distinguish between selecting a particular behaviour for investigation and standard techniques for recording social interaction. In the former, it is useful to distinguish between different types of data. You may count how many people do something or how often they do it and therefore have 'objective' data. Qualitative approaches that draw on 'grounded theory' techniques to 'saturate' all observed categories often have this objective flavour (Strauss and Corbin, 1990; Henwood and Pidgeon, 1992). Alternatively, you may have a more subjective form of data, such as estimates of the frequency or magnitude of some behaviour.

TABLE 6.1. *The main techniques used by psychologists for obtaining data*

Category	Examples	Type of data
Physiological measures		
	Galvanic skin response	Amplitude; frequency
	Eye movements	Fixation duration; frequency
Performance measures		
Time		Milliseconds
Accuracy		Number of errors; number correct
Perceptual/sensory accuracy	Psychophysical methods	Estimates of 'greater' or 'lesser'; jnd; PSE
	Signal detection	'Hits' and 'misses'; d'
Standardized tests	Intelligence test	Percentiles; standard scores; IQ
Self-report measures		
Attitude scales	Attitude to women scale	High or low score
Questionnaires		
specific	Assessing drug use	Qualitative and/or quantitative data
standardized	Personality inventory	Scores on extroversion
Interviews		
structured		
semi-structured		
ethnographic		
Repertory grids		
Q-sort		
Diaries		
Verbal protocols		
'Natural behaviour' measures		
Specific		
structured	People obeying a road sign	Number counted
	Aggressiveness	Ratings
unstructured		Verbal descriptions
Standard procedures	Interaction process analysis	
Participant observation		
Action research		
Text analysis measures		
Discourse analysis		
Focus group discussions		
Semi-structured interviews		
Ethnographic interviews		

The final group contains the textual analysis techniques such as discourse analysis, which was described in Chapter 5, which have recently been applied in psychology. These take as their subject matter the language which people use, and this can be obtained from existing written or spoken text, or from situations deliberately intended to produce appropriate utterances. Approaches within the discourse analytic, qualitative tradition make a virtue of subjectivity (Hollway, 1989; Walkerdine, 1991).

The different areas of psychology vary in the extent to which they tend to use the different measures. Cognitive psychology relies heavily on specific tasks to measure performance, while social psychology makes more use of self-reports and observation. But all areas use all the measures some of the time, so do not fall into the trap of thinking that the different types of measure reflect different topics within the discipline.

Faced with Table 6.1, you may wonder which technique and which measure you should choose as the dependent variable for your investigation. There are no simple rules; you have to select ones which are relevant to the topic you are investigating, which is likely to answer the questions you are asking, and in most approaches this means that it must be reliable and valid. Reliability here means that the dependent variable, the measuring instrument you are using, gives the same readings when it is used by different researchers (inter-observer agreement), or when one researcher uses it on different occasions (observer consistency). The concept has been especially prominent in the development of psychometric tests (Chapter 7), but bear it in mind whatever form of measure you are using.

Validity is whether the dependent variable is truly an index of the underlying psychological attribute (attention, motivation, memory, social skill, etc.) that you are assessing. It is not easy to know whether your dependent variable is valid, and you may have to rely on 'face validity' – does it seem reasonable to assume that your dependent variable is valid?

Another aspect to bear in mind is the sensitivity of the dependent variable. For most purposes, it is no use giving people a task that they can all do without mistakes in the time allowed or a task that none of them can do. In either case you end up with a set of scores that shows no difference between the participants, and so are unable to relate performance differences to anything else. If everyone is doing the task perfectly, you have a ceiling effect, and if everyone is scoring zero it is a floor effect: both are likely to make your study useless. In most research you want to compare people's performance under different conditions, and this means that the scores must be able to reflect variation in performance. Ideally, you hope to use a performance measure where most of the respondents score about 50%; any effect of the independent variable then has the greatest chance of being revealed.

6.1 Physiological measures

Measurements of physiological processes are used not only in the subdiscipline of physiological psychology, but also more widely to measure such features as people's level of arousal. The main techniques for this are the measurement of the galvanic skin response (the electrical conductance of the skin, which varies with minute changes in the amount of moisture on the body surface), heart rate, eye pupil dilation and electrical activity in the brain. All these require special recording apparatus, which is rarely available to the student beginning psychology. Consequently these measures will not be considered here; accounts of their use can be found in textbooks such as Carlson (1994) and Kalat (1992).

Eye movements in reading have been the subject of considerable research over the last 20 years, but again it is unlikely that you will have access to the equipment needed, even though this has become far simpler than used to be the case. The work is surveyed by Rayner and Pollatsek (1989).

6.2 Performance measures

Investigators frequently create their own tasks for measuring someone's performance, using their own procedure to create an operational definition of the construct they are investigating. For example, Box 2.1 describes an experiment on memory for faces in which Morris *et al.* created their own tests of memory for comparing the groups of participants.

There are two major ways to measure people's performance: either you can measure how long they take to do a task, or you can measure their accuracy (which is often expressed as how many errors they make). It is, of course, possible to do both, but this poses a problem if the two sets of results show dissimilar trends. People may respond faster but make more errors, or they may make few errors but take longer to do the task. This is referred to as the speed/accuracy trade-off. Suppose you have two groups of participants, and group A responds faster than group B but also makes more errors. You then have to decide which is the better level of performance – responding quickly or making few errors. One way to avoid this dilemma is to ask people to respond as fast as they can while keeping errors to a minimum. You use the time taken as the index of performance, and any participants who make more than a certain number of errors which has been specified beforehand are excluded and their data ignored. Or you can adopt the converse procedure, and ask participants to be as accurate as possible but to respond within a certain time; any who fail to meet the deadline are then excluded. The third possibility is to construct a task which reflects both the time taken and the accuracy of the response: look at SAQ 6.1.

6.2.1 Response time

If you have the facilities, you can measure the time people take to make a single response, such as deciding the colour of a word (see Box 6.1). When it is not feasible to measure individual reactions, you can present a series of items or tasks, and record the time taken to complete the whole set (see Box 6.1). Measuring response times can readily be done using a computer to present the stimuli and

---

SAQ 6.1. Speed or accuracy when measuring reading?
The problem of measuring time or accuracy has been particularly severe for researchers investigating reading performance. If you measure only how long people take to read a passage, there is no guarantee that they have understood it. So measuring reading speed alone has dubious validity. If you want to measure how well people have understood a passage they have read, you can give some test of comprehension and obtain an accuracy score. But you need to control the amount of time the participants have for reading the text: if they have unlimited time, they might not just read the passage but try to learn it off by heart! Scores on the comprehension test would not then be a valid indication of reading performance. So if you are measuring reading, you need to have some way of dealing with variation in both reading speed and comprehension level. What suggestions can you make about how this could be achieved?

---

record the response, especially if you have access to an experiment generator, described in Chapter 13.

Simple reaction time (RT)
Simple RT is measured when the participant is presented with a stimulus and has to respond to it as rapidly as possible. RT is the time between the stimulus being presented and the respondent completing a response which stops the clock. It includes the time for the sense organ to accept and respond to the stimulus, the time for the impulses to be conducted to and from the brain, the time to move the muscles and, most importantly, the time taken in the brain to decide to make the response.

The only uncertainty in a simple RT task is when the stimulus will occur. Typical RTs are about 250 milliseconds, but simple RT is influenced by features of the stimulus (such as its modality and intensity), and features of the participant. These include peripheral factors, such as the condition of the sense organ, central factors, such as arousal level, and global characteristics, such as age.

Disjunctive and choice reaction time
This is when the participant is faced with a number of alternative stimuli and/or a number of alternative responses, and has to decide not only when to make a response but also which response to make. You might, for example, present a string of letters and ask the respondent to press one key when they form a word and a different key when they do not. (This is known as the lexical decision task.)

Donders initiated the use of reaction times to reveal underlying components of cognitive processing in the mid-nineteenth century. He distinguished between simple RT, disjunctive RT and choice RT. Disjunctive RT is when two stimuli are presented, but the participant must only respond to one of them and ignore

---

Box 6.1 Using reaction time to measure the Stroop effect

The Stroop effect occurs when people are presented with a colour name, such as RED, printed in a different colour, such as green, and have to state as quickly as they can the colour of the ink. People find this task difficult – it is hard to ignore the meaning of the word and just react to the colour of ink it is printed in. So they take much longer to respond than they do if the word is printed in the congruent colour (the word RED printed in red ink), or if they are just asked to say the colour of a green neutral stimulus such as an asterisk.

The Stroop effect is very reliable but still defies full explanation, although there have been hundreds of studies of it. A recent example is provided by the Spanish psychologists Fuentes and Ortells (1993). In their study (experiment 1) they showed the respondents a rectangular frame which was blue, green or red. In the frame or displaced to one side they also showed a neutral word or a colour word printed in black. The colour word was either compatible with the colour of the frame or incompatible. Respondents were asked to state the colour of the frame, and the time taken to do this was measured. When the word was neutral, the mean RT was 628 ms; with a compatible colour word the mean was 584 ms; and when the colour word was incompatible it was 669 ms. So even when the colour word was separate and printed in black, if it was incompatible with the required response (the colour of the frame), reaction times were lengthened. A compatible colour word led to faster responding, a facilitation effect.

Fuentes and Ortells recorded the reaction time on each occasion a stimulus pattern was shown, which requires apparatus to measure times very precisely. The original work by Stroop (1935) used simpler materials. He gave people lists of items: one list consisted of colour words printed in compatible colours, another had colour words printed in incompatible colours. Respondents were simply asked to go down the list naming the colour of the inks used for each item, and the total time taken to do this for the whole list was measured. With this procedure you can measure reaction time with just a stopwatch.

---

the other. In choice RT, two stimuli are presented individually and a different response has to be made to each one. Donders argued that simple RT requires viewers to detect the stimulus and make the response, disjunctive RT requires them to detect the stimulus and make the response but also to identify which of the alternative stimuli was presented. Choice RT requires them to detect the stimulus, make the response, identify the stimulus and also decide between the alternative responses.

So each task includes an additional stage of processing, and you can find out how long each stage takes by subtraction. If disjunctive RT is 450 ms and choice

RT is 650 ms, then the additional stage of deciding which response to make takes 200 ms. This is a very neat idea. Unfortunately the argument is invalid, because the three types of task do not differ simply in the presence or absence of the additional stage, as Donders had argued. The disjunctive RT does involve making a decision – about whether to give or withhold the response. So you cannot use the difference between disjunctive and choice RT to measure decision time. Eysenck and Keane (1990) observe that Donders' method assumes that each stage of processing is completed before the next one begins (serial processing).

Donders' method fell into disuse, but was revived and modified by Sternberg (1967), who put forward the 'additive factor' method of analysing reaction times to reveal the way the stages of cognitive processing operate. Responding to a

---

Box 6.2 The additive factor method for investigating stages of processing

If you carry out an experiment where you manipulate two independent variables, you can see whether they affect different stages of information processing. For example, Sternberg (1967) gave people a 'memory scanning' task: they were presented with a target list of digits (3 and 7, perhaps), known as the positive set, and then another test digit. They had to decide as quickly as they could whether the test digit was one of the positive set. RT increased as the length of the target list increased, as illustrated in Fig. 6.1. This suggested that people successively compared the test item with each member of the positive set in succession.

Sternberg repeated the study, using degraded versions of the digits for the test stimulus. The degraded versions consisted of digits with a chess-board pattern superimposed over them, so they were harder to identify. The effect is shown as the upper line in Fig. 6.1: it increased RT by a constant amount however long the target set was. The line for the degraded digit condition is parallel to that for intact digits, but intersects the left-hand scale higher up. Sternberg argued that this meant that the two variables of positive set size and stimulus degradation influenced different stages of the processing system. Degradation affects the stimulus identification stage, while target set size influences the stage of comparing the test digit and positive set items.

Sternberg argued that if the effects of two independent variables interacted and produced non-parallel lines on a graph, this would indicate that they affected the same processing stage: 'The additive-factors method is particularly interesting because it provides an elegant and powerful technique for disentangling the component stages of a serial process. But [it has] somewhat limited applicability; many processes of interest do not fit the simple model of a sequence of clearly independent mental operations' (Bower and Clapper, 1990, p. 261).

---

reaction time task includes substages such as detecting the stimulus, identifying it, selecting the response and executing the response. The additive factor method reveals whether two independent variables that affect RT influence the same or different substages. An example is described in Box 6.2.

Practical aspects of measuring RT

If you measure respondents' RT, you will find wide variations in the measurements. You get large individual differences, and people also differ from trial to trial. A momentary lapse of concentration or a sudden attack of confusion about which response to make will give readings which are very much longer than most but which are 'rogue' results, quite unlike most readings. There are a number of ways of dealing with this problem. One strategy is to argue that any respondent who took more than a certain time to respond was not performing the task properly, and to exclude the data from that trial. Goodrich *et al.* (1990), for example, rejected very short and very long RTs: 'RTs under 100 msec were rejected as anticipations. A failure to respond was registered if no response ensued within 3000 msec of the signal' (p. 765).

You can just exclude the result on those trials where the responses were excessively long or excessively short and present those trials again later. Or you can calculate the average of all the trials and exclude any respondents whose average RT exceeded the criterion you had specified. Another technique is to give respondents plenty of practice so that they are less likely to make errors such as getting confused about which response to make. The responses on the practice trials are not used. In the Fuentes and Ortells experiment described in

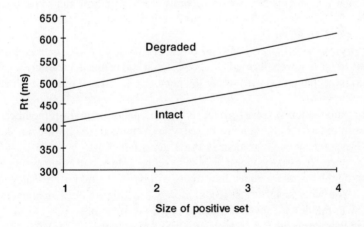

FIG. 6.1. *Sternberg's (1967) results for the memory scan task with degraded and intact stimuli*

Box 6.1, for example, there were 24 practice trials before the 'experiment proper' began.

You also need to decide in advance what to do if the person makes the wrong response, such as pushing the 'yes' button when the correct response was 'no'. Should you discard these trials? If you do, you may end up with an imbalanced experiment, so it is often better to present these trials again later. If possible, they should be included in the remaining trials of the experiment rather than being given as a separate set at the end, when the respondent may be able to anticipate the conditions coming up.

When you collect a set of reaction times, you may find that you have a few readings which are much longer than the others. This is known as a skewed distribution (see section 11.2). If this happens, the arithmetic mean, which is obtained by adding up all the readings and dividing by the number of readings you have, is not an accurate estimate of the central tendency. You should use the medians instead of the means; section 11.3 explains how to find the median. Alternatively, you can transform the data and then calculate the mean: Fazio (1990) suggests calculating the reciprocal, $1/x$, or, if all the reaction times are less than 1 second, $1/[x+1]$. So if you had a reading of 1.60 seconds, you would calculate the reciprocal $1/1.60 = 0.625$. If the reading was 0.25 seconds, you would calculate $1/[0.25+1] = 0.80$.

6.2.2 Accuracy of performance

The measure of accuracy of performance depends, of course, on the specific task the participant is given. In memory research, you may want to assess how accurately the person has remembered the material; in reasoning research it might be how many problems the person solved correctly or how many people can solve the problem; in skill learning it may be how frequently performance falls below a specified level.

Memory experiments pose special problems. Will you ask for recognition, where the items that were learned are shown again and people have to say whether they recognize them, or recall, where the person is asked just to recall whatever had been presented?

Recognition often involves giving the participants items to remember and then presenting a list of these items mixed with distracters which were not shown before. Respondents have to identify those items which had been shown at the learning stage. It usually yields a higher score than recall. One problem is determining the distracter items: how many will be used, and how are they to be selected? You would expect that recognition will be higher if the distracters are dissimilar to the targets: given a list of countries to remember, you are likely to recognize them all if the test consists of a list of the countries mingled with a list of chemicals. The distracters should be plausible, similar to the targets in their main attributes. So if you were testing people's memory for a list of countries, your distracters would also be countries. If your original list were African

---

SAQ 6.2 Scoring free recall
If you give people a list of separate items to remember, you can count how many of them are recalled. But if you have presented meaningful text or pictures, how can you score the responses? What are the problems likely to occur?

---

countries, your distracters would also be African countries. The aim is to give a task which is not too easy: if everyone scores near to 100% on a recognition test, you have an insensitive experiment in which the effects of any independent variable are obscured by a ceiling effect.

If you ask for recall, there are problems in scoring. Try SAQ 6.2 to see if you can anticipate what they are and how to deal with them.

6.2.3 Dual-task methods

This means that participants are asked to do two tasks simultaneously. It is assumed that one task occupies a certain amount of cognitive processing capacity. When someone has to perform another task at the same time, this requires additional cognitive processing capacity. Using this logic, you can investigate 'how much' of the second task has to be added before there is a decline in performance on the first one, which indicates how much capacity is taken up by the first task. An illustration is given in Box 6.3.

Results from the dual-task method have also been interpreted as identifying subsystems within the cognitive structure. If adding task B has no effect on the performance of task A, the two tasks do not interfere with each other, and this may be because they are performed by independent cognitive subsystems. If they are difficult to do simultaneously, this may be because they require the same cognitive subsystem, which gets overloaded and so performs inefficiently. Box 6.4 describes an example of this argument.

A difficulty with the dual-task procedure is that people may be undecided about which task is the more important. They may concentrate on doing as well as possible on task A and not bother about task B, or they may concentrate on task B. They may try to do both tasks as well as possible, or their strategy may fluctuate during the experiment. One way of dealing with this is to instruct them to concentrate on doing the main task as well as possible, and to monitor how well they do on the secondary task. If performance on task B falls below some predetermined level, respondents can be eliminated because they were not actually doing both tasks. Box 6.3 describes how the authors of that study interpreted performance on the secondary task to conclude that respondents had not switched their priorities when the main task (measuring simple or choice RTs) was altered.

We have looked at ways of assessing people's performance by recording how quickly or accurately they can do a task. Another way of investigating people's ability is to ask them to report *how* they do it, rather than just looking at *what*

Box 6.3 Example of a dual-task study and its interpretation

Goodrich *et al.* (1990, experiment 1) measured simple reaction time (SRT) and two-choice reaction time (CRT). In one condition respondents had to shadow a text. This means that they had to repeat verbally what they heard over headphones. For SRT, Goodrich *et al.* found the mean latency without shadowing was 222 (standard deviation (s.d.) 36) ms, whereas with shadowing it was 416 (s.d. 225) ms. For CRT the means were 280 (s.d. 49) ms and 396 (s.d. 172) ms in the non-shadowing and shadowing conditions, respectively. Giving participants the secondary shadowing task slowed reaction time, and this had a greater effect on SRT than CRT.

The research had been prompted by the fact that when no secondary task is given, SRT is typically faster than CRT. It had been suggested that this is partly because the respondent can prepare for the SRT stimulus before it is shown. This preparation takes some attention capacity, and therefore can be disrupted by giving respondents a secondary task. The results were consistent with this argument.

Goodrich *et al.* recorded performance on the secondary shadowing task and found a slight tendency for there to be more errors (hesitations and speech errors) in the SRT condition than in the CRT condition. 'We can therefore confidently reject the possibility that the greater interference effect with SRT latencies is attributable to a shift in priorities between the tasks' (p. 768).

---

they do. Asking for reports on their thinking processes as people do a task is now referred to as collecting verbal protocols, which are discussed in section 8.6.

6.2.4 Perceptual accuracy: psychophysical methods

If you want to assess someone's sensory ability, there are some standard tests you can use, such as the Ishihara test for colour blindness. But you may want to know how accurately people can judge the appearance of a stimulus or how well they can discriminate one from another. Standard procedures have been developed for measuring perceptual accuracy and related phenomena, such as the magnitude of illusions.

Method of adjustment

What is the physical magnitude of a comparison stimulus which seems the same as the standard? The easiest way of finding out is to present observers with two stimuli, one a fixed standard and the other variable. Observers are asked to adjust the variable until it appears to be the same magnitude as the standard. This is

---

Box 6.4 Example of the use of dual tasks to reveal the structure of cognitive subsystems

Baddeley developed the notion that short-term memory should be thought of as a working memory containing a phonological loop, which he described as follows (1990, p. 72): 'The phonological loop is assumed to comprise two components, a phonological store that is capable of holding speech-based information and an articulatory control process based on inner speech. Memory traces within the phonological store are assumed to fade and become irretrievable after about one-and-a-half to two seconds. The memory trace can however be refreshed by a process of reading off the trace into the articulatory control process which then feeds back into the store....' With the articulatory process, items are remembered when you say them to yourself using 'internal speech'; the mental instructions, or codes, used to control how you would say them aloud are what you remember.

A prediction from Baddeley's theory is that memory will be disrupted if the person trying to remember items is prevented from creating their articulatory code. This prediction can be tested using a technique known as articulatory suppression: people are presented with items to remember, but asked to say over and over again a simple series of words such as 'one two three'. The idea is that this second (dual) task occupies the learners' articulatory system and disrupts their ability to record the articulatory code of the items they are trying to remember. So they will make more errors when trying to remember items presented with articulatory suppression than they will with items presented without articulatory suppression. The prediction has been fulfilled (e.g. Baddeley *et al.*, 1984). So the evidence is consistent with the theory that memory involves articulatory coding.

---

repeated a number of times, and the average of the physical magnitudes of the variable stimulus judged as equal to the standard gives the 'point of subjective equality' (PSE). An example of applying this method to measuring a visual illusion is described in Box 6.5.

Method of limits and method of constant stimuli
The method of adjustment cannot be used if the stimulus is not continuously adjustable. Suppose you want to know the difference threshold for judgements of number: if people are briefly shown 38 dots, how many have to be shown to appear just more than 38? Present people with a standard display containing 38 items, and a series of comparison stimuli, containing 34, 36, 38, 40 or 42 items. If these comparison stimuli are presented in a regular ascending and descending sequences, this is the method of limits. If they are presented in random order, it

---

Box 6.5 Using the method of adjustment to measure a visual illusion

Visual illusions occur when the apparent characteristics of a stimulus differ from the physical characteristics, and their study has generated an enormous literature. An example is a study by Hotopf and Brown (1988), who investigated the illusion illustrated in Fig. 6.2. The pointer, the oblique line on the left, is aligned with the target dot at the foot of the vertical (induction) line on the right, although most observers do not see them as aligned: they judge the target dot as too low.

Hotopf and Brown (experiment 1, condition c) measured the magnitude of the misalignment effect as the gap between the target dot and the induction line was increased. Respondents were shown displays similar to Fig. 6.2, with the pointer line initially above or below the true alignment position. They moved the pointer line up or down until they judged it to be aligned with the target.

Hotopf and Brown measured the actual position of the pointer when respondents had adjusted the display so that it seemed to be aligned with the target. By subtracting this from the position where the pointer and target were actually aligned, they obtained a measure of the magnitude of the illusion. The illusion declined as the distance between the inducing line and the target increased.

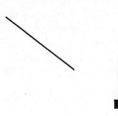

FIG. 6.2. *The attraction misalignment illusion studied by Hotopf and Brown (1988)*

is known as the method of constant stimuli. By asking the observer to say for each comparison stimulus whether it appears to have fewer or more items than the standard, the difference threshold can be calculated by analysing how many times the observer reported 'fewer' and 'more' to each one. (How this is done is explained in Box 6.6.)

The classical methods can be used to measure difference thresholds, PSEs or the magnitude of a stimulus that appears a particular fraction or multiple of the standard. This involves the development of scales of psychological magnitude: how many pennies will seem to weigh twice as much as 50 one-penny pieces? You might think the answer must be 100, but this is not the case. Simple ways of investigating these types of question were devised by Stevens, whose work is summarized in Stevens (1975). One of his procedures is magnitude estimation.

Box 6.6 Using the method of limits to measure a visual illusion, find PSEs and obtain difference thresholds

Measuring an illusion
When observers look briefly at an array of dots, their estimates of the number of dots are affected by whether the dots are arranged in a regular pattern or not. Alam *et al.* (1986, experiment 1) measured this effect, using the method of paired comparisons, a variant of the method of limits.

They showed their respondents regular patterns, consisting of a central dot with further dots arranged round it in concentric circles, and irregular patterns. On each trial, respondents saw a standard pattern containing 37 dots, and one of a series of comparison stimuli, which varied from 28 to 46 dots. The series of comparison stimuli were shown in ascending or descending sequence, and on each presentation respondents had to say which of the two patterns shown contained more dots. PSEs, the number in the comparison pattern which appeared equal to the standard of 37 dots, were calculated. When the stimuli were shown for 160 ms, the mean PSEs obtained are shown in Table 6.2. Alam *et al.* repeated the procedure, exposing the stimuli for 2 s. Taking the data for all conditions, they state: 'there is significant overestimation of the regular patterns relative to the irregular ones' (p. 885).

Finding the point of subjective equality and difference threshold
The responses from the method of limits or the method of constant stimuli give a response table like Table 6.3. Each row corresponds to one size of comparison stimulus, and the columns show the responses obtained in each series of trials. The entries indicate whether the respondent said 'fewer', 'equal' or 'more' to that comparison stimulus in that series of trials.

The lower threshold (LT) is the point where the respondent switched from using fewer to equal, and the upper threshold (UT) is the point where the respondent switched from equal to more. In the first series of trials in the table, the LT is between 32 and 34, so is recorded as 33. The UT is between 42 and 44, so is recorded as 43. Finding the LT and UT values for each series of trials and then the averages gives the best estimate of these thresholds. For this set of data, the mean LT is 34 and the mean UT is 37.4.

The PSE is the value of the comparison stimuli which appears equal to the standard, and is the mean of the upper and lower thresholds, so in Table 6.2 it is 35.7. The interval of uncertainty is the difference between the mean LT and mean UT values (here 37.4 - 34 = 3.4) and the difference threshold is half the interval of uncertainty, 1.7 in this example.

TABLE 6.2. *Number of dots appearing the same as 37 dots*

	Regular patterns	Irregular patterns
Ascending	38.03	36.16
Descending	38.03	35.19

Data from Alam *et al.* (1986)

TABLE 6.3. *Example of responses from a method of limits experiment*

Number of dots in comparison	Series of trials									
	1	2	3	4	5	6	7	8	9	10
28	F	F	F	F	F	F	F	F	F	F
30	F	F	F	F	F	F	F	F	F	F
32	F	F	F	E	F	F	F	F	F	F
34	E	E	E	E	M	M	F	F	F	E
36	E	E	E	M	M	M	M	F	F	M
38	E	E	E	M	M	M	M	F	M	M
40	E	E	M	M	M	M	M	E	M	M
42	E	M	M	M	M	M	M	M	M	M
44	M	M	M	M	M	M	M	M	M	M
46	M	M	M	M	M	M	M	M	M	M
LT	33	33	33	31	33	33	35	39	37	33
UT	43	43	39	35	33	33	35	41	37	35

Magnitude estimation

Here observers are presented with two stimuli, a standard and a comparison. They are told that the standard has a psychological strength of a certain number (say, 100), and asked to say how great the comparison stimulus is on the same scale. The method can be used with stimuli that do not have an underlying physical attribute. For example, if murder has a value of 100, what is the value of rape? If a murderer deserves a prison sentence of 15 years, how long a sentence should be given for causing death by dangerous driving? Although the method has drawbacks, such as people being influenced by the number assigned to the standard (known as the modulus), it has been widely used. Box 6.7 describes two examples. When you have read Box 6.7, try SAQ 6.3.

The classical psychophysical methods have a major drawback: people may make an incorrect response and say they can detect a stimulus or the difference between stimuli even if none is presented. 'Catch' trials can be used to try to

---

Box 6.7 Examples of magnitude estimation

Is stealing £10,000 twice as serious as stealing £5,000? Stevens (1975, pp. 258–9) describes experiments in which people were asked to indicate the seriousness of stealing various amounts of money. The magnitude estimates of seriousness were related to the amount stolen by a power function: seriousness = (amount stolen) raised to the power of 0.17. 'The value of the exponent, 0.17, suggests that, in order for one crime to be considered twice as serious as another, the amount stolen must be about 60 times as large.' So someone would have to steal £300,000 for the crime to appear twice as bad as stealing £5,000!

You may have noticed that people who do not like the type of music you like tend to complain that you play it too loudly. One way of investigating this is to ask people to judge the loudness of bursts of music of a kind that they like and of a kind that they dislike. Fucci *et al.* (1993) used magnitude estimation to do this. Two groups, one of people who liked rock music and another of people who did not, had their auditory sensitivity measured using the method of limits described in Box 6.6. They were then presented with bursts of rock music at different loudnesses above their threshold, and asked to give a number which represented how loud it seemed on each occasion. Geometric means were calculated, and it was found that those who disliked rock music gave higher estimates than those who liked it: 'well-liked music may be perceived as less loud than music that it is not liked when both samples are played at the same intensity' (p. 1174).

---

prevent the observer merely giving the same response on every trial, but there is little one can do except urge the observer to be as conscientious as possible. A different approach is to use signal detection theory, which has been widely used in studies of perception and memory.

If you shut your eyes, you 'see' internally generated sensations that come from the random neural activity within your sensory system. This background of internal 'sensations' is known as noise. When a very weak stimulus (a signal) is presented to you, your internal sensory system has both the noise and whatever neural activity is set up by the signal. So to detect a stimulus, you have to

---

SAQ 6.3

Box 6.7 describes how magnitude estimation has been used in studying the judged seriousness of thefts and the apparent loudness of music. List three more 'real-life' topics which could be studied using this psychophysical method.

---

discriminate those occasions when only the noise occurs from those on which both the noise and the signal occur.

A signal detection experiment involves presenting on a number of trials one of two conditions: noise, or signal and noise. The observer has to say on each occasion whether a signal was presented or not. If only noise was presented, but the observer wrongly says there was a signal, this is a 'false alarm'. A 'hit' occurs when a signal is presented and the observer correctly reports there was a signal. In signal detection theory the ability to detect the signal is defined in terms of the difference between the rate of hits and the rate of false alarms, this difference being expressed as d' (d prime). A d' of zero occurs when the hit rate equals the false alarm rate, and means that the observer is failing to distinguish between signals and noise. As d' increases, better performance is demonstrated. The d' measure of performance can be used to show how well people have remembered a set of items. For example, Baddeley and Woodhead (1982) investigated memory for faces by presenting people with a set of faces to remember and later showing these same faces mixed with a set of new faces. Observers had to say whether each of the faces had been in the first set. The number of hits and false alarms was found, and d' calculated for each respondent.

Psychological techniques: psychometric tests

7.0 Basic principles

Psychometric tests are standardized instruments for assessing people's ability, aptitude, attitude or personality. They are standardized in that they have fixed items, and rules about the way they are administered. Also, the performance of a standardization sample of people is known. The results of any individual can be compared with this standardization sample.

Psychometric testing is a specialty in its own right, and before you consider using psychometric tests you need to be familiar with the underlying issues. We give only a brief account here; for detailed treatment, you should refer to texts such as Kline (1993).

Psychometric tests of ability can be divided into speed tests, in which the person is presented with numerous simple questions and you record how many are answered in the time allowed, and power tests, in which items of increasing difficulty are presented and you record the level of difficulty that the person attains. In practice, tests combine the features of speed and power, but each can be seen as predominantly one or the other. You can also distinguish group tests, where a number of people can be tested simultaneously, from individual tests, which require each person to be tested on their own.

The criteria by which you judge a test, apart from its relevance to the aspect of the person you want to assess, are its reliability and validity.

7.1 Standardization and norms

Standardized tests are accompanied by a test manual, which will report the scores of the people who were used in the standardization process. You find out how well participants have done by comparing their 'raw scores', the number of items they answered correctly, with the norms, the performance of the standardization sample. The raw score only means anything when it is compared with the norms. For example, if you scored 18 out of 30 on a test, you have no way of knowing whether this shows a high level of performance or not. But if you know that 60%

Box 7.1 Example of a section from a table of test norms

A norm table, such as Table 7.1, shows how a standardization sample performed on a test. In Table 7.1, two groups of respondents were tested. Group W were managers from small and medium-sized companies, and group X were technical supervisors from public-sector organizations.

The figures in the body of Table 7.1 are raw scores. To use the table you decide on which standardization group you wish to use for evaluating the responses from the person you have tested, and find the raw score in the appropriate column of the table. Suppose you have tested a manager from a small company and found that he scored 12 on the test. You want to find whether this score means he has done well or badly. Since he is a manager in a small company, you compare the score with those of similar people, group W's scores. In the column headed 'Sample W', find the position of a raw score of 12 (it is in the band 11–14), look along the row and find the entry in that row for the column headed 'Percentile'. The entry is 5, and this means that the raw score of 12 corresponds to a percentile position of 5. Five per cent of the standardization sample scored at or below this level.

You can see from Table 7.1 that the meaning of the raw score varies according to which standardization sample you are using. A raw score of 12 is equivalent to a percentile of 5 when sample W is used, but a percentile of 15 when sample X is used. This emphasizes the point that a raw score alone means nothing; it gains meaning when it is compared with the performance of the appropriate standardization sample.

TABLE 7.1. *Example of part of a table of test norms*

Sample W	Sample X	Percentile	Range of percentiles
0–6	0–3	1	1
7–10	4–5	3	2–3
11–14	6–8	5	3–7
15–17	9–10	10	8–12
18–19	11–12	15	13–17
20–21	13	20	18–22

of a sample of 2000 people of your sex and age scored less than 18, you know that you have done well. Box 7.1 illustrates part of the norms from one ability test and explains how it is used. When you have read it, check your understanding with SAQ 7.1.

If people are tested a number of times, they will not necessarily always get exactly the same score: as ever, there is variability. So an observed score can be

---

SAQ 7.1

Margaret Brown, a technical supervisor in a public health laboratory scores 13 on a test of ability. Part of the table of norms for this test are shown in Table 7.1. How well did Ms Brown score compared with other people?

---

thought of as an estimate of a 'true' score. Confidence limits to the estimate of the true score can be obtained using the standard error of measurement (SEm), which is related to the reliability of the test. (SEm = sd/$\sqrt{(1-r)}$, where r is the reliability coefficient and sd is the standard deviation of the test.) We will not go into the details here, but broadly you can set up confidence limits. Given a test score you can say there is a 95% probability that the true score is within the limits of the obtained score ± 2 SEm.

7.2 Reliability

In the context of psychometric tests, reliability refers to the consistency of the test results. There are a number of types of reliability, and each is measured in its own way. *Test–retest reliability* means that people obtain the same scores if they take the test on two occasions. It can be assessed by giving the test to the same people on two occasions and seeing whether they score the same. (In practice, to prevent the respondents simply remembering the answers they gave the first time, you may have two versions of the test with slightly different items. The two versions are known as parallel forms.)

Another aspect of reliability is ensuring that all the items measure 'the same thing'. This is assessed by comparing the scores on any item with the total score on all the items. If one item does not correlate with the total score, it is eliminated so that the test has homogeneity of items. Another procedure is to divide the test into two halves and see how far the scores on each half correlate. This *'split-half' reliability* indicates the internal consistency of the test.

Inter-scorer and *inter-administrator agreement* mean that the test gives the same results whoever is marking or administering it. You would not have a lot of faith in a test if you knew that people scored 80% when Mr Jones marked it but only 40% when Ms Collins did!

A test needs to be reliable, but reliability is not a fixed quantity: a test that has high inter-scorer reliability may not have high test–retest reliability. The range of respondents tested is another influential factor: a test of intelligence may be reliable when applied to a wide range of people but less reliable if it is used only on people who are very intelligent. Reliability also depends on the length of a test: the more items it has, the greater the reliability can be.

High reliability in all senses is not always a 'good thing'. High inter-scorer agreement is always desirable, but high item homogeneity is not. If you are measuring intelligence, you want to be sure that all aspects of intelligence are tested, and so you will not want all the items to show a very high correlation with each other.

Information about the reliability of a test will be included in the test manual, and is usually expressed as a correlation coefficient. (Correlation coefficients are explained in Chapter 11. Briefly, they can vary between -1.00 and +1.00. If two sets of scores are quite unrelated, the coefficient is 0.00.) You may come across the terms KR20 and Cronbach's alpha. These are measures of internal consistency, based on the notion of split-half reliability, which involves dividing the test into two halves. But there are many ways you can construct the two halves. If you had a test of 40 items, you could take the first 20 and the final 20, or you could take the odd-numbered ones and then the even-numbered ones, or you could take items 1–10 and 21–30 as one half with the others forming the other half, and so on. Perhaps the best thing would be to take every possible way of forming two halves, correlate the scores of the halves and then find the average of the correlations. This is essentially what Cronbach's alpha does. Alpha is easily calculated by computer, and is one of the standard ways of expressing a test's reliability.

You may ask what is an acceptable level of reliability, but there is no simple answer. For tests of cognitive ability (such as intelligence tests), reliability coefficients of about 0.8 are usually expected. But tests of personality often have much lower values, partly because personality is a broader construct.

7.3 Validity

This means 'Does the test measure what it claims to measure?' Does a test of driving ability really measure driving ability? There are different kinds of validity and a number of ways of measuring it. We shall use the example of a driving test to explain them.

Concurrent validity means that people who are known to differ on the construct that the test is measuring score differently. To show the driving test had concurrent validity, you would take two groups of people, one known to be competent drivers and the other known not to be competent drivers. Both groups would take the test, and you would expect the competent drivers to score higher than the non-competent group.

Predictive validity means the test can predict how well people will perform later. If you wanted to show that your driving test had predictive validity, you would take a number of people who could not drive, give them the test, and save the scores. You then teach everyone to drive and measure how well people learn. (You might record the number of lessons they needed before they reached a certain level of competence.) You then examine their test scores and see whether those who learnt fastest had obtained higher scores than those who took longer to learn.

Content validity means the test covers all aspects of the construct it is measuring. So you would look at your driving test to see whether it contained items covering all aspects of driving, which might include (among other things)

SAQ 7.2
Why is it that 'A test that is reliable may or may not be valid'?

---

the ability to judge accurately how long an approaching vehicle will take to reach you, the ability to understand road signs, the ability to start on a hill without rolling backwards. Deciding on content validity is a more subjective procedure than determining concurrent or predictive validity.

Construct validity refers to the extent to which the test measures the underlying construct which it claims to measure, such as driving competence, and is the sum of all the evidence that the test relates to the construct. It may include demonstrating that the test correlates with other tests of the same construct, and that it does not correlate with other tests which measure different constructs. So, for example, a test of driving skill should correlate with other indices of driving competence: you would expect people who scored higher on the test to have on average a lower number of insurance claims. Conversely it should not be related to musical aptitude, which you would not expect to be correlated with driving skill.

None of these should be confused with *face validity*, which means whether the test content looks as though it is relevant to the attribute being measured. A test that claimed to measure driving competence would have face validity if it actually involved driving. If it consisted only of a written examination, face validity would be lacking. Face validity can be important for gaining the cooperation of people being tested, but is of little technical value: a test may have high face validity but not really measure the underlying construct adequately.

7.4 Relationship between reliability and validity

A test that is unreliable cannot be valid. A test that is reliable may or may not be valid. If you have found a reliable test, you need to examine the manual to find out what evidence there is for its validity. Confirm that you understand this point by answering SAQ 7.2

7.5 Regulations regarding the use of psychological tests

There are strict rules about who can purchase and use psychometric tests, and people have to gain qualifications such as The British Psychological Society's Certificate of Competence before they are allowed to do so. (There are different certificates for ability tests and personality tests.) Most psychological tests are not available to students, and it would be both dangerous and unethical if they were used by untrained people. You should not, therefore, expect to be able to use them until you have undergone a recognized training procedure.

Psychological techniques:
self-report measures

8.0 Introduction

Self-reports are most commonly used to investigate people's attitudes or opinions. You can ask people to tell you what they think by giving them direct questions, but they may not be consciously aware of their attitudes and you may want to use a more subtle technique, such as the Q-sort procedure. Self-reports also cover what used to be known as introspection, reporting on how you do a task while you are doing it. This is now referred to as collecting verbal protocols.

8.1 Self-report measures: attitudes

8.1.1 What is an attitude?

An attitude is: 'predispositions to respond to some class of stimuli with certain classes of response' (Rosenberg and Hovland, 1960, p. 3) and has three components: cognitive, what you believe about the object; affective, how you feel about it; behavioural, how you act towards it. Evidence for attitudes comes from a pattern of consistency in responses: if you regularly avoid dogs, refuse to have one in the house, fail to support charities for dogs, and say that all dogs should be put down, then an observer may conclude that you have a negative attitude towards them.

8.1.2 Measuring attitudes

Psychologists often want to measure attitudes so that they can put a numerical value on them, and then submit those values to statistical manipulation. For example, you may want to know the 'average' attitude of particular groups of people to some particular topic. There are many ways to assess attitudes. You might draw inferences from overt behaviour: presumably people who attend church regularly have a positive attitude to the church. But an attitude may not be reflected in behaviour: some people with a positive attitude to the church do not attend. Conversely, some people may indulge in the behaviour but not have a strong positive attitude. Perhaps you go to church simply to keep your partner company.

You could use physiological reactions to assess attitude: arachnophobia may be shown by increased heart-rate, sweating, etc., when the person sees a spider. Or you could study people's reactions to partially structured material. For example, you may give someone a sentence-completion task including items like this: 'Rover, the Yorkshire terrier, ran up to John and ...'. If your respondent completes the sentence with 'bit him', this may imply a negative attitude to dogs, whereas completing the sentence with 'dragged him from the burning wreckage' may indicate a positive attitude.

The most common technique for measuring attitudes is to use self-report scales, and a large number of these have been created.

8.1.3 Sources of established attitude scales

There are well-known scales for measuring some attitudes; sometimes, as in the case of job satisfaction, there is an embarrassing number of alternatives. If the attitude you wish to measure has been investigated before, it is sensible to use an existing scale. This saves you all the preliminary work, data on the scale's reliability and validity should be available, and you have an authority to cite if anyone challenges you. The problem is how to find it. If you are examining a well-known construct such as job satisfaction, you should be able to trace existing scales through textbook references or journal papers. Less common scales may be located if you have the facilities for a thorough search of the literature.

If you cannot obtain an existing scale, you will need to develop your own. There are a number of procedures for constructing an attitude scale, which is a standard list of statements to which the subject responds. The most common is the Likert method.

8.1.4 Developing your own attitude scale using the Likert procedure

An attitude scale is a set of statements about some topic or object, where some are 'pro' and some 'anti'. Respondents indicate their level of agreement with each statement on a scale (often a five- or seven-point scale), from 'Strongly agree' to 'Strongly disagree'. With a five-point response scale, the responses are given numerical values from 1 to 5. 'Pro' items are scored 1–5 and 'anti' items are scored 5–1. The person's score is simply the total of the responses.

In developing the scale, any items which show a low correlation with the total scores are deleted. The final scale is made up by selecting items which cover a range of positive and negative views and which show a high correlation with the total score, so that item homogeneity is maximized, or which discriminate between high and low scorers. Box 8.1 explains how to develop a Likert attitude scale, but how can you demonstrate its validity? When you have read Box 8.1, try SAQ 8.1

Box 8.1 Example of creating a scale rating attitude towards dogs
In this example, only a very few statements and respondents have been used, but that is simply to keep the exposition simple. In practice you would start with 20–30 statements and about 40–50 respondents. The final scale would typically contain 10–20 items.

(1) Assemble a number of attitudinal statements on the topic, varying from very 'pro' to very 'anti'. If you were developing a scale to measure attitude to dogs, you might have statements like these:

1 Dogs are 'man's best friend' (+)   SA A N D SD
2 I will always want to have a dog (+)   SA A N D SD
3 A dog is a rewarding companion when
       you are feeling lonely (+)   SA A N D SD
4 Many people are bitten by dogs every year (-)   SA A N D SD
5 Dogs are a serious health hazard to people (-)   SA A N D SD
6 People in cities should not be allowed to
       have a dog (-)   SA A N D SD
7 Guide dogs are a great help for blind
       people (+)   SA A N D SD

   (2) Ask a number of respondents to indicate their response to each statement using a five- or seven-point scale of agreement. They can be asked simply to circle the appropriate alternative answer: strongly agree (SA), agree (A), neither agree nor disagree (N), disagree (D) or strongly disagree (SD).
   (3) Categorize each statement as pro or anti. This is usually straight-forward. If it is hard to decide whether a statement is pro or anti, make an arbitrary choice; the responses will show whether it correlates with the pro statements or with the anti ones. In this example, statements 1, 2 and 3 are classed as positive (+) and 4, 5 and 6 as negative (-). Statement 7 is hard to classify, but put into the positive group.

— — *Continued* — — — — — — — — — — — — — — — — —

TABLE 8.1. *Example of response table used for studying item homogeneity in an attitude scale*

Statement	Respondent number								Mean	Corrected item–total correlation
	1	*2*	*3*	*4*	*5*	*6*	*7*	*8*		
1	5	1	2	1	5	1	4	1	20/8 = 2.50	0.93
2	4	1	2	2	5	3	5	1	2.875	0.91
3	4	2	1	3	5	2	4	1	2.75	0.90
4	4	3	2	3	4	2	4	2	3.00	0.89
5	5	2	2	1	5	2	5	2	3.00	0.91
6	4	1	2	3	5	1	5	1	2.75	0.92
7	5	5	5	5	4	5	5	5	4.875	-0.56
Total	31	15	16	18	33	16	32	13		

— — Continued —

(4) With a five-point scale, responses to 'pro' statements are scored so that strongly agree counts 5 and strongly disagree counts 1. Responses to 'anti' statements are scored with the opposite allocation of numbers, so that strongly agree counts 1. With this scoring scheme, a high score on the eventual scale will indicate a strong 'pro' attitude. So the scores for each response to each question are like this:

	SA	A	N	D	SD
1 Dogs are 'man's best friend'	5	4	3	2	1
2 I will always want to have a dog	5	4	3	2	1
3 A dog is a rewarding companion when you are feeling lonely	5	4	3	2	1
4 Many people are bitten by dogs every year	1	2	3	4	5
5 Dogs are a serious health hazard to people	1	2	3	4	5
6 People in cities should not be allowed to have a dog	1	2	3	4	5
7 Guide dogs are a great help for blind people	5	4	3	2	1

(5) Examine the item homogeneity of the scale. This is easily achieved if you have access to an appropriate computer program. The program is presented with a table, such as Table 8.1, showing the responses of every one of the judges to every one of the statements. The program calculates the total score for each respondent and then for each statement the corrected correlation between the responses to that statement and the adjusted total scores. (The adjusted total scores are the totals with the scores on the item being examined removed. So when calculating the correlation for statement 1, take the totals but subtract the scores for item 1 before calculating the correlation.) The mean score for each statement is also found.

Two ways of selecting items for the final version of the scale are widely used. One is based on maximizing the extent to which the items correlate (item homogeneity). Using this method, you delete those statements showing a low correlation with the adjusted totals. From the remaining statements, select a set so that you end up with some 'pro' and some 'anti' items. In the example shown here, you might select statements 1, 2, 5 and 6.

The other procedure for selecting items is to choose those which discriminate most clearly between high and low scorers. Find the 25% of respondents who had the highest scores and the 25% who had the lowest scores. In the example, the highest 25% of scorers are respondents 5 and 7, the lowest 25% are respondents 2 and 8. For each statement, calculate the total of the responses from the high scorers and then from the low scorers. For example, for statement 1, the total of the high-scoring group (respondents 5 and 7) is 5 + 4 = 9; the total for the low-scoring group (respondents 2 and 8) is 1 + 1 = 2. The difference between the two totals (7) is the index of discriminatory power. When you have calculated this index for every statement, you select for the final version of the scale those which have the highest index values.

SAQ 8.1

The procedure explained in Box 8.1 produces a reliable scale, but this does not mean the scale is valid. What type of validity needs to be established and how could this be done?

8.2 Self-report measures: questionnaires

Questionnaires and interviews have obvious appeal as a direct way of discovering what people believe or do: you simply ask them! A psychologist should have experience at using both these methods, and be aware of their pitfalls as well as their benefits. Some types of interview are similar to a questionnaire, in that a predetermined series of questions is asked and the answers recorded. Other types of interview are less constrained. Questionnaires and interviews can be used in a quantitative or a qualitative manner, and which approach you are using will determine the way they are conducted and how the results are dealt with.

8.2.1 Quantitative use of questionnaires

A questionnaire is a set of questions which are presented to the respondents, usually in a printed form although they can be administered via a computer. There are standard questionnaires for some purposes; personality inventories are an example. But in the vast majority of cases, investigators interested in a particular topic have to construct their own questionnaire.

The first step is to decide just what it is you want to find out. Robson (1993, p. 228) notes that you can distinguish between finding out what people know, what they do, and what they believe: facts, behaviour, and beliefs. Although you might think that finding out about facts is straightforward, careful planning of the questions is important whichever type of information you are seeking.

Free response or multiple choice?

Having decided on the precise aim of the study, the next stage is writing appropriate questions and answers. In free responses, respondents have the opportunity to write whatever they feel is the appropriate answer. The multiple-choice answer format means that you provide a set of alternatives and ask the respondent to indicate which one or ones are appropriate.

Free responding creates problems for the investigator. Respondents have the chance to explain their answers, and are not limited by a set of alternatives which they may feel do not allow them to express just what they want to say. But you then have to code the answers and reduce them to some manageable set, which usually means being able to sort them into a small number of categories and count how many you have in each category. This is both time-consuming and raises problems of reliability. If you have a number of people coding free responses, you have to ensure they are being consistent, which means you need a clear set of guidelines based on actual examples of the responses. If you have just one person doing the coding, you still need to ensure consistency: there is a danger of criteria changing as you work through a lengthy set of responses. Robson (1993, p. 243) makes the telling point that 'The desire to use open-ended questions appears to be almost universal in novice researchers, but is usually rapidly extinguished with experience'. This may be unfortunate, as open-ended questioning may be seen as less scientific simply because it is more difficult. Qualitative approaches tackle this head on, rather than trying to avoid it.

As a rule, it is wise to use multiple-choice responses whenever one can, but leave respondents the opportunity to add their own comments as well. This can leave them feeling less frustrated, even if you do not actually use the free-response part of the answer when analysing the outcome. Many respondents get annoyed if they are only offered yes/no as the alternatives, and it is sensible to add a 'no opinion' or 'does not apply' option, which may be shown as a question mark: 'Do you agree? Yes ? No'.

There are different types of multiple-choice answer systems. The commonest is a set of exclusive alternatives: the person selects just one answer from those offered. It is crucial that there should be a complete set of alternatives. Asking people whether they are married or not is inadequate, as many people may be unclear about what you mean by 'married': do those who are separated count as 'married'? What about the divorced, the widowed, people with a partner who are not legally married?

You can have non-exclusive sets of alternatives, where the person can tick more than one of the alternatives. For example: 'Which of the following led you to use this product? Price; Reliability; Reputation; Recommendation by a friend'. Someone might tick any number of these, and you can have difficulty in coding the responses, because there are so many possible response patterns. This emphasizes the need to be clear about the purpose of the question. In this case, are you wanting to know how many people took each attribute into account in deciding on their purchase? If that is the aim, you could just count how many times each attribute was ticked, remembering that the total number of ticks will be more than the total number of respondents.

Ranking
In many cases you want people to indicate their opinion about the magnitude of whatever the question is concerned with: how important was price, reliability, etc., in persuading you to buy this item? One way of obtaining this type of information is to ask people to rank the alternatives, putting a 1 against the feature that was most important, a 2 against the next most important, and so on. You can then find the average rank score of each alternative. The problem with rankings is that they only show how an alternative compares with the others which were presented. Suppose you asked someone to rank people in terms of how good they were as leaders, and offered them the alternatives of Napoleon, Hitler, Ghandi and de Gaulle. Whichever one got the top rank is top only in that

set; the respondent may have thought that all of them were rather poor leaders. To avoid this problem, you may decide to use ratings.

Rating
Here respondents are asked to estimate the magnitude of the subject on a scale; so you might ask people to indicate how good a leader Napoleon was by giving a figure from 1 to 9. There are two main ways of presenting the task. One is to use a graphic or numerical rating scale. The end-points can be labelled with drawings indicating 'happy' and 'sad' faces (useful if you are using young children) or with verbal labels at the end-points like these:

Extremely good ___:_:_:_:_:_:_ Not at all good
Extremely good   1 2 3 4 5 6 7   Not at all good

Using a marker (:) to separate steps on the graphic scale means that responses can easily be coded as numbers, the left-most space being 1 and the right-most 5, 7 or 9, depending on how many markers you use. An odd number of steps is preferable as the middle one allows the respondent to indicate a neutral position. But numerical and graphic scales are inherently ambiguous: what does a rating of 3 mean? Why should you suppose that a rating of 3 from one respondent means the same as a 3 from another?

The alternative is to offer a list of verbal quantifiers indicating increasing levels, as in these questions:

'How important was the product's reputation in your decision to purchase it? Extremely important; Very important; Important; Quite important; Not at all important.'

'How often do you have head-aches? Very frequently; Often; Sometimes; Rarely.'

The phrases are usually presented in an orderly sequence from strongest to weakest (or the other way round). Various studies, for example those by Hartley *et al.* (1984) and Gaskell *et al.* (1993), have shown that the particular phrases used affect the way people react to the question. If you want people to indicate how often they do something, Hartley *et al.* recommend using 'All of the time; Three-quarters of the time; Half the time; One quarter of the time; None of the time' rather than the less precise 'Always; Quite often; Sometimes; Very infrequently; None of the time'. These verbal phrases have ill-defined limits (how often is 'quite often'?) and their meaning varies according to context: to say I eat chips 'quite often' might mean two or three times a week, whereas going abroad for my holidays 'quite often' may mean two or three times a decade.

The response alternatives must be meaningful and relevant to the question. Consider this example: 'How often do you use bottle banks? Always; Sometimes;

Never'. The alternatives here seem irrelevant because the question is not sufficiently precise. It needs a more definite context to explain what is meant by using a bottle bank, and so could be expanded like this: 'When you are getting rid of empty bottles, how often do you use a bottle bank?' This example also demonstrates the need to think carefully about the alternative responses. 'Always' is very precise: if I fail to use the bottle bank on one occasion, I am not really truthful in claiming to use them always. A better alternative might be to use the scale recommended by Hartley *et al.* or at least to include the option 'usually'.

Ratings are widely used, but Oppenheim (1992, p. 230) has reservations about them: 'The use of ratings invites the gravest dangers and possible errors, and in untutored hands the procedure is useless'. He notes that ratings suffer a number of drawbacks. Their reliability is doubtful. People may exhibit a halo effect, which means they decide they generally like or dislike whatever is being rated and then mark it up or down on every scale. Another problem is response sets, where people tend to use just the left or just the right end of the scales, or avoid the extreme categories. The way people carry out ratings has become a research topic of its own (Poulton, 1989), and you should take care in the way you present them and the way you interpret the responses.

Writing questions

There are a number of principles to remember when writing questions and answers, and these are described in Box 8.2. But even when you have conscientiously tried to follow them, you are very likely to have made some errors. A pilot study is vital.

Many questionnaire items are intended to obtain information about people's behaviour, and ask respondents how often they have done something in the recent past. We have already commented on the problems associated with using verbal quantifiers, such as 'often' and 'rarely'. But even when you use more precise types of response alternative such as 'once a week', 'once a month', there are doubts about the truthfulness of the responses. This may be deliberate: respondents tend to understate the frequency of socially disapproved behaviours such as drinking, smoking or breaking the speed limit when driving. Or it may arise even when people are trying to be cooperative and truthful.

Schwarz (1990) makes the point that the traditional distinction between 'opinion questions' and 'factual questions' is misleading: answering factual questions requires a considerable degree of inference and judgement, just as opinion questions do. Asking respondents to recall how often they have performed some behaviour means relying on the accuracy of their memory. People's memory suffers from many sources of error, so that it is not reasonable to expect them to be able to recall and count accurately all the instances of them doing something over the previous month, year or longer. Schwarz (1990) suggests that it may be better to break a global question down into several more specific ones. Rather than asking people how often they had eaten out in a restaurant in the previous three months, you could ask how often they had eaten at a Chinese restaurant, a

---

Box 8.2 Rules for writing questionnaire items

(1) Avoid jargon or technical terms unlikely to be familiar to your respondents.

    Poor item: Do you worry that you may have halitosis?

    Better item: Do you worry that you may have bad breath?

(2) Avoid ambiguous questions and answers.

    Poor item: Do you frequently consult your doctor?

    Better item: How many times have you consulted your doctor in the last six months? None; 1 or 2 times; 3–5 times; more than 5 times.

(3) Avoid 'combination' questions: do not include the word 'and' in case a respondent wants to respond 'yes' to one and 'no' to the other part of the question.

    Poor item: Do you believe in fairies and elves?

    Better: Do you believe in fairies?

                Do you believe in elves?

(4) Avoid negatives. Double negatives in the question or in the question and answer combination are especially likely to confuse your respondents.

    Poor item: I do not trust politicians to tell the truth. Yes No.

    Better item: Do you believe politicians usually tell the truth?

        Yes   ?   No

    Better still: In general, how often do you think politicians tell the truth?

    All the time; Three-quarters of the time; Half the time; One quarter of the time; None of the time.

— *Continued* —

'fast-food' restaurant, an Italian restaurant, etc. But specific questions do have the drawback that instances which do not match the particular question will not be reported. So an estimate of how often people have eaten out will be wrong if the specific questions fail to include one of the types of eating establishment respondents have used.

Piloting

In writing questions you must never be satisfied with your first attempts and you should always pilot the questions on a small group of people from your target set of respondents. Bear in mind that although you may know what you are talking about and want to find out, your respondents probably do not. They may be quite unfamiliar with the topic, and you need to ensure questions (and alternative answers if you are providing them) are clear and unambiguous to your respondents and not just to you. Oppenheim (1992) recommends that multiple-choice questions should be piloted as free-response questions first, so that you can find out which alternatives should be offered.

— — *Continued* — — — — — — — — — — — — — — — — — — —

(5) Do not use leading questions which imply the response that is wanted.

Poor item: Do you agree with most people that capital punishment should be restored? Yes   No

Better item: Do you believe that for some crimes capital punishment should be restored, should not be restored, or do you have no opinion? Should be restored; Should not be restored; No opinion.

(6) Include a 'no opinion' option when asking about people's beliefs or attitudes. An example is given in point 5 above.

(7) Avoid loaded questions containing emotive words which may bias the responses.

Poor item: Do you agree that racist organizations such as the ABC should be banned?

This is a poor question because it labels the target organization as racist; the respondent might not have considered it as racist without this suggestion.

(8) The way people are asked to show their response should be simple. Ask them to tick what does apply, rather than delete what does not. Ticking or circling is more definite than underlining. You can ask people to put a cross (X) against the alternative which applies, but this may cause problems if people think of X as indicating 'wrong': a tick is less confusing.

Poor item: Are you aged between 20 and 30? Delete whichever does not apply: Yes   No

Better item: Are you aged between 20 and 30 inclusive? Tick the appropriate answer: Yes (   ) No (   )

(9) If you are asking about a number of different topics, questions on one topic should be grouped together and as a rule they should go from the general to the particular. Questions referring to demographic information such as the person's age, sex, and income bracket can be placed at the end.

When the first draft of the questionnaire has been prepared, pilot it on people who come from the eventual user population. Piloting involves asking them to complete the questionnaire and as they do so note any difficulties, ambiguities, etc., that they come across. It is important to emphasize to the respondents at this stage that the pilot is a test not of them but of the questionnaire, and that you are asking for their help – they should not feel that if they do not understand something this is because they have failed or are being stupid. Relying on written comments is not very fruitful. It is better to ask people to complete the questionnaire and tell you what they are doing as they fill it in or ask them to complete the questionnaire and as soon as they have finished ask them to go through it with

SAQ 8.2

Devise a short questionnaire on some topic of interest to you, following the advice given in Box 8.2. Try it out on three or four friends, asking them to complete the questionnaire and then describe how they reacted to each question, and whether they found any ambiguities or other difficulties. A few practice sessions like this will help you develop skill at questionnaire construction.

you explaining what they did at each point. Observing them as they fill it in can indicate where there are difficulties in individual items or in navigating their way through the questions.

The results of the pilot can be used to revise the items and structure of the questionnaire. If it required a major revision, another pilot study is needed; if the alterations were minor, you may decide not to run another pilot. It is up to the investigator to judge what constitutes a major revision. Gain some practice by trying SAQ 8.2.

Analysing the responses

When the completed questionnaires are returned, the responses have to be coded and recorded. Coding means transforming the responses into numbers, such as assigning a 1 if the person is female and a 2 if he is male. For each question, every response needs to be represented by a unique number so that you can readily find the number of times each answer was given. You will have devised a coding scheme at the earliest stages of devising the questionnaire. The analysis will typically involve frequency counts (how many respondents gave which response to each question?), cross-tabulations (e.g. how many men and how many women gave each of the alternative answers to question 14?), and correlations (are the responses to question 4 correlated with the answers to question 10?).

For a survey of any size, you will want to use computer analysis, preferably using one of the specialized programs, such as Minitab or SPSS. Once the data are on disk, these let you carry out whichever analyses you want with minimal effort; analyses that would be impractical by hand can be done in a few moments.

8.2.2 Qualitative use of questionnaires

Qualitative research with questionnaires must start with the collection of sensible open questions. If the questions do not give the respondent space to interpret the question, then all that will be fed back to the researcher are agreements or disagreements with the propositions that have been put. The advantage of qualitative questionnaires is that the assumptions of the interviewer can be laid open to scrutiny. This is unlike standard questionnaires, where a particular view is often introduced and the respondent is powerless to challenge it (Roiser, 1974). It is important to make sure (1) that the questions taken together do ask all the things you want to know about: do not hope that they will bring in information which you did not specifically ask for; (2) that the questions will make sense to your respondents: do not ask questions about things they will know nothing about; and (3) that the questions are phrased in a way that will invite an answer: do not ask about things that will be offensive.

The analysis should be flexible and interpretative. We go into this process of analysis in more detail in Chapter 12, but the idea that the researcher should be attempting to get inside the respondents' frame of reference should be borne in mind from the start of the study. Some of the warnings that apply to questionnaires in quantitative studies can be approached slightly differently. For example, ambiguity in questions needs to be avoided, but you have to distinguish between an ambiguous question and one where you have left opportunity for different responses. The watchwords here are reflection and anticipation. A pilot study is still absolutely necessary.

8.3 Self-report measures: interviews

Interviews are face-to-face interactions but not normally just a conversation: they have their own rules about the roles of the participants. There are various ways of dividing interviews into types – for example, one can distinguish between formats (unstructured, structured, etc.) or between aims (assessment, guidance, etc.). There has been a huge amount of investigation into whether the interview is a reliable and valid method of obtaining information, especially in the context of the employment selection interview (e.g. Weisner and Cronshaw, 1989). Recent work suggests that a structured interview can be more reliable and valid than was previously believed.

8.3.1 Quantitative use of interviews

Interviews when used with a quantitative approach resemble questionnaires in having a set aim of obtaining information using a series of questions. It is conventional to distinguish between a structured interview, where there is a list of questions to be asked, and an unstructured one, where there is a set of topics to be covered but not a formal set of precise questions. Structure is really a dimension, and most interviews will contain structured and unstructured sections where the interviewer can follow up responses and ask for further explanations.

Because it involves face-to-face contact, the interview has additional sources of possible bias that are not so prominent in a questionnaire. One factor is the similarity of the interviewer and interviewee: if they are of different sexes, racial groups, or ages, the interviewee may be less willing to be truthful. The presence of the interviewer may tempt respondents to give socially approved answers even if these do not reflect their own views.

The similarities between the questionnaire and the interview mean that many of the points covered in the section on questionnaires, especially regarding question wording, are also pertinent to interviews. You should devise an interview schedule, a plan of what you are going to say during the interview and how you are going to record the responses, and you should pilot this by running the interview on a few people who are taken from your target group. This will allow you to see whether the questions are comprehensible, whether your method of recording the responses is practical, how long the interview is likely to take and generally allow you to rehearse what is after all a social presentation of yourself (assuming you will be carrying out the interviews).

If at all possible, you should make a complete record of the interview on audio or video tape, so that you can review what was said. During the interview itself, making verbatim notes will be impossible if you want the interaction to be continuous. You will have to obtain the permission of the interviewee, of course, before making a recording. With a completely structured interview, many or even all of the questions will have a predetermined set of possible answers, as in a multiple-choice questionnaire item, so recording responses is simpler. But the point of an interview is to allow respondents to amplify their responses, and this really means having a record of exactly what is said.

Interviewing is a skill: the interviewer must establish rapport with the interviewee, so that she or he is relaxed and willing to provide the information requested, but must control the encounter to ensure that all the desired information is obtained, in a form which can be interpreted or aggregated. At first, the interviewer may well find the situation stressful, embarrassing, 'uncomfortable'. But it is a technique which all psychologists should be able to handle competently. Practising on colleagues, and asking for honest comments from them on your performance, can be a relatively unstressed way of gaining initial experience and training.

8.3.2 Qualitative use of interviews

The issues that apply to the qualitative uses of questionnaires (the importance of open-ended questions, the flexibility of analysis, the attempt to work within the research participant's frame of reference) also apply to interviews. In addition, the interview is a peculiar social occasion in which a person who is usually seen to have some expertise (the interviewer) enjoys some power over a person who is expected to speak (the interviewee).

Interviewing has been described as 'a conversation with a purpose', and the purpose should be made clear before the interview takes place. It should be emphasized, however, that this is no ordinary conversation, and the researcher has a responsibility to be clear about what the parameters of the conversation will be (Spradley, 1979). The question of whose purpose is being served is a key preoccupation in recent discussions of the interview process. This is explored in Box 8.3.

Box 8.3 Four approaches in qualitative interviewing

In recent years four broad approaches within qualitative interviewing have been identified (Banister *et al.*, 1994):

(1) Ethnographic interviewing looks to the expertise of the interviewees in accessing rules which structure their lives. The goal of the ethnographic interview is to get within their frame of reference, and a prerequisite for this type of approach is some prior engagement with the life world of the interviewees by working alongside them or spending time participating in their activities and closely observing what is going on (Spradley, 1979).

(2) New-paradigm research looks to the interviewee as someone who should be involved in framing the research question. This means that the topic and task of the interview should be negotiated beforehand, and the changes in the agenda traced as the interview proceeds. This approach asks the interviewee to become, in some senses, a researcher too.

(3) Feminist approaches emphasize the power of the interviewer and the ways in which that power is reproduced moment by moment in the interview itself. There is a particular concern with gender here, but this does not mean that this attention is appropriate only when men are interviewing women. The particular dynamics of questioning, negotiation and response that occur between men or between women can be part of the reflective work that the researcher undertakes (Finch, 1984).

(4) Postmodernist approaches take a further step in considering the anxiety about professional control that is displayed by the other three approaches. There is a concern with the variety of different agendas and meanings that pervade the research, and the way each act of interpretation does some violence to something else that the interviewee may mean to say (Gubrium and Silverman, 1989).

These four approaches often overlap, but it is worth thinking through which approach or approaches you will want to adopt before the work starts.

Qualitative interviewing should not be seen as a licence for simply having a chat with someone you like, and you should take care in setting up the interview in such a way that you will get what you intended and the interviewee will not feel that information has simply been 'extracted'. As with any other variety of research, you should be clear about the scope of the research topic, and, following from this, you must be able to justify interviewing particular people. Sampling, as discussed in Chapter 4, is not always appropriate here, but some consideration must be given as to why your potential interviewees are able to access or represent the salient issues. When you first contact the interviewee you should say how the interview will be recorded, how the information will be kept, who will see it, and what level of anonymity can be assured. Each of these points should be discussed with interviewees, and they should be given the right to see transcripts, ask for certain sections to be deleted, or to withdraw from the study at any stage. You may want to offer them a copy of the final report. It is helpful to discuss with the interviewee the range of questions that you will be focusing on. This is not a test, and you are not trying to catch anyone out. Their thoughtful reflection upon the issues will make for a better interview, and sight of the open-ended questions beforehand can only make that easier.

It is worth doing a practice interview first. It is surprising how often interviewers find out too late how stressful the situation is, and a complete run through with a colleague or friend is invaluable. It is also worth having 'prompts' to hand such as 'can you say a bit more about that', 'can we look at that a bit more', 'is there anything else on that you would want to add'. The stance you should take is of someone who is struggling to understand something different, and you should show respect for the other person's account as he or she speaks.

8.4 Repertory grids and Q methodology

Quantitative and qualitative approaches in psychology often seem to come into conflict because they have arrived from quite different places. Quantitative approaches appear to come from a way of looking at things, specifically at behaviour, that is derived from the method of the natural sciences, and qualitative approaches focus on processes, specifically at meaning in people's lives, that owe much to social or human sciences. There is often a confusion between these different scientific frameworks, and a strong debate as to which framework is the more appropriate to understand individual psychology, as Box 8.4 illustrates.

In the case of repertory grids and Q methodology, however, the story is a little different. Both of these methods contain within them quantitative and qualitative aspects that can fruitfully be used together. There is still a debate among researchers as to which aspect should predominate, and it is a measure of the impact of qualitative research in psychology in recent years that the quantitative part of the procedure should be seen as a step towards a fuller qualitative picture. After some initial attempts to treat them only as quantitative methods, researchers are starting to reclaim the original spirit of each framework, which was to understand the complexity of experience rather than simple behaviour. Repertory grids and Q methodology helps the researcher to structure data, and then to produce a powerful illuminating description of what is going on.

8.4.1 Repertory grids

Repertory grids were developed by George Kelly (1955) as part of an attempt to make psychology respect the variety of ways people actually understand themselves. He was opposed to what he called the 'accumulative fragmentalism'

Box 8.4 Is psychoanalysis scientific?

The debate over quantitative and qualitative research in psychology has consequences for the way in which we might view one of the rival disciplines to psychology, Freudian psychoanalysis. It has often seemed to psychologists to be a clear-cut issue, and Freud's theory is typically treated in psychology courses as the best example of non-science around, or as a joke, or both. One problem that has confounded psychology's understanding of Freud has been the systematic misrepresentation of his ideas in textbooks. Students will quickly learn, for example, that Freud believed in innate aggression and called it the 'death drive', and that little girls have a difficult relationship with their father which is called the 'Electra complex'. As one textbook copies the next, such mistaken accounts of Freud's ideas get circulated around our discipline (Richards, 1989). The theory of the 'id', 'ego' and 'superego' warring against one another, and the mysterious work of 'cathexis' in the 'mental apparatus' all make Freud seem very object-ive, and at the very least (or worst) 'pseudo-scientific'. The description of the 'Oedipus complex', in which every son is assumed to want to kill his father and make love to his mother, also makes it seem as if people have no power to change their lives or social relationships.

Both Kelly (1955) and Stephenson (1953) reacted to the attempts of psychology to provide an 'objective' description of human experience, and developed humanist approaches as alternatives to traditional laboratory experimentation in the discipline. The irony is that they were also very suspicious of Freud, because they saw him as another 'objective' writer who failed to respect individual meaning. This was at the same time as psychoanalysis failed every experimental test to check whether its account was true. It is only quite recently that a new picture of Freud is emerging which brings him close to humanism and, at the same time, to a version of 'science'.

The new picture is presented in Bettelheim's (1986) account of the two models of science that were around in German culture when Freud was writing. The natural sciences (the *Naturwissenschaften*) were seen as appropriate to such enterprises as chemistry and geology, but a different type of science, human sciences (or *Geisteswissenschaften*), was seen as necessary to understand human matters. Translators of Freud wanted him to appear to be scientific in the Anglo-American sense of the term, the natural-science sense. In the process, the meaning of Freud's terminology was radically distorted. Freud used everyday terms to describe experience ('id', 'ego', 'superego' and 'cathexis' were inventions of the translators). The phrase 'mental apparatus' is a very mechanical translation of the German term '*Seele*', which should be translated as 'soul'. Bettelheim also shows how the story of Oedipus is a story of self-knowledge, and an attempt to avert the catastrophe of murdering and marrying the parents. The title of Bettelheim's book, *Freud and Man's Soul,* tries to recover a humanist and scientific psychoanalysis. If Bettelheim is right, psychology is in error when it applies quantitative tests to a qualitative approach.

of much psychology, by which he meant the gathering of meaningless bits of data about behaviour, the sum of which would tell us nothing. He looked instead to a psychology informed by a philosophy of 'constructive alternativism' in which many accounts flowered. Repertory grids capture aspects of experience, the 'elements', organized around what Kelly called 'personal constructs'. The elements can be people, situations, feelings, or any discrete set of experiences that can be identified by the research participant. The constructs organize the elements in relation to one another, in a variety of complex oppositions. The

---

Box 8.5 Repertory grid technique

First, choose some elements. Imagine that you want to look at how you view different social situations. You may identify your work room at home, the student common room, the pub, your kitchen, the train carriage, etc., as among the important elements. Around ten elements will produce an interesting picture; in Fig. 8.1 we have used five simply to illustrate what the format of the grid looks like. List these elements along the top of sheet of paper.

Choose three elements and think about how one differs from the other two. The pub and the kitchen may feel cosy, for example, and the student common room unwelcoming. That distinction between 'cosy' and 'unwelcoming' will then operate as your first construct. Put the side of the construct that summed up the similarity between two elements on the left, and the side that summed up the element which was different from the other two on the right. You can now go along the other elements putting 0 for those that are cosy and putting a cross against those that are unwelcoming. It is important to remember that there is no correct set of oppositions here. If you feel, for example, that your kitchen and student common room are 'spiteful' and the train carriage is diametrically opposite to these because it is 'like mum', then you have arrived at a personal construct that is a meaningful way of structuring your personal world. Between 10 to 15 constructs will usefully differentiate elements and give a sense of how a person subjectively organizes his or her world. We have restricted the number to six in our example.

Sometimes quite extraordinary clusters of meanings are revealed. In Fig. 8.1, this person finds the home work room boring, but it is also felt to be spiteful and cosy. A further exploration would look into the tensions and conflicts that underlie this picture, and sometimes such an exploration borders on the therapeutic (see Box 12.2. **p. 169**). It is possible to explore the relationships between elements in much more detail, and to identify factors using a computer package. Our concern here, though, is with the use of the repertory grid technique as phenomenological tool. A fuller description of the process of constructing a grid is contained in Bannister and Fransella's (1989) introduction to Kelly's work.

repertory grid is a way of representing the ways in which a person organizes elements along the bipolar construct dimensions. The technique is explained in Box 8.5.

Related techniques

The repertory grid is a powerful way of drawing out the constructs that people use to organize their perceptions of self and others. Other methods are also used within the personal-construct tradition to flesh out the meanings of the various different bipolar dimensions. One such method is 'self-characterization', in which the research participants are asked to provide a simple, one-page description of how they see themselves. They could then be asked to provide a simple description of how they were once, or how they would like to be. The different self-characterizations can be analysed in terms of the constructs that structure each account. Another related method, which takes us further into the participant's personal world, is 'laddering', in which the opposite poles of each construct are divided into a new set of overarching ('superordinate') constructs. This research process can then be used therapeutically, and there is a tradition of 'personal-construct therapy' which uses these techniques in a qualitative way to assist change.

Elements				
1	2	3	4	5
Home work room	Student common room	The pub	Your kitchen	The train carriage
Constructs (similarity pole)				Constructs (contrast pole)
1 cosy				unwelcoming
0	X	0	0	0
2 spiteful				like Mum
0	X	0	X	0
3 like				dislike
0	X	X	0	X
4 crowded				empty
0	0	0	X	0
5 tense				relaxed
0	0	0	X	X
6 exciting				boring
X	0	X	X	0

FIG. 8.1. *A rudimentary repertory grid*

8.4.2 Q methodology

Q methodology was developed by Stephenson (1953) as a reaction to psychologists' apparent obsession with testing large numbers of people and then imagining that this could tell them something about one particular person. The method of Q-sorting was meant to pick up the ways in which individuals made sense of the ideas that were available to the community, not with measuring each individual against one ideal standard.

A good simple description of the process of constructing a Q-sort is provided in Curt (1994). The first task is to generate a set of statements about the topic. Around 80–90 propositions should be prepared from a sampling of the 'concourse' of talk about the topic. A bottom limit is 40 for a reasonable coverage. This is quite similar to the first stage of sampling for the production of a questionnaire. The statements are then put on to different pieces of card, and the person is asked to 'sort' this collection along a normal distribution, a bell-shaped curve. Most statements will then be in the central neutral category (0), with the statements which are agreed with put at one side (+5) and the statements disagreed with at

---

Box 8.6 Cue: lesbian identities

Q methodology is useful for exploring alternative forms of identity, for it gives the participants in the research a method by which they can define how they understand themselves. A striking account of Q methodology research is Kitzinger's (1987) study of lesbian identity.

A number of different mechanisms have been identified by researchers, usually men, to describe how oppressed minorities cope with their position. These mechanisms, which Kitzinger drew upon to frame the statements in the Q-sort, include 'deviance disavowal' (refusal to acknowledge membership of the category), 'minstrelization' (behaving in accordance with stereotype), 'role inversion' (attempting to behave against stereotypical expectations), 'concern with in-group purification' (attacking members of the minority that are blamed for the problems they face) and 'fear of group solidarity' (looking to individual solutions to escape stigmatization). Kitzinger took these various descriptions seriously, and so was able to use existing traditional psychological research.

Sixty-one statements were typed on to individual cards and numbered randomly. Forty-one women who defined themselves as lesbian were then asked to arrange the cards along a dimension ranging from agree (+5) through to disagree (-5), in such a way as to conform to a normal distribution (with the bulk of the statements falling around the neutral, zero position). A note was then made of the numbers from the statement cards, and where they fell on the +5 to -5 scale. Factor analysis revealed seven factors, and in this way clusters of identity

— *Continued* — — — — — — — — — — — — — — — — — —

---

the other side (-5). Each statement should be numbered, and the participant is then asked to fill in the Q-pack, putting the numbers of the statements against the normal-distribution scale points (ranging from +5 to -5). A factor analysis then pulls out clusters of statements that different participants have seen as appropriate or inappropriate to describe the topic. Box 8.6 illustrates how this operates in practice, and how the method then works within a qualitative approach.

Repertory grids and Q methodology are rigorous techniques for dealing with self-reports. The form of self-report that everyone will already be familiar with is the keeping of a diary. This seems much looser than the methods we have discussed so far, but diaries can be turned to advantage in the research process.

8.5 Diaries

We have commented earlier about the dangers in relying on questionnaire items that ask people to remember how often they have done something in the past. One way to avoid these problems is to ask people to keep a diary and record in it

— — *Continued* —

statements were highlighted. This step of the research is quantitative, of course, but lays the basis for an exploration of how these clusters express different forms of identity. Kitzinger was able then to connect the sets of factored items with accounts the women gave of their lives and relationships. In this way, the study became a thorough piece of qualitative research.

It is worth noting that this study did not pretend to be 'neutral' or 'objective'. Kitzinger's own lesbian identity played a powerful role in the social construction of the voices that emerged in her research. The argument that runs through her book is also an argument against the ways in which lesbians have been marginalized and pathologized by psychology. It was only in 1973, for example, that the American Psychiatric Association removed homosexuality from its list of psychopathological conditions in the *Diagnostic and Statistical Manual of Mental Disorders*. Kitzinger also wants to show that it is not sufficient to incorporate lesbian psychology into another pluralistic list of 'happy lifestyles', but that it is necessary to take seriously lesbians' own perceptions of their identity as a political challenge to 'hetero-patriarchy', the organization of society around the power of men and the subordination of women in sexual relationships with them (Kitzinger, 1990). The study is a good example of how research that draws on the subjectivity of the researcher as a resource, rather than trying to hide it away, can be more fruitful than much 'objective' work. It is then possible to turn back and reflect upon heterosexuality, something which society and psychology usually takes to be self-evident, natural and universal.

SAQ 8.3

Investigate your own tendency to make slips and lapses by keeping a diary in which you record all occurrences as they happen. Slips are actions-not-as-planned, such as making a pot of tea but forgetting to put the tea in, while lapses are failures of memory which may only be apparent to the person who experiences them, such as forgetting where you put something or forgetting somebody's name.

any examples of the behaviour you are studying. People's mistakes and errors are an intriguing area of study, highlighted by their potential for huge costs in lives as well as money when 'pilot error' causes a plane crash or when a disaster occurs at a nuclear power station. Reason (1990) surveys the ways in which psychologists can study human errors, and refers to the use of extended diaries. Reason and Lucas (1984) comment that diary studies are likely to include biases, because the volunteers may be atypical, because the diarist may select only particularly noteworthy examples to include, and because the diary entry is likely to be made after the event and so will be a shortened account of what happened. Nevertheless, they argue, cognitive diaries can serve a valuable function as 'wide-guage trawl nets, picking up the more salient type of lapse' (p. 56). They used an 'extended' form of diary, in which people not only recorded examples of the type of behaviour being studied but also answered a series of standard questions about each occurrence so that they were cued to note aspects which might otherwise have been omitted. It is worth gaining first-hand experience of the diary technique by doing SAQ 8.3.

8.6 Verbal protocols

Verbal protocols are the reports people give of what they are doing as they do a task or solve a problem. For many years they were ignored, but have become prominent in recent years. There is an argument about their validity: do they give an accurate indication of people's thought processes while they are solving a problem, or are they rationalized justifications for the outcome of processes that are unavailable to conscious awareness (Nisbett and Wilson, 1977; Ericsson and Simon, 1993)?

Ericsson and Simon (1993) assert that 'The accuracy of verbal reports depends on the procedures used to elicit them and the relation between the requested information and the actual sequence of heeded information' (p. 25). They distinguish between three types of verbal report: talk aloud, think aloud, and retrospective reports.

Giving verbal protocols while performing some complex task is not easy: respondents are likely to fall silent, and if you ask them what they are thinking they may well tell you that verbalizing their thoughts prevents them thinking properly!

To reduce this problem, Ericsson and Simon recommend the use of warm-up exercises. They are able, from their experience, to recommend how to obtain verbal protocols. For talk aloud, they use these instructions (p. 376): '...we will ask you to talk aloud as you work on the problems. What I mean by talk aloud is that I want you to say out loud *everything* that you say to yourself silently. Just act as if you are alone in the room speaking to yourself. If you are silent for any length of time I will remind you to keep talking aloud.' They recommend giving some simple problems, such as multiplying 24 by 34, as a warm-up.

For think aloud and for retrospective reports, they use these instructions (p. 378): 'I am going to ask you to think aloud as you work on the problem given. What I mean by think aloud is that I want you to tell me *everything* you are thinking from the time you first see the question until you give an answer. I would like you to talk aloud constantly from the time I present each problem until you have given your final answer to the question. I don't want you to try to plan out what you say or try to explain to me what you are saying. Just act as if you are alone in the room speaking to yourself. It is most important that you keep talking. If you are silent for any long period of time I will ask you to talk.' They then present the practice problem and continue: '...now I want to see how much you can remember about what you were thinking from the time you read the question until you gave the answer. We are interested in what you actually can remember rather than what you think you must have thought.... I don't want you to work on solving the problem again, just report all you can remember thinking about when answering the question.' In think aloud, as opposed to talk aloud, people are encouraged to verbalize information that was encoded in non-verbal form.

Respondents who have had a little practice can provide verbal protocols, but this leaves you with the task of analysing them. Ericsson and Simon discuss the techniques and give examples. The first step is to divide the protocol into statements or segments, which may just be a phrase rather than a complete sentence. Each segment is then encoded, which means that it is expressed in a special shorthand notation indicating its category. For example, 'I'll move disc number 3 from position A to position B' might be encoded as 'Move 3(A, B)'. 'I'll have to put disc 2 in position C' is expressing an intention and might be encoded as 'Goal (2 in C)'. The creation of the coding scheme is a crucial, and time-consuming, part of the preparatory work. Its structure will depend on the task that respondents are given: the aim is to reduce the protocol to a much smaller set of elements, each of which may be expressed verbally in a number of different ways. You can then examine the sequence of elements, count up the number of times different elements occurred, and compare the protocols from different respondents.

Any scoring or coding scheme raises the issue of reliability: do different encoders agree on the way the contents of a protocol should be coded? One way of assessing reliability is to find out how often coders assigned segments to the

---

SAQ 8.4

Try using protocol analysis on yourself and on one or two respondents by presenting a reasoning task. (You could use the task of deciding whether syllogisms like those mentioned in Box 3.3, page 28, are valid.) First, ask a friend to devise a set of problems and present them to you so that you act as respondent. Then ask one or two other friends to act as respondent while you administer the task. Ask them to talk aloud, as explained in section 8.6, and record what they say.

---

same elements, although this has the drawback that it is too heavily influenced by the more common coding categories (Ericsson and Simon, 1993, p. 299).

Protocol analysis is a complex procedure. In broad terms, you need to construct a coding system and assign segments of the protocol to categories. If possible, have two encoders do the task independently. Where they are found to disagree, ask them to negotiate and come to an agreed categorization. Protocol analysis is not easy, takes a lot of time, and requires practice. But it can provide valuable insights into how people dealt with a task, and is a useful complement to performance measures. Use SAQ 8.4 to gain some experience with it.

Psychological techniques: 'natural behaviour' measures

9.0 Introduction

Some of the techniques that psychologists use may seem rather contrived, likely to produce atypical behaviour. So there is an argument for observing how people behave in natural situations. But simple observation has its own difficulties, and is not so simple as you might imagine.

9.1 Observing behaviour

A distinction is made between participant observation, where the observer joins the people being observed, and non-participant observation, where the observer remains external to the people under observation. In either case, it is important to have a clear aim so you can identify what is and what is not pertinent to the study.

Usually you will be able to observe people only in a situation where they expect to be observed, such as in a public place. The target of an observational study obviously depends on the topic being investigated, but you have to decide how many people to observe, and how you will select them. You have to consider whether the people present at the time you are making the observations are likely to be representative. If you observe people in a shopping centre on a weekday morning, you are likely to see fewer employed people than you would on a Saturday, as many of them will be at their place of work.

Even short sequences of behaviour include so many different kinds of action and interaction that it is impossible to record everything, so you have to decide in advance which parts of behaviour will be observed and which ignored. You also need to plan how you are going to record what you observe. This refers both to the physical recording of the observations (video, audio, written notes) and to the encoding of what has taken place. In the study of TV advertisements described in Box 4.2 on page 53, a coding system was applied, and you will need to use an existing one or devise your own.

When you adopt the quantitative approach to observations, there are two types of data you may record in addition to the characteristics (sex, age, etc.) of the people being observed. You may *count* the number of occasions when a certain behaviour occurs. This provides frequency data, telling you who did what and how often. The other form of data comes from *rating* the magnitude of the behaviour you observe; you might, for example, rate the level of aggressiveness of boys and girls in a school playground.

You would expect counting to be easier than judging magnitude, and different observers to show more agreement when counting. But even counting is liable to error, especially if you are observing a number of people and trying to extract only some parts of behaviour. To obtain a clear record of what happened, you will usually need a checklist which lists the types of behaviour: verbal (what is said), paralinguistic (such as the tone used in saying something), nonverbal (bodily movements, such as touching someone), physical movement. You can then fill in the columns with tally marks to show how often each behaviour occurred and/or measures of duration. You may create your own checklist, making it appropriate to the particular area you are investigating. This will usually be devised in the light of pilot observations, which will indicate the number and range of categories that are needed to encapsulate the topic of interest. Alternatively, there are standard coding schemes which you can use; one of these is described in section 9.2.

Robson (1993, p. 213) notes that among other things a coding scheme needs to be objective (requiring little inference from the observer), explicitly defined, exhaustive, mutually exclusive (so that the observer can readily assign an observed item of behaviour to one category) and easy to use. Observers need to be thoroughly familiar with the coding system they are using so that they apply it consistently and, if making the records while the behaviour is actually happening, fast enough to keep up with what is happening.

9.1.1 Rating observed behaviour

Rating the severity or magnitude of behaviour is a more subjective procedure than recording its presence or absence, and it is more difficult to be consistent. Ratings are affected by the number of steps on the scale; people differ in terms of their tendency to use the extreme categories, and raters are affected by the magnitude of other items they have rated. If rating is used, it is best to have a video or audio recording of the behaviour so that it can be studied a number of times, and the whole series can be viewed so that the range can be seen before individual items are given a rating. It is wise to have at least two observers carry out ratings independently, so you can then check on the amount of agreement they show. If possible, the raters should be unaware of the aim of the study, so they are less influenced by expectation effects.

9.1.2 Sampling in observation work

When you set out to observe people, especially if they are interacting with each other, it is impossible to keep track of everything that happens, so you have to sample the behaviour. There are a number of alternatives. In *time-interval sampling*, you take a series of separate short intervals and record what happens during those periods. Cardwell (1992), for example, describes how students could carry out an observational study comparing the amount of aggressive behaviour shown by boys and girls, using 15-second time samples. His recommended method is for the observer to record whether or not a case of verbal or physical aggression occurred during each period, disregarding how often it occurred.

Time-point sampling is when you make observations at predetermined time intervals, such as at the end of every two minutes, and record whether a particular type of behaviour is occurring at that moment.

Event sampling is useful if the behaviour to be observed is comparatively infrequent. In event sampling, behaviour that meets some previously specified definition is observed. For example, suppose you were interested in people's ability to understand maps of the building they are in; you might decide to observe how many people looked at the map, how often they looked at it, how they tried to remember its contents (did they make written notes, or repeat a series of instructions to themselves such as 'turn left then second right'?). You would observe the behaviour only of people who looked at the map, and record only behaviour concerned with reading, understanding and remembering the map: this would be event sampling.

Situation sampling means that behaviour is observed in a number of different situations. If you were observing some common behaviour, such as the way people avoid eye contact in lifts, you might decide to make observations at different times of day and in different kinds of building.

The aim of these different types of sampling is to increase the extent to which you can generalize the findings. If you observe that people in crowded lifts on their way to work in the morning tend to look over the heads of the other people in the lift, is this also found when the lifts are less crowded, when people are leaving work in the evening, when the lift is in a public shopping centre rather than an office building, or when the lift has glass sides? The more widely you have sampled the observations, the more justification you have for claiming that the findings are not restricted to the particular situations and times when you made your observations.

9.1.3 Assessing the reliability of observations

Reliability here means the extent to which different observers who have observed the same behaviour agree with each other, and the extent to which one observer is consistent over time. Authorities recommend that more than one observer should be used to encode the observations, so that a check on reliability can be made. The way you can assess inter-observer reliability depends on the type of data. Examples are described in Box 9.1.

9.1.4 The ecological validity of observations

Part of the appeal of the observational method is its claim to observe natural behaviour in real situations. Real situations can readily be arranged, but ensuring

Box 9.1 Assessing the inter-observer reliability of observations

If the observers have counted the frequency or rated the magnitude of what they saw, you can calculate a correlation coefficient. For example, suppose that two observers have counted the number of times each of a number of children have shown aggressive behaviour. The data table will show the counts of each observer for each child, and these values can be correlated.

In some studies, observers simply record whether or not a certain type of behaviour occurred in each of a number of time periods. You might have them observing a group of children and recording whether aggressive behaviour had occurred in each of 8 two-minute periods, for example. Examining the responses from two observers will show whether they agreed on their yes/no responses for each time interval. You might suppose that you can assess reliability by calculating percentage agreement:

formula 9.1a:

$$\frac{\text{No. of times two observers agree}}{\text{No. of time intervals (opportunities to agree)}} \times 100$$

But as Neale and Liebert (1986) point out, this formula gives an inflated measure of agreement: if the critical behaviour happened only rarely, the observers will agree on the many occasions when it was not observed. Neale and Liebert suggest that those cases where the observers agree that the critical behaviour did not occur should be ignored, and one should calculate:

formula 9.1b:

$$\frac{\text{No. of agreed occurrences}}{\text{No. of agreed occurrences} + \text{No. of disagreed occurrences}} \times 100$$

Suppose that two observers have observed the behaviour of a group of children for 8 two-minute periods and recorded whether aggressive behaviour did or did not occur during each one. Table 9.1 gives an example of the results.

Using formula 9.1a, you would count up the number of time periods where the two observers agreed, the number of Ys in the 'Agreement?' column, and divide it by the number of time periods to get a percentage agreement of $7/8 = 87.5\%$. But in time periods 5–8 the two observers agreed only in that aggressive behaviour did not occur. Using formula 9.1b these instances are ignored, and you calculate the amount of agreement by taking the number of cases where the two observers agreed that the behaviour did occur. In the example, there are three cases (time periods 1,2 and 3). This is divided by the number of agreed occurrences (3) plus the number of disagreed occurrences. These are the periods where one observer said the aggressive behaviour had occurred while the other said it had not. In the example, this situation arose on trial 4. So using this formula on the figures in the table, the index of agreement is $3/(3+1) = 75\%$.

— — *Continued* — — — — — — — — — — — — — — — —

— — *Continued* —

In some observational studies, observations are categorized. In a study of TV advertisements such as that described in Box 4.2 (p. 53), for example, the arguments presented for buying a product might be categorized as 'scientific', 'non-scientific' or 'other'. If you have two observers do the categorization independently, you can draw up a confusion matrix, such as Table 9.2, which shows how the advertisements were categorized by each observer.

Each cell of this table contains a figure showing how many advertisements fell into each grouping. The number which had been put into the same category by both observers can be found by finding the total of the entries in the cells marked with an asterisk (28). This can then be expressed as a percentage of the total number of advertisements categorized, giving the index of agreement: 28/40 gives 70%.

There are other ways of expressing the amount of agreement, such as Cohen's Kappa, which take into account the proportion of agreements expected by chance. Robson (1993, pp. 222–223) illustrates how to calculate this index.

If you had more than two observers, assessing reliability becomes more complicated. With three or more sets of rankings, you could use Kendall's Coefficient of Concordance, as described in Siegel and Castellan (1988).

TABLE 9.1. *Example of data from two observers*

Time period	Observer A	Observer B	Agreement?
1	Y	Y	Y
2	Y	Y	Y
3	Y	Y	Y
4	Y	N	N
5	N	N	Y
6	N	N	Y
7	N	N	Y
8	N	N	Y

TABLE 9.2. *Example of a confusion matrix for observational data*

	Observer A			Total
	Scientific	Non-scientific	Other	
Observer B				
Scientific	10*	2	1	13
Non-scientific	1	8*	3	12
Other	1	4	10*	15
Total	12	14	14	40

SAQ 9.1

Plan and carry out a small-scale observational study. Bearing in mind the ethical issues underlying observations, you should observe people only in a public place. Driver behaviour, pedestrians' ability to find their way, and use of road crossings are topics which lend themselves to observational work. You will need to conduct a pilot study to determine what you are going to record, how you are going to record it, and how you will decide on the samples to use. If you can, have two different observers working independently and then assess the reliability of the observations, as explained in Box 9.1.

---

the behaviour is natural is not so straightforward. People who are aware that they are being observed may well act in an unnatural manner, and this is not at all what is wanted. There are two main ways of dealing with this. One is to prevent the people becoming aware that they are being observed. Current opinion holds that this is rarely acceptable unless people are being observed while they are in a public place. The other procedure is to repeat the observations over a series of sessions so that the people adapt to the situation and revert to their 'usual' way of behaving. You might, for example, observe a group of people for ten sessions, but only use the recordings of the last five, when you hope they have overcome any tendency to 'act' specially for your benefit.

There is no substitute for actually trying out a technique if you want to discover its benefits and problems. We recommend you try SAQ 9.1.

9.2 Standard procedures for recording observations

There are a number of established schemes for coding observed behaviour. For small-group interaction, Bales' interaction process analysis (IPA) (Bales, 1950) is well known. It allows for 12 categories of verbal behaviour divided into task relations and social-emotional relations, as shown in Table 9.3. As you can see, it is a symmetrical scheme, with each category in each area being balanced by a complementary one. Manstead and Semin (1988) describe its use as follows: 'The observer's task in using this system is to concentrate on the verbal interaction taking place between members of a group, and to place individual statements or "thought units" into one of the 12 categories, noting at the same time who made the statement and to whom it was directed' (p. 76). Using a scheme like this demands practice. Manstead and Semin comment that IPA ignores nonverbal behaviour.

9.3 General conclusion on psychological techniques

Psychology is such a diverse discipline that specialists in one area may have little understanding of what specialists in other areas do. Each area has its own

TABLE 9.3. *The categories of verbal behaviour in small-group interaction used in Bales' interaction process analysis*

Social-emotional relations: positive reactions
    shows solidarity
    shows tension release
    agrees

Task relations: answers
    gives suggestion
    gives opinion
    gives information

Task relations: questions
    asks for information
    asks for opinion
    asks for suggestion

Social-emotional relations: negative reactions
    disagrees
    shows tension
    shows antagonism

---

preferred methods and techniques. Cognitive psychology, for example, makes considerable use of the experimental approach to investigate the speed with which people can perform a task, and less use of interviews or self-reports. Industrial psychologists, on the other hand, make considerable use of questionnaires and attitude measures, and rarely have the opportunity to perform formal experiments. But do not assume that any method is only applicable within one specialism. It is misleading to think 'This is cognitive psychology, so I must do an experiment; this is social psychology, so I must not do an experiment'. The choice of methods and techniques should depend on the purpose of the investigation, not its subject matter. Understanding is likely to be increased when a number of methods, not just one, are employed.

Chapter 10

Planning the investigation

10.0 Introduction

When you first undertake investigations in psychology you will be provided with detailed guidance on what to do, with support such as that given in the *BPS Manual of Psychology Practicals* (McIlveen *et al.*, 1992). But you will soon be faced with planning and carrying out your own studies. In this chapter we provide some hints on how to go about this, and how to avoid some of the more common errors. The various steps are summarized in Box 10.3.

10.1 Stating the aim

The first requirement is that you should have a clear aim for your study. You may begin with a preference for a general area of the discipline ('I want to do something on memory/advertising/children'), but you cannot make progress until you have a more definite goal. So a preliminary step is to read round the topic or area in which you are interested, acquire an awareness of the topics that have been studied, and the ways in which investigators have approached them. You will then be able to make a more precise statement of what it is you want to investigate. Initially, this may still be rather general, but you must be able to state it with sufficient precision that it suggests both the method(s) you could use and the type of outcome you can expect (a table of numerical scores, a series of verbal protocols, interview transcripts, etc.). So you may narrow your interest down to 'memory for music', 'the effects of anxiety on performance', 'children's ideas of God' – a more precise title like this will provide a framework for further reading, in which you try to discover what has previously been done on the topic.

A major consideration is the need to select a topic that is feasible with the resources available to you. Resources include your time, physical apparatus, and access to appropriate types of respondent: there is no sense planning a study of offenders' moral judgements if you have no opportunity of meeting any offenders! It is also necessary to consider ethical issues. Some topics may not be ethically acceptable because they increase the risk of the participants experiencing physical or mental harm, because it is impossible to obtain real consent, or for some other reason covered by the ethical principles discussed in Chapter 2.

10.2 Finding relevant literature

There are two difficulties you are likely to face: you cannot find relevant material or you find far too much! The latter is especially likely if you choose a popular topic, such as face recognition, teaching reading, or racial attitudes. The lack of relevant studies is much rarer: psychologists have been filling journals with reports of research for over a century, and almost everything you can think of has been studied by someone somewhere, even if you cannot find it!

You are likely to have two immediate sources to start you off in finding literature on your chosen topic: one is your teachers, who may be able to give you a starting point of relevant journal papers or books, and the other is the secondary literature of textbooks. Suppose you want to find out what research has been reported on people's memory for music: where would you start?

Start with your basic textbook and then any more specialized books on your chosen topic which you know of or which are mentioned in your basic text. Then go to your academic library. You should be able to find where any books on the topic you are pursuing are located on the shelves from the library catalogue or by asking the librarian. It is often useful to find how a book on your topic is classified in your library and then look on the shelves around that class number for books on similar topics.

From an early stage in your studies you will be needing to consult the original research reports, rather than relying on the second-hand summaries in textbooks. Once you have the reference to an original journal paper, you may be able to find it in your library or request a copy of it through the Inter-Library Loans service. You will need to ask your teachers how deeply you are expected to go in surveying the existing literature on the topic of your investigation. A final-year undergraduate project will need a much fuller summary than an A-level practical.

If you have a number of references to journal papers, you must be selective about which ones to consult: there is a temptation to chase up all relevant work, which is extravagant of both time and money. So concentrate on those most likely to be useful to you. How can you decide which these are? There are four clues. (1) Papers which are cited in many textbooks are likely to be the important ones. (2) Longer papers are likely to provide further references. (3) Some journals, such as *Behavioral and Brain Sciences*, *Psychological Review*, *Psychological Bulletin* and the *Annual Review of Psychology*, specialize in review papers which survey the research on a given topic. So a paper that appears in one of these is likely to be a valuable source of information. (4) The title of the paper may indicate that it is a review paper summarizing a topic. So if you were chasing material on memory for music, you would look out for papers with titles such as 'Memory for music: A review of research in the 1990s' or 'A meta-analysis of research into memory for music'.

If you need to search through the journals for papers on a specific topic, the least efficient method is to read through the contents pages of the actual journals. (Although this can bring to your notice interesting work which you would not otherwise have come across, a phenomenon known as serendipity.) If there is one available, it is better to use an abstracting service. *Psychological Abstracts* prints the abstracts of thousands of papers published each year, and almost anything you are likely to require will be summarized in its pages. Many university libraries now have a CD-ROM version of *Psychological Abstracts*, PsycLit. You type in key words, such as 'memory', and the computer then searches through its thousands of abstracts and creates a subset of abstracts which contain this key word. You can ask it for abstracts containing another key word (such as 'music') and then ask for those abstracts which contain both 'memory' and 'music'. You can search for particular authors, journal titles, dates, etc., so that there is enormous power at your finger tips. You can then have the selected abstracts displayed on the screen, printed and even saved on your own floppy disk. Your library may have access to other computer-based databases which can provide valuable reference material.

When you have read a number of papers or book extracts, you should be able to state the aim of the particular study you intend to perform.

10.2.1 Meta-analysis

Meta-analysis is a technique which combines statistically the results of different investigations on one topic. There is no single procedure of meta-analysis, as the experts argue about the details of what should be calculated and how. Technical expositions can be found in such texts as Hunter *et al.* (1982), but the technicalities do not need to concern you until you reach advanced undergraduate level. Even if the statistics are beyond your comprehension, you will find meta-analyses provide very full reference lists on the topic, summaries of what the research on the topic has demonstrated, criticisms of the area, and suggestions for further research. For some topics, such as the use of interviews in selecting people for jobs, meta-analyses appear quite regularly. But if you cannot trace a meta-analysis for your particular research area, you will have to rely on the discursive review paper such as those in the *Annual Review of Psychology*.

Meta-analyses are usually based on a computer search of the journals, and the references yielded by the computer search will be given in the report. Remember that the meta-analysis will be out of date before you read it: to find the most recent studies, concentrate on searching the journals after the date of the meta-analysis.

10.3 Selecting the method and technique

Reading previous work will have informed you not only about what researchers have found, but also the way they investigated the topic. You may decide to follow their example, or you may decide to apply a different method or use a different technique of gathering data. In many instances a range of methods could be used, and it is necessary to decide on which one or ones are most likely to provide the most useful information. Whether you decide on an experiment, survey, observational study, correlational study or case study will determine the next set of decisions you have to make.

10.4 Stating the hypothesis

This section is written in the context of designing a quantitative study, such as an experiment, but the principles of knowing precisely what you are examining and expecting to occur apply whichever method you have chosen.

It is important to distinguish between the aim of the study and the hypothesis. The aim might be quite general; the hypothesis is much more specific. As the example described in Box 10.1 indicates, stating the hypothesis means you have to have made decisions about the method and techniques you will use, and your hypothesis may appear very constrained and narrow compared with the aim you started with. The hypothesis is a precise prediction of what will be the outcome of the particular study you are performing. You must be clear about whether you are predicting a difference between the sets of scores, or a relationship (correlation) between them. In an experiment the experimental hypothesis predicts the effect on the dependent variable of the manipulations of the independent variable – that there will be a difference in the scores (on the dependent variable) of the groups of respondents. The null hypothesis states that there will be no difference between the scores of the groups. Make sure you know whether your experimental hypothesis is directional or nondirectional. If you are saying there will be a difference between the conditions, you have a nondirectional hypothesis. If you predict which condition will be superior, then you have a directional hypothesis.

In a correlational study, your hypothesis will predict a relationship between sets of scores. An example is: 'People who score highly on a questionnaire of Attitude to Study will have higher scores on a questionnaire measuring academic achievement'. The null hypothesis is that there will be no correlation ($r = 0$).

Remember not to design a study to confirm the null hypothesis because a failure to obtain a difference or relationship is ambiguous. It may arise because the independent variable has no effect on the dependent variable, or it may arise from other causes, such as an inadequate procedure.

In planning your study do not be too ambitious. It is particularly important not to proliferate independent variables. You may begin with a simple experiment, comparing memory for coloured and black-and-white photographs of faces, and then think it would be interesting to see whether the effects (if there are any) are influenced by the respondent's sex, so you will run the experiment separately on males and females. You might then decide that age may be an important factor, and decide to test people of three age groups (children, young adults, older adults). This would give you at least a $2 \times 2 \times 3$ study; the analysis and interpretation of experiments with three factors is likely to strain your statistical abilities to their limit.

Box 10.1 Case study in designing an investigation: effects of music on studying

Stage 1: Stating the aim
A group of students were required to carry out a study in any area they chose, and decided they wanted to look at the effects of background music on studying. They all had music in the background when they were studying, but knew that some people asked 'How can you concentrate with that din going on?' So their initial aim was to see whether music affected people's ability to study.

Stage 2: Finding relevant literature
The next step was to see what research had already been done on this topic. From lectures they had already had, they thought there were two areas of research which might be relevant. One was the study of attention and the effects of distraction on performance. The other was that part of memory research known as cue-dependent learning; this in very broad terms suggests that if you learn something in one environment then you are likely to remember it better if you return to that environment. They conducted a literature search, looking for information under the headings of 'music' and 'memory'. This yielded a list of references which seemed from their titles as though they would be relevant to the question of how background music affects learning.

Stage 3: Selecting the method
There are a number of ways one could investigate the topic of background music and studying. A correlational study could be used to compare the performance of those who study with music and those who study without, an interview/survey could be used to find out how many students used background music, what types of music, how loudly they had it, etc. This group decided they were interested in discovering whether background music had an effect on people's learning from a text, as this seems to have ecological validity, resembling the real-life student situation. They therefore decided to carry out an experiment in which participants would be asked to perform a study task with or without background music, and the amount learned would be compared.

Stage 4: Stating the hypothesis
Having decided on carrying out an experiment to investigate the effects of background music on studying, it is necessary to decide on the particular procedures to use, how the independent and dependent variables are to be manipulated and measured. Only when this has been done is it possible to state the experimental hypothesis.

In this example, the students predicted that there would be a difference between the learning of those studying with background

— — *Continued* — — — — — — — — — — — — — — — — — —

— — *Continued* — — — — — — — — — — — — — — — — — — —

music and those without. They had to decide what exactly was meant by background music (what type of music, how loud, etc.) and what operational definition of 'learning' they would use. It is here that compromises have to be made, and you have to narrow the study down to a particular set of conditions. Should you use music that the participants like, the kind they typically have when they are studying? If you use one type of music, some people may detest it and find it distracting, others not. There are various issues regarding the material to be learnt. If you use a within-subjects experiment, you need two separate learning assignments. If you use a between-subjects design, individual differences may obscure any effects of the independent variable. How will 'learning' be measured: what is the dependent variable going to be?

The students decided to use a between-subjects experiment, so that everyone could be presented with the same learning task, and to assess the amount learned by giving a post-test using the free-recall procedure. Their experimental hypothesis was: 'Readers who read the text for 5 minutes with background music will score differently on the post-test from those readers who read the text for 5 minutes without background music.'

They had to decide on the reading/learning text to use, how to score the post-reading recalls, the time to elapse between the reading and the recall, and how this time was to be occupied. They also had to consider how extraneous variables were to be dealt with. Who were to act as participants? How would they be allocated to conditions? How could they ensure that no one had an unfair advantage by knowing the text content beforehand?

They planned the statistical analysis by drawing up a data table like Table 10.1. They concluded they could apply a test to compare the means of two groups.

In planning the experiment, they had had to narrow down their original idea so that they had a testable experimental hypothesis. This illustrates the benefits and limitations of using experiments: the procedures and hypothesis have to be very precise, but it is unlikely that one small experiment will let you draw any general conclusion about the topic that initially sparked your interest.

TABLE 10.1. *Example of a data table used in planning a study – table of recall scores*

Participant	Condition with music	Participant	Condition without music
1		2	
3		4	
5		6	
:		:	
x		x	
$\bar{x}$		$\bar{x}$	

As a general rule, when planning an experiment, keep to a simple design. We recommend no more than two independent variables in a single study; three might be acceptable if you understand how to analyse the data, but any more than that will render the study too complicated. You may feel that this omits potentially important variables, but bear in mind that you are not likely to answer the major theoretical problems in the discipline. If you want to know how other factors influence the outcome of the study, it is often best to carry out a series of separate studies rather than try to incorporate numerous conditions in a single investigation.

You need to know before you obtain any data which tests of statistical significance you intend to use. It is not uncommon for students to turn up with sets of data and ask 'What should I do with this now?' It cannot be stated too strongly that this is the path to potential disaster! Often, the numbers are useless because variables were confounded, or the measurements were on too coarse a scale, or the attempt to manipulate an independent variable failed. It is no use deferring the problem by saying 'I will use the appropriate statistical test': you must know which test, how to calculate it, and how to interpret the outcome. If your calculations show that the Mann–Whitney test gives a $U = 17$ when you had two groups of 10 respondents, what does this indicate about the statistical significance of the results? If the result is statistically significant, what does this mean with regard to your hypothesis? (The Appendix at the end of this book explains how to calculate tests of statistical significance, and the notion of statistical significance is dealt with in Chaper 11.)

You may find that the data make you alter your plan: you intended to use a *t*-test, for example, but found that the data do not meet the assumptions which that test requires. So you have to use a non-parametric alternative. But this is no excuse for failing to be very clear in advance about the analysis you intend to apply.

Draw up a data table and list the tests you will apply, indicating which figures will be used in the calculations. If you cannot do this, stop! Either your study is beyond your level of statistical competence, or you have not thought through how you will apply your statistical competence. In the latter case, careful thinking should solve the problem. If it does not do so, you have the former situation, and proceeding beyond your level of competence can be disastrous. If you do not understand how to analyse the results, you must do one of two things. Either increase your understanding of statistical analysis so you can approach your data confident that you know how to analyse them. Alternatively, redesign the study so that you do understand how to analyse the results. Box 10.2 describes an example.

10.5 Selecting the respondents

Which respondents you will use depends upon the aim of the study and people's availability. The benefits of randomly sampling respondents from a population are emphasized in all methodology books but, in practice, you may find that you

Box 10.2 Example of redesigning a study

One group of students planned to tackle the problem of the effects of music on studying described in Box 10.1 using a before-and-after design. They intended to test their participants' knowledge of a particular topic before they read a passage about it, and then test them again afterwards. There were to be three groups, one with quiet music, one with loud music and one with no music. So there would be six sets of scores:

	Quiet music	Loud music	No music
Before reading			
After reading			

How would a set of data like this be analysed? This is a 3 × 2 design with repeated measures on the second factor, and really needs the analysis of variance. But the students had not learnt how to apply a two-way analysis of variance. To cope with this, they decided that for each participant they would calculate the difference between the scores obtained on the 'before' and 'after' tests. Then each participant would have just one score. But there would still be three sets of scores. The students knew how to apply a t-test to two sets of scores, but not how to compare three sets. So they decided they would have to drop one of the conditions, and just use the loud-music and no-music conditions. They would then be able to use the t-test, which they had learned, to analyse the results.

have to use respondents from a small pool such as personal friends, colleagues at work, or fellow students. A key issue is how far you wish to generalize the result of the study. An experiment is based on comparing the groups of respondents' results, and it is acceptable to use quite small numbers of people with no attempt to make them representative of the general population. If there is any reason to suspect that the results do not apply to other types of people, the experiment should be replicated on other groups.

Remember that the validity of an experiment depends on using proper techniques for allocating respondents to conditions. A survey requires a representative sample of the population, and the people available to you will limit how far you can generalize the outcome. Correlational studies are like surveys in that respect. As a general rule, there are weaker grounds for generalizing from field studies and case studies: the results may be true only for the people who took part.

10.5.1 How many respondents are required?

Students, particularly when they are planning an experiment, often ask how many participants they need. There are two ways of answering this. As a rule of thumb, at least ten respondents per group in a between-subjects experiment is the minimum to aim at in a practical. If you are using a within-subjects design, aim for ten people. For a correlational study, about 30 respondents is a reasonable target.

The proper answer to the question, which gives some justification for the recommendations made in the previous paragraph, uses the notion of the power of a statistical test. It depends on advanced issues unlikely to trouble you while you are learning the basic skills of research, but it is important to appreciate that the question of how many participants to use can be estimated in advance. A detailed consideration is provided by Howell (1992, Chapter 8).

10.6 Designing an experiment

Designing an experiment requires a number of decisions, as the example described in Box 10.1 illustrates. What will be the dependent variable? How will you manipulate the independent variable and how many levels will you use? Will you have a control group? How will you control extraneous variables? Remember that there are different types of extraneous variable: all need to be considered and kept constant, randomized or counterbalanced. It is particularly important to use a proper procedure for allocating respondents to conditions and to deal with possible order effects, as we discussed in Chapter 3. Some of the questions you will have to answer are included in Box 10.3.

10.7 Designing quantitative studies using nonexperimental approaches

If you are planning a study which does not count as an experiment or quasi-experiment, you still have to decide on the dependent variable (what are you going to measure?), the participants to be used (how many and how will they be chosen?), the procedure you will use, and the way you will summarize and analyse the data. If you are expecting to find a relationship between scores or differences between groups of participants, you will be able to formulate a hypothesis stating what you predict the outcome will be. Although nonexperiments are less restrictive, it is still essential for you to know what you are hoping to find (aim), how you are going to find it (procedure), who you are going to study (participants), and how you are going to summarize what you found (statistical analysis).

10.8 Designing a qualitative study

As with a quantitative study, a qualitative investigation must start with a clear definition of the scope of the research. Unlike quantitative research, however, the precise focus of the eventual report will emerge during the process of carrying out the study, interpreting the 'data' and writing the report. We deal with the analysis and writing up stages and the ways in which you should handle the changes in research focus in Chapters 12 and 14. At this point, we want to emphasize the importance both of (1) setting an initial research question and (2) narrowing this question down as the design proceeds.

With respect to (1), you should define the question, the participants, the process, and your expectations. Let us take each of these in turn.

(a) Delimit the boundaries of the question. Perhaps you are interested in the way people talk about mental health. Here you have to specify what you mean by 'mental health'. To focus it, such a broad topic will need to be related to another particular issue.

(b) You need to be clear which 'people' you are concerned with. If you are interviewing mental health workers about their views of mental health and 'community care', for example, you should say exactly what group of mental health workers you are concerned with (psychiatric social workers, community volunteers, etc.), how many, and why. Why this group particularly? It is necessary to define exactly who will be interviewed (in the case of an interview study), which texts are to be used (in the case of a discourse analysis), or which social world is to be studied (in the case of ethnographic or action research).

(c) What exactly are you intending to do? Will you interview people once, for example, and then analyse the transcripts, or will you interview them and take the transcripts back for comments?

(d) What do you expect to be said (in the case of interviews), or to appear (in the case of discourse analysis, qualitative personal construct research, or ethnographic study), or to happen (in the case of action research)?

These four aspects of the research define your aims, and while you will not be testing 'hypotheses', you have to be clear what your starting point is so that you can be clear in your report about how your view of the phenomenon in question changed in the course of the research.

As the study proceeds, you may discover that the questions that structured your interview, reading or observation do not make sense to your interviewees or that other things are going on in the text or social world you chose. You must trace the ways in which you discover that your starting choices and assumptions have to be adapted. If psychiatric social workers were uninterested in community care for people with mental health problems, for example, you need to consider why that may be the case. If your participation in a drop-in centre had to stop because the organizers or users were hostile to the research, you should look to why that may have happened. As with quantitative research, each problem is material for discussion in the report. In a qualitative study, though, you take this further and turn each problem into an opportunity for reflection on the nature of the question you initially posed. The report is then

Box 10.3 Checklist when planning a study

(1) Decide on the general area.

(2) Read background material.

(3) Decide on the specific area.

(4) Check on feasibility: do you have the resources, time, participants? If not, go back to step 3.

(5) Consider ethical issues by using the checklist in Chapter 2 (p. 15)

(6) Find and read relevant literature.

(7) Specify the aim of this particular study.

(8) Decide on the method(s): experiment, survey, observation, etc. See Chapter 3 for a description of the various methods. Will you use more than one method?

(9) Decide on the technique, the kind of measure (dependent variable) you will use. See Table 6.1 (p. 71) for a list of some of the possibilities.

(10) Specify the independent variable and the number of levels you will have.

(11) State the hypothesis. Check you are not trying to test a null hypothesis.

(12) Design the experiment, quantitative non-experiment or qualitative method investigation.

If you are using an experiment, you need to decide on whether to use a within-subjects, between-subjects, matched-groups or mixed design, and how to control extraneous variables, as covered in Chapter 3. Allocating respondents to groups is covered in step 14. Here you need to be able to answer the following questions:

    (a) Are there any confounding variables? If so, remove them.

    (b) Which factors will you keep constant for all participants? These should include the instructions and amount of practice they receive, and the physical conditions under which the study occurs.

    (c) Which variables do you need to control by counterbalancing? These might include experimenters, so that each experimenter tests the same number of each group of participants. The time of day when the testing occurs may need to be counterbalanced if it cannot be kept constant for everybody.

Order effects definitely need to be considered. If you have a within-subjects design, you need to counterbalance order. With two tasks, A and B, half the people should have them in the order AB while the other half have them in the order BA.

If you have three tasks, A, B and C, there are six possible orders: ABC, ACB, BAC, BCA, CAB, CBA. So you need six subgroups if

— *Continued* — — — — — — — — — — — — — — — — — —

— — *Continued* —

every possible order is to be used. If this is not practical, or you have more than three tasks, you can use a separate, random order of tasks for each participant, so that any order effects should average out. Table N2 (p. 243) can be used to give you random orders of conditions. (There are more precise ways of dealing with order effects, using Latin squares, but these are for more advanced work.)

With a between-subjects design you need to control the order in which groups are tested. Do not leave one group to the end, as the experimenter may be more skilled or less interested in carrying out the study conscientiously by the time this group is tested. Balance the order of testing, so that with two groups, A and B, half of A are tested first, then group B, then the other half of group A. If you have three groups, A, B and C, divide them into halves and test them in the order ABCCBA.

(13) Decide on how you will analyse the outcome. If you are using a quantitative method, draw up the tables in which you will show the data and specify which statistical tests will be needed.

(14) Select the respondents. Allocate them to the various conditions using an appropriate procedure such as random group formation (see Box 3.4, p. 30) or a matching procedure (see Box 3.5, p. 33).

(15) Create any materials you require and ensure you have any equipment you need such as computers, stopwatches, etc. Write out the instructions for the respondents. If there are two or more investigators, they need instructions too.

(16) Run a pilot study on two or three people to check that everything proceeds as planned. If it does not, revise the procedure and run another pilot study.

(17) Carry out the main study. Be prepared to stop, revise and run it again if it soon becomes clear that there is a problem such as people failing to follow the instructions or it proves impossible to record the data as the study is happening.

(18) Collate the data and fill in the tables you created at step 13.

(19) Analyse the data and interpret the outcome. (See Chapters 11 and 12.)

(20) Write the report. (See Chapter 14.)

(21) Submit the report.

(22) When the report is returned, bask in the glory of the marks achieved, or read carefully through the comments you get to see where you could have done better....

an account of what you have learnt, and how your readers may also learn from what occurred.

10.9 Preparing the materials

Obviously you need to ensure you have appropriate materials for your respondents, whether these are questionnaires to complete, printed sets of items to remember, or whatever. But in addition you should go to some trouble to prepare in advance written instructions for your respondents. These should include statements about their right to withdraw from the study, as was explained in the discussion of ethics in Chapter 2. You may read these to them, but a verbatim copy of the instructions is valuable for the report later. It is also crucial if different investigators are being used, since it is important that everyone follows the same procedure.

You may also need an interview schedule, coding sheets for observations or content analysis, or other appropriate 'hard-copy' materials for each member of the investigating team.

We have already advised you to prepare in advance the data tables so that you can see what the data will look like and which statistical procedures will be appropriate.

10.10 Running a pilot study

Before undertaking the study proper, you should always run a pilot on one or two respondents. This allows you to see whether the instructions and task are understood, and you can make any alterations that are needed. Run your pilot as though you were running the study proper, but at appropriate points ask respondents whether it is clear what you are asking them to do, how they should carry out the task, etc. When they have finished the task, ask them to tell you how they approached it, and what difficulties they encountered. Debriefing pilot respondents is a dialogue, in which you explain what the study was intended to do, and they tell you whether it did! The aim is to obtain a full account as possible of how the situation appeared to the respondent, so that you can be reasonably sure that when you run the study proper it is doing what you planned.

It is very likely that the pilot study will reveal the need to make changes to the instructions, procedure or recording techniques of the study. When you have made the changes, you really need to run another pilot to ensure that the revised procedure works successfully. If the changes you have introduced are minor, this may be unnecessary. But if they are significant, a second pilot is important. It is difficult to say exactly what is 'significant', but if your original instructions left the respondent confused and you have rewritten them, a second pilot to check that the revised version is clear is definitely necessary. Similarly, if you found that you were unable to record the responses under the conditions you had devised, you will need to check that the revised procedure does let you do so.

10.11 Carrying out the study

You are now ready to carry out the study proper. By this stage you should be confident that you know what you are going to do and how you expect respondents to behave. As you gather the data from your respondents do check that the study seems to be functioning as intended. If you find all the first few participants are scoring 100%, for example, do not be afraid of halting the study, revising the procedure and starting again.

10.12 Interpreting the outcome

When the data-collection phase is complete, you move to the analysis stage. Dealing with quantitative data is covered in Chapter 11, and the analysis of qualitative data in Chapter 12. The interpretation of the outcome of the study will obviously depend on the data you obtained. Was the hypothesis supported? How many respondents of each category gave a particular score or response? There are some particular points to bear in mind.

First, avoid the temptation to assert that you have proved a hypothesis or theory. In Chapter 1 we pointed out that science does not, according to Popper's model, establish proof. If the hypothesis has been supported, that is how you should express the outcome.

Second, avoid the temptation to argue that if the respondents did not do something, they cannot do it.

Third, if you have followed our advice you had a clear idea of how to analyse the data before you collected any. You knew that to test your hypothesis, you needed to apply, say, a Mann–Whitney test to the scores from the two groups of participants. Begin the analysis with this idea. You may find other aspects worth commenting upon and following up with subsidiary analyses, but ensure these do not obscure the main outcome which prompted the study in the first place.

10.13 Writing and submitting the report

These stages will, at least when you are a beginner, be a major drain on your time. Detailed advice is given in Chapters 14 and 15.

Quantitative data analysis

11.0 Introduction

When students first come to psychology they are often surprised, even appalled, at the amount of statistics they have to master. This mastery is required because the quantitative approach to psychology assumes that you measure phenomena. Measurement involves assigning numbers – the size of the number representing the magnitude of whatever it is that you are measuring, and this means you need statistical analysis.

There are two approaches to teaching statistics to psychologists. One is sometimes referred to, rather disapprovingly, as the 'cookbook' method: students are told what to do, but given little explanation of why they should follow the rules. The other, purist approach, argues that psychologists need to *understand* statistics – not only how to calculate them, but also the underlying theory which explains why the various procedures are used. In this book, we adopt a compromise position. This chapter covers the basic principles underlying statistical analysis, but does not attempt to provide a full account of the technical background. If you need that, you should refer to a text such as Howell (1992). You will probably have access to a computer program which will carry out calculations for you, and so the main thing you need is to understand which calculations you require and what the outcome means when the computer presents it to you. In case you do not have a computer available, a 'cookbook' describing the steps needed to calculate the statistics you are most likely to need is given in Appendix 1 at the end of this book.

11.1 Fundamental concepts

11.1.1 Population and sample

In carrying out research you obtain data from a number of people, but usually want to argue that what you find with this small number is also true of other people. The people you actually employ in the study form your sample, and the 'other people' form the population. (Do not confuse this term with the population of a country or the world. In statistical analysis, a population is usually a specified set of individuals, such as the women of France aged under 30, or Australian nine-year-olds.) Whether it is valid to generalize from the sample to the population depends upon whether it is representative: does it have the same characteristics as its population?

11.1.2 Descriptive and inferential statistics

Descriptive statistics describe and summarize sets of data. Table 11.1 shows the time people took to recognize faces seen either in full-face view or profile view. The averages tell you something about those sets of scores: group A had an average of 0.46 seconds and group B an average of 0.60. But usually you want to generalize and say that what was true of your sample is true of a wider population. This is when you have to use inferential statistics.

Inferential statistics are used in two ways. One is to infer characteristics of the population: if the mean of a sample is known, we can use this to estimate the mean of the population. The measure that applies to a whole population is known as a parameter, and the same measure calculated from a sample is a statistic. The second use of inferential statistics is testing hypotheses. When you carry out an experiment to test a hypothesis, you obtain scores from different groups of respondents. In this situation, you want to know whether one group scored differently from another. You are not interested in whether the specific scores from your respondents can be generalized to the population at large, but in the difference between the scores of the groups. If the two sets of scores are really different, they can be thought of as coming from two different populations, corresponding to the two experimental conditions. If they are not really different, they all come from one population.

Students are often confused over this, and say that an experiment is suspect because it did not use a representative sample of people, and so one cannot generalize the results. But whether the people who took part are representative of a wider population is not really the issue. The aim of the branch of statistical analysis known as significance testing is to establish whether the scores from the various groups in the experiment are truly different, so that you can argue that the independent variable affected performance. If the independent variable did affect performance in the experiment, you assume that it would also affect performance if other people did the experiment. Of course it is only an assumption that the results generalize to other people, and sometimes this assumption is challenged: this is the issue of 'population validity', mentioned in section 3.6.2.

11.1.3 Scales of measurement

Measurement involves assigning numbers, but there are different ways in which the numbers can be related to whatever is being measured.

In a nominal scale, the numbers are simply used as labels, to divide the respondents into categories. In Table 11.1, for example, the full-face group could

TABLE 11.1. *Time (seconds) to recognize faces in full-face or profile view*

	Group A: full-face view (n = 9)	Group B: profile view (n = 10)
	0.37	0.80
	0.38	0.59
	0.38	0.36
	0.38	0.75
	0.44	0.49
	0.50	0.58
	0.52	0.58
	0.54	0.68
	0.59	0.59
		0.58
	$\Sigma x = 4.10$	$\Sigma x = 6.00$
$\bar{x}$ = mean	$\Sigma x/n = \bar{x} = 0.46$	$\Sigma x/n = \bar{x} = 0.60$

be called group 1 and the profile group group 2. But the size of the numbers has no meaning: 2 is not bigger or better than 1. We could just as easily use 1 to indicate the profile group and 2 the full-face group.

In an ordinal or rank scale, there is some correspondence between the size of the numbers and the magnitude of the quality represented by the numbers. A common ordinal scale is position in a race. One knows that the person who came first (position 1) was faster than the person who came second (position 2). But the numbers 1 and 2 do not tell you anything about the size of the differences between the runners. Number 1 may have been well ahead of number 2, or only just ahead.

With an interval scale, the numbers do represent the magnitude of the differences. A frequently cited example is the Celsius temperature scale, where the difference between 20 and 30 degrees is the same as the difference between 30 and 40 degrees. But in an interval scale the ratio of the numbers does not reflect the ratio of the underlying attribute: something with a temperature of 40 degrees is not twice as hot as something with a temperature of 20 degrees.

In ratio scales, there is a true zero point and the ratio of the numbers reflects the ratios of the attribute measured. For example, an object 30 cm long is twice the length of an object 15 cm long; similarly, 10 seconds is twice as long as 5 seconds.

The distinction between types of scale is important because it determines which statistics you can use. For example, when recording data from a number of respondents, it is common to use numbers to represent sex; you might give all the females the 'score' of 2, and all the males a 'score' of 1. This is a nominal scale. Sex is a categorical variable, and you are just using the numbers to label the categories. The size of the numbers is meaningless, and you could have used 1 to indicate female, 2 for male. If you want to find out how many men and women there are, you count them up: you do *not* calculate the average of the 'score' on sex. If you did, the average would be nonsense since it is simply not relevant to a nominal scale.

11.1.4 Why do psychologists need statistics?

In Table 11.1, everybody gave a different reaction time, even those in the same condition. This result is typical: whenever we measure the performance of a group of people, or measure one person's performance on a number of occasions, they almost never give exactly the same reading, even when there has been no deliberate change in the situation. This variation in scores is the basic reason why psychologists have to rely on statistical analyses.

11.2 Frequency distributions

When you have a set of scores, you can draw a histogram showing the frequency distribution, where the scores (x values) are laid out along the horizontal axis with the number of times a score occurred in each group represented by the height of the vertical bars. Sometimes you will find the distribution is very asymmetric, like that shown in Fig. 11.1, which shows the frequency of road accident casualties in an English city between 18.00 and 24.00 hours. This is a skewed distribution: the frequencies tend to bunch up at one end. When the scores bunch to the left, as in Fig. 11.1, the distribution is positively skewed. If they bunch to the right, the distribution is negatively skewed.

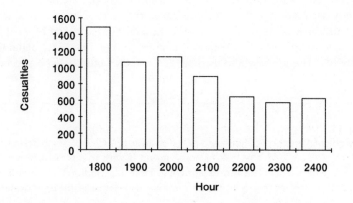

FIG 11.1. *Histogram of road accident casualties by time of day*

11.3 Measures of central tendency: mean, median, mode

Measures of central tendency provide a single figure which represents a set of scores. In common speech, we talk about the average score, which is found by adding up all the scores and dividing the sum by the number of scores there are. This average is the mean. In statistics, any individual number is referred to as x, and adding up a set of numbers is represented by Σ. So Σx tells you to add up all the numbers. The number of scores in the set is represented by n, so the formula for the mean is $\Sigma x/n$, which is represented as $\bar{x}$. The values of Σx and $\bar{x}$ ($= \Sigma x/n$) for each group are shown in Table 11.1. $\bar{x}$ is the arithmetic mean. There are other types, such as the geometric mean and the harmonic mean, but they are rarely used. The geometric mean is the nth root of the product of n numbers. The harmonic mean is $n/\Sigma(1/x)$.

The *median* is the value that divides the distribution of scores in half. To find the median, put the scores in ascending order, as in group A in Table 11.1. If there are an odd number of scores, the median is the middle score. If there are an even number of scores, average the two middle scores. In either case, half the scores in the set will be above the median and half below it. In group A of Table 11.1, the median score is the fifth one in the ascending order, which is 0.44: four of the nine scores are less and four are larger than this median value. In group B there are ten scores, so the median is the average of the fifth and sixth ones when they are in ascending order: 0.36, 0.49, 0.58, 0.58, 0.58, 0.59, 0.59, 0.68, 0.75, 0.80. The fifth score is 0.58 and the sixth is 0.59, so the median is the mean of these: 0.585.

The *mode* is the most frequently occurring value in a set of scores. In group A of Table 11.1, the mode is 0.38, and in group B it is 0.58.

Check that you can find the mean and median by doing SAQ 11.1.

11.3.1 When to use which

For a set of scores measured on an interval or ratio scale, the mean is the most commonly used measure of the central value. But if you have a few scores that are very different from the others (outliers), then the mean can be misleading. For example, suppose the last respondent in group A of Table 11.1 had a time of 1.50 seconds. The mean would then be 0.56, which would only be exceeded by

---

SAQ 11.1
In a study of the effects of noise and music on an arithmetic task, an experimenter had group A perform the task in noise, group B with background music, and group C with silence. The scores, shown in Table 11.2, indicate the number of problems solved correctly in three minutes. Calculate the mean and median score of each group.

TABLE 11.2. *Hypothetical data on problems solved with different auditory backgrounds*

Group A: noise		Group B: music		Group C: silence	
S1	8	S9	14	S17	22
S2	9	S10	9	S18	21
S3	10	S11	3	S19	15
S4	13	S12	25	S20	20
S5	15	S13	8	S21	26
S6	18	S14	16	S22	28
S7	22	S15	18	S23	17
S8	25	S16	27	S24	19
Median:		Median:		Median:	
Σx:		Σx:		Σx:	
$\bar{x}$:		$\bar{x}$:		$\bar{x}$:	

one of the scores. But the median would remain the same at 0.44. So if your data are clearly skewed, use the median.

If you have measured performance on an ordinal scale, so that you have rank scores, the median is the appropriate measure of central value.

The mode is not commonly used in psychological statistics except for reporting the results of surveys or the standardization of psychological tests, when it can be useful to know which response or score was given most frequently.

11.4 Measures of variability

11.4.1 The concept of variability

Central tendency is one feature of a set of numbers. Another is the spread, or variation of the scores in the set. In Table 11.2, the means for groups A and B are the same, but the scores in group B are more variable than the scores in group A: in group B scores vary between 3 and 27, whereas in group A scores vary from 8 to 25. How can we express the variation within a set of scores as a number?

11.4.2 Range and interquartile range

The range of a set of scores is simply the difference between the highest and lowest scores. So for group A of Table 11.2 the range is 25 - 8 = 17, and for group B the range is 27 - 3 = 24.

Range gives an indication of the spread of the scores, but depends completely on just two figures from the whole set, the highest and the lowest. One very low or very high score will produce a large increase in the range, and this might be quite misleading. So we need a measure of variation that is less influenced by a single aberrant score.

One measure is the interquartile range, which is used if scores have been measured on an ordinal scale. You will remember that the median is that score which divides the set into two halves, with half the scores falling below the median and half the scores falling above it. The median is the 50th percentile, which means 50% of the scores fall below it. We can also have a 25th percentile, which is the score below which 25% of the scores fall, a 75th percentile, a 90th percentile, etc. Group A of Table 11.2 has eight scores. The 25th percentile is the value below which 25% of the scores fall. Since there are eight scores, and 25% of 8 is 2, the 25th percentile corresponds to the point below which two of the scores in this group fall. In the table, the figures are in ascending order, and you can see that the first three are 8, 9 and 10. The 25th percentile is the mean of the second and third score, which is $(9+10)/2 = 9.5$. The 75th percentile is found in a similar way: 75% of 8 is 6, so the 75th percentile is the value below which 6 of the 8 scores fall. For the data we are using, the 75th percentile is between the sixth score (18) and the seventh score (22), so is $(18+22)/2 = 20$. The interquartile range is the difference between the 25th and 75th percentiles. In our example it is $20-9.5 = 11.5$. You may come across the semi-interquartile range, which is the interquartile range divided by 2; in our example it is $11.5/2 = 5.75$.

The interquartile range is not affected by a single extreme outlying score, as the range is. But like the range, it only uses two figures from the set to express the variability in the set, and so it ignores most of the numbers. A better measure of variation would be one that used all the numbers in the set, not just two of them.

11.4.3 Variance and standard deviation

The problem is tackled by taking the difference between each score and the mean. Table 11.3 lists the differences between each score and the mean $(x-\bar{x})$,

TABLE 11.3. *Deviations of scores for group A from Table 11.2*

Group A: noise			
	x	$(x-\bar{x})$	$(x-\bar{x})^2$
S1	8	-7.00	49.00
S2	9	-6.00	36.00
S3	10	-5.00	25.0
S4	13	-2.00	4.00
S5	15	0	0
S6	18	+3.00	9.00
S7	22	+7.00	49.00
S8	25	+10.00	100.00
	Σx: 120	$\Sigma(x-\bar{x})$: 0	$\Sigma(x-\bar{x})^2$: 272
	$\bar{x}$: 15		$\Sigma(x-\bar{x})^2/n$: 34

known as the deviation, for group A of Table 11.2. The total of the deviations is zero, so this total is not very helpful as an indication of the variation in the set of scores!

The way round this is to square each of the numbers in the $(x-\bar{x})$ column, which gets rid of all the negative numbers, and then add them up. This has been done in the final column of Table 11.3. In order to get an idea of the variation in the set, it is sensible to take the mean of the squared deviations, which is the *variance* of scores. In Table 11.3 it is $272/8 = 34$.

Earlier we pointed out the difference between descriptive and inferential statistics, the latter being used to estimate the characteristics of a population from the data obtained from a sample. When you are describing the variance of a set of data, the sum of the squared deviations is divided by n to give the variance of the sample data. But if you are using the sample data to estimate the variance of a wider population, you get a better estimate of the population variance if you divide the sum of the squared deviations by $n-1$ rather than n. In practice you are almost always using the sample data to estimate the population parameter and so divide by $n-1$. Check that you understand how to find the variance by doing SAQ 11.2.

In calculating the variance, the deviations of each score from the mean are calculated, squared and summed. To get back to the original scale of numbers, it

---

SAQ 11.2

Fill in the differences between the mean and each score $(x-\bar{x})$ for group B in Table 11.4, then find $(x-\bar{x})$ and $(x-\bar{x})^2$, the sum of the deviations squared. Calculate the mean of this column, the variance of the scores.

TABLE 11.4. *Group B: music*

	x	$(x-\bar{x})$	$(x-\bar{x})^2$
S9	14		
S10	9		
S11	3		
S12	25		
S13	8		
S14	16		
S15	15		
S16	27		
	Σx: 120	$\Sigma(x-\bar{x})$: 0	$\Sigma(x-\bar{x})^2$:
	$\bar{x}$: 15		$\Sigma(x-\bar{x})^2/n$:
			$\Sigma(x-\bar{x})^2/n-1$:

would seem fair to 'unsquare' them by taking the square root. The square root of the variance is the *standard deviation*, the number most frequently used to express the variation in a set of scores. The standard deviation of the scores in Table 11.3 is $\sqrt{34} = 5.83$.

The standard deviation is sometimes known as the root mean square deviation, which reminds us that it involves taking the deviations, squaring them, finding the mean, then taking the square root. But there are simple ways of calculating it. The three formulae below give identical results. Dividing by $n-1$, as we usually need to estimate the standard deviation of a population, formula (a) expresses the way we have calculated standard deviation so far; formulae (b) and (c) give the same answer rather more easily.

(a)   s.d. $= \sqrt{[\Sigma(x - \bar{x})^2/(n - 1)]}$
(b)   s.d. $= \sqrt{[(\Sigma x^2 - (\Sigma x)^2/n)/(n - 1)]}$
(c)   s.d. $= \sqrt{[(n(\Sigma x^2) - (\Sigma x)^2)/n(n - 1)]}$

In (b) and (c) you do not have to calculate the deviations at all, but you do need the sum of the squared x values, Σx^2, as well as the sum of x all squared $(\Sigma x)^2$. The first of these, Σx^2, is obtained by taking each score, x, squaring it, and finding the sum of these squared values. Be careful not to confuse it with $(\Sigma x)^2$, which is obtained by taking the sum of the x values and then squaring that total. Read and write all statistical formulae carefully! Check that you can use formulae (b) and (c) by doing SAQ 11.3.

SAQ 11.3
Using formula (b) or (c) calculate the standard deviation for the data for group C in Table 11.2.

11.4.4 Plotting means and standard deviations

It is often useful to display the means and standard deviations of the scores from groups of respondents on a graph so that you can see not only how the means of the groups compare, but also how far the scores from the various groups overlap.

Fig. 11.2 displays the data from the three groups of Table 11.2. The centre of each line represents the mean of each group, and the lines extending above and below the means each represent one standard deviation.

11.5 The normal distribution curve and z scores

11.5.1 The normal distribution curve

The normal distribution curve, which is fundamental to statistical analysis, is illustrated in Fig. 11.3. It is a frequency distribution, with the frequency of a

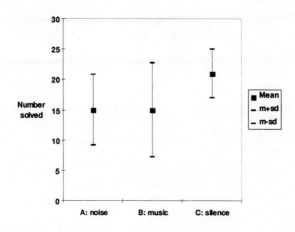

FIG. 11.2. *Plot showing means and s.d.s of groups A, B and C from Table 11.2*

score on the vertical axis, and the scores along the horizontal axis. If we take large sets of data for biological functions such as body height, we often find that the resulting frequency distribution is close to a normal curve.

11.5.2 Standard deviation of the normal curve: z scores

There are three major aspects of the normal curve that you should be aware of. First, it is symmetrical, with the 'middle' being equal to the mean. Secondly, normal curves vary in their 'spread', which is related to the standard deviation of the scores. Thirdly, one can measure off the horizontal axis in standard deviations.

Assume we have measured the breadth of hand of 500 British men aged 19–45 years. The measurements form a normal distribution, with a mean of 85 mm and a standard deviation of 5 (Pheasant, 1986). The frequency distribution is shown in Fig. 11.4a, where the horizontal axis indicates hand breadth in mm and

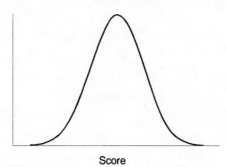

Score

FIG. 11.3. *Normal distribution curve*

145

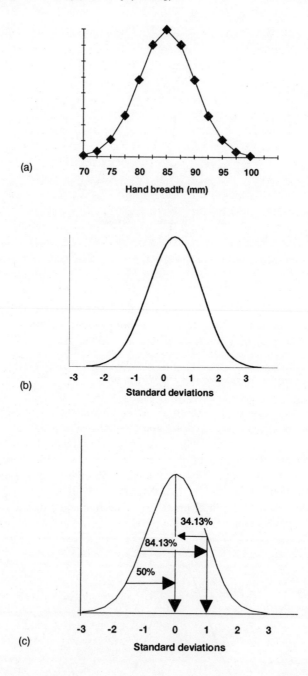

(a)

(b)

(c)

FIG. 11.4 *(a) Distribution of hand breadth measurements. (b). Normal distribution with horizontal scaled in s.d. units (c). Normal distribution with s.d. along x axis and showing proportions of curve within specified s.d. limits*

the vertical axis indicates frequency. We can plot the measurements along the horizontal axis in terms of the number of standard deviations they are away from the mean; a score of 90 mm is 1 standard deviation above the mean, so the 90 mm point can be expressed as +1 s.d. Similarly, a score of 75 mm is 2 standard deviations below the mean, so can be expressed as -2 s.d. Fig. 11.4b shows the horizontal axis scaled in s.d. units.

There are a number of points to note. First, very nearly all the distribution lies between -3 s.d. (70 mm) and +3 s.d. (100 mm) from the mean. For a perfect normal distribution curve, the precise location of standard deviations along the horizontal is known.

A vital property of the normal distribution curve is that it is known what proportion of the curve lies between any given positions along the horizontal axis, when the horizontal is in standard deviation units. One way to appreciate this is to remember that the normal curve is symmetrical. This means that 50% of the curve is above the mean, and 50% is below. (Taking the area under the curve as 1.00, we can say that 0.50 of the distribution is above the mean and 0.50 is below it.) The mean corresponds to a value of 0 when the horizontal is in standard deviation units, because it is 0 standard deviations away from the mean. So we know that 0.50 of the curve is below the position where the horizontal score in s.d. units is 0.

Statisticians also know how much of the curve lies below +1 s.d., -2 s.d., +1.96 s.d. and any other value we care to suggest. For example, it is known that 0.8413 of the area under the curve falls below +1 s.d. So how much is included in the area between the mean (0 s.d.) and +1 s.d. (i.e. 1 s.d. above the mean)? You can see from Fig. 11.4c that the answer is 0.8413 - 0.500 = 0.3413, or 34.13%.

When we express a score in standard deviation units from the mean, they are known as z units. So +1 s.d. = +1z, -2.46 s.d. = -2.46z.

11.5.3 Using normal curve (z) tables

To find the area under the curve for any z value, use the table of the normal curve (Table A1 in Appendix 3). An example of one line in that table is

z	Mean to z	Larger portion	Smaller portion
1.00	0.3413	0.8413	0.1587

The meanings of these entries is illustrated in Fig. 11.5. In the z table there are entries for values of z from $z = 0$ (i.e. where z equals the mean) to $z = 3.9$. The entries are the same whether z is + or -, so only one set of values is given.

The z table lets us answer various questions about how one score compares with others. Remember that the z table uses s.d. units, so if we are dealing with ordinary scores, we have to transform them into z units before we can use the table. Here is an example. The mean for hand breadth is 85 mm and the standard deviation is 5 mm. So what proportion of the men measured had a hand breadth less than 95 mm? To answer this question, transform the score of 95 mm into z units by finding the difference between the mean and the score (95-85) and

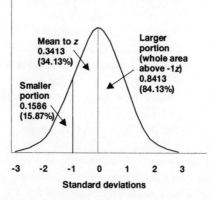

FIG. 11.5. *Portion of the normal distribution curve between -1z and x̄*

dividing the result by the s.d. (5). In this case, you get a value of 2. So 95 mm is +2z (2 standard deviations above the mean). In the table of z, you will find that when z = 2 the area in the larger portion of the curve is 0.9772; therefore the proportion of men who had a hand breadth less than 95 mm is 97.72%.

Check that you understand this use of z tables with SAQ 11.4.

11.5.4 Comparing scores using z values

Using z scores, we can compare the scores of tests where the mean and standard deviation differ. If Joseph Smith has a hand breadth of 90 mm, we know he has a large hand, because his hand is larger than 84.13% of the population. (90 mm is 5 mm or 1 standard deviation above the mean, and the z table tells us that the proportion of the population falling below this value is 0.8413 or 84.13%.) Suppose Katherine Smith has a hand breadth of 81 mm. Is this a large hand? When you know that the mean hand breadth for British women is 75 mm and the standard deviation = 4 mm, you can find out how many of the population of British women have a smaller hand than Katherine Smith. Her hand is 6 mm wider than the average; as the standard deviation for women's hands is 4 mm, Katherine's is 1.5 standard deviations larger than the mean. From the z table you will find that this means Katherine's hand is larger than 0.9332 or 93.32% of British women's hands. So Katherine has a larger hand, compared with other women, than Joseph, compared with other men.

SAQ 11.4

1 Given that the mean hand breadth for men is 85 mm with a standard deviation of 5 mm, what proportion of men had a hand breadth less than 80 mm?
2 The mean score on a test of IQ is 100, with s.d. = 15. What proportion of the respondents have an IQ between 85 and 115?

The z tables are particularly useful when you are dealing with the results of standardized tests. Once you know the mean and s.d. of the normative sample who were used to standardize the test, you can use z tables to discover whether any particular score is 'high' or 'low' by finding out the proportion of the normative sample who scored less than the score of the person you have tested.

In section 11.4.2 we mentioned percentiles: when a score is at the 84th percentile, 84% of people score below it. So you might expect that percentiles can be related to z scores, and indeed this is the case. The z table shows that when $z = +1.00$, the portion of the curve below z is 0.8413 (84.13%), i.e. if someone scores at $+1z$, he or she has surpassed 84% of the population. So the percentile score is 84.

11.5.5 Standard error and confidence limits

Inferential statistics involve estimating the characteristics of a population, such as the mean, from the data obtained from a sample of that population. If you took a large number of samples from the population, the means of the samples would themselves form a normal distribution. The standard deviation of that distribution is given by taking the standard deviation of the sample and dividing it by the square root of n, the number in the sample. This is the standard error. It allows you to state the probability that the true mean of the population is within specified limits.

From the z table, it is known that there is a 95% probability that the true mean of the population is within plus or minus approximately two standard errors of the sample mean. Suppose you have taken a sample of 100 respondents from a population and found that the mean of the sample is 50, and the standard deviation is 8. The standard error is $8/\sqrt{100} = 0.8$, so there is a 95% probability that the true mean of the population is within the limits $50 \pm$ two standard errors $= 50 \pm 1.6$, i.e. between 48.4 and 51.6. These values are the 95% confidence interval, meaning that there is a 95% probability that the true mean is between these limits.

11.6 Statistical significance

11.6.1 The concept

Statistical significance is fundamental to statistical analysis. Although students sometimes find it hard to grasp, the basic ideas are quite straightforward.

You are already familiar with the notion of variability in scores, and the use of the standard deviation or variance as indices of the amount of variability. Look back at the data in Table 11.1. The question that the experimenter asks is whether there is a difference between the scores of groups A (full face) and B (profile).

Group A has the smaller mean, and so you might wish to conclude that these respondents responded faster. But look at the third respondent in groups A and B:

the group B member had a faster response than the group A member. So if you took just those two respondents, you could not say that group A had the quicker response.

Now let us approach the problem from a slightly different viewpoint. If the view of the faces had no effect on the respondents' speed of recognition, the scores from groups A and B would be the 'same'. This does not imply, of course, that all the scores would be identical, because responses almost always show some variability. This random, unexplained variation is due to chance. For example, the variation in the scores for group B in Table 11.1 is variation due to chance. In that group, the mean for respondents 1–5 is 0.598 and the mean for respondents 6–10 is 0.604. The difference between these two means is simply due to chance, random variation in the data; it arises even though both these subgroups come from one 'population', the complete set of scores given by group B members.

Our question now is whether the difference between the means of group A and group B is also simply due to chance. If it is, groups A and B are samples from the same 'population', just as respondents 1–5 and 6–10 of group B are samples from one population.

How can you decide whether groups A and B are samples from one population or are 'really' different and come from different populations? You make the decision by applying a test of statistical significance, which lets you estimate how likely it is that the data from the separate groups come from one population. If it is unlikely that they came from the same population, you can conclude that they did not, and that they came from separate populations.

When you carry out the appropriate significance test, you look at the difference between the means of the groups and compare it with the amount of variation in the scores which arises through chance. If the chance variation is likely to have produced the difference between the groups, the difference is said to be nonsignificant, and you have to conclude there is no 'real' or statistically significant difference between the groups: they are both from the same underlying population.

If, however, the difference between the sets of data is unlikely to have arisen through chance variation, you state that there was a statistically significant difference: the two sets are not from the same population.

But what do we mean by unlikely? It is conventional in psychology to use the 5% probability level (also referred to as alpha level). What does this mean? If there is a 5% (also written as 0.05) or smaller probability that the difference between the groups arose from chance variation, we conclude it did not arise from chance and that there is a 'real' difference. If there is more than 5% (0.05) probability that the difference arose from chance, we accept that the difference we have found may have been due to chance and therefore conclude the difference is not a real one.

When you set out to do a quantitative study, you will have stated an experimental hypothesis that there will be a difference between the groups' scores. If the statistical test shows a 'significant difference', then you reject the null hypothesis of no difference and accept the experimental hypothesis (sometimes known as the alternative hypothesis). If the test turns out to be not significant, you have to accept the null hypothesis that the sets of scores did not differ.

You may ask why we use the 5% probability level; and the answer is that it is merely convention. We could use 10% (0.10), 1% (0.01), or 0.5% (0.005). As MacRae (1994, p. 4) points out, a significance level of 0.05 means you are accepting a 1 in 20 chance of being misled into thinking that there is a real effect when there is not. A smaller significance level is chosen if you are particularly anxious to ensure that you do not make that mistake. Unless you have good reason, rely on the 5% level, even though this may seem arbitrary.

When you carry out significance tests, you find out what is the probability the difference between the groups is due to chance. If the probability is 5% or less, it is written as: $p < 0.05$. Note that this means the difference is significant at the 5% level. If you find the difference is not significant at 5%, you write NS, or $p > 0.05$. Make sure you get the appropriate < or > !

11.6.2 Type I and type II errors

A significance test allows us to say how likely it is that the observed difference between the sets of scores is due to chance. If there is a 5% or smaller probability that the difference is due to chance variation, we conclude that it was not caused by chance. But we can never be sure: there is always a possibility that the difference we find was due to chance even when we conclude that it was not. Conversely, we may find a difference and conclude that it is not significant (that it was due to random or chance variability in the scores) when in fact it was a 'real' difference. So there are two types of error we may make. These are referred to as type I and type II errors.

A type I error occurs when we reject null hypothesis when it is true, i.e. we say there is a 'real' difference between the groups when in fact the difference is not 'real'. The probability that we shall make a type I error is given by the significance level we use. With an alpha or significance level of 0.05, on 5% of occasions we are likely to make a type I error and say the groups differ when they do not.

We can reduce the probability of making a type I error by using a more stringent level of significance: 0.01, say, rather than 0.05. But as we reduce the chances of making a type I error, we increase the likelihood that we shall make a type II error, which is where we say there is no difference between the groups when there is one.

11.6.3 Directional and nondirectional hypotheses

A nondirectional hypothesis states that there will be a difference between the scores of the groups of participants. It does not say *which* group will score higher or lower than the other, merely that the groups will differ.

If the experimental hypothesis says that group A will score less than group B (i.e. if we predict the direction of the difference between the groups), this is a directional hypothesis. Similarly, if the hypothesis were that group A would score higher than group B, it would also be a directional hypothesis, because it still predicts the direction of the difference between the groups.

The distinction between directional and nondirectional hypotheses is important when applying significance tests. A result that is not significant when you are testing a nondirectional hypothesis may be significant if it had been a directional hypothesis, so you need to know which one you are testing. But you must state the hypothesis, and therefore know whether it is directional or nondirectional, *before* you analyse the data, not afterwards!

There is another important point to remember. Sometimes you state a directional hypothesis, that group A will score higher than group B, but find that the results are in the opposite direction: group B has the higher score. MacRae (1994, p. 8) writes that in these circumstances 'any outcome in the direction opposite to the one predicted will be interpreted as a chance result however great the effect turns out to be'.

Assume that you have a nondirectional hypothesis unless you have a clear understanding of why it is directional. If you are wrong, you will err on the side of caution: you are not likely to commit a type I error and wrongly claim that you have found a difference when it is not statistically reliable.

Check that you can tell which is a directional and which a nondirectional hypothesis by completing SAQ 11.5.

11.6.4 Interpreting the outcome of a significance test

Understanding what a significance test tells you is crucial: doing all the proper tests and getting the correct answers is no good if you then misunderstand what the outcome means! Try to remember some basic principles.

(1) If the test tells you the difference between groups is not significant, you must conclude there is no difference, even though the mean scores are not identical.

SAQ 11.5
1 Jones predicted that a group of children would behave more aggressively after viewing a particular film. Is this a directional hypothesis?
2 Klein carried out an experiment on facial recognition and compared the scores of 17 people in two conditions in a within-subjects experiment. She predicted that condition A would yield different scores from condition B. Is this a directional hypothesis?
3 Dobbs compared 24 students' scores on a scale of attitude to drugs before and after they had a lecture on drug-taking, predicting that scores would increase. Is this a directional hypothesis?

---

(2)   If the result is not significant, this does not mean the null hypothesis is true and only chance affected the results. Earlier we pointed out that you should not try to confirm a null hypothesis because finding no difference between sets of scores is ambiguous: it may be the result of a flawed procedure.

(3)   If the difference between groups is statistically significant, this does not necessarily mean that it is practically meaningful or significant in the everyday sense. For example, Mackinnon *et al.* (1990) report a study of people's ability to remember car licence plates. One group's score remained the same on two test occasions so the increase was 0, whereas another group's score increased from 3.22 to 3.42, an increase of 0.20; the difference was statistically significant. But whether the increase of 0.20 for the second group has any practical importance is a subjective judgement, not a statistical one.

(4)   The assumption behind the experimental method is that one can conclude that significant changes in the dependent variable are caused by the changes in the independent variable. But the validity of this assumption depends on having a properly designed and controlled experiment: just because one has a significant difference between group A and group B does *not* mean you can necessarily conclude the difference was due to the changes in the independent variable. If the experiment had confounded variables, you may well get significant results but they would not give you grounds for concluding that the independent variable brought about the changes.

(5)   Avoid the temptation to take the level of significance as an index of the magnitude of the experimental effect. Psychologists normally use the 5% significance level, but can use a more stringent one, and find that a difference between groups is significant not only at 5% but also at 1% or 0.1%. Really one should specify the significance level in advance and keep to it. But it is common practice to cite the strictest level of significance against which the outcome is still significant, so you will see reports in which researchers state that the effect was significant at $p<0.01$, $p<0.001$, etc. But this should not be interpreted as meaning that an effect significant at $p<0.001$ is larger than one significant at $p<0.05$.

11.7 Which test of statistical significance?

To identify which significance test to use, you need to answer a number of questions.

(1)   Have your data been measured on an interval, ordinal or nominal scale?

If you have scores or measurements (interval or ordinal data), there are a number of alternatives you can use, and you need to go on to the other questions listed below. If you have counted frequencies, the number of people falling into certain categories, you have used a categorical variable and a nominal scale. In this case you will be looking at the chi-square test, which is used to compare observed frequencies with expected ones. The basic concepts underlying the chi-square test are described in section 11.10.

(2)   Differences or relationships?

Are you looking for a difference or a relationship between sets of scores? Do not just answer 'yes': you must know which one! If you are using correlations, there are some underlying issues covered in section 11.11.

(3)   Parametric and nonparametric tests?

Tests of statistical significance are divided into the parametric and the nonparametric. (The terminology is confusing, and some writers such as MacRae (1994, p. 13) argue that it is best avoided and one should use the terms 'distribution-dependent' and 'distribution-free' instead. But we use it here because it is so common.) There has been a lengthy debate among the experts about their relative value. Parametric tests are more powerful, meaning they are more likely to reject a false null hypothesis. If the data are 'interval', such tests are usually preferred. But they depend upon you being able to make certain assumptions about the population of data. (The data you have obtained in your study are viewed as a sample of this population.) These assumptions are:

(a)   You have interval data. Remember that ordinal (rank) data or frequency counts are not measured on an interval scale.

(b)   The data in the population from which you have drawn your sample of respondents are normally distributed. If the data are highly skewed, it is safer to use a nonparametric test.

(c)   The sets of data you are comparing have equal variances, referred to as homogeneity of variance.

If you cannot make these assumptions then you should use nonparametric tests. So if you have the rank order of people on a measure of performance, you need a nonparametric test.

If you are in doubt about which type of test to use, the nonparametric test is the 'safe' bet (so long as you choose the appropriate one, of course!). Interval data can be converted into ordinal or nominal data (but it does not work the other way round): scores such as those shown in Table 11.1 can be ranked (making them ordinal data) and a nonparametric test used.

(4)   How many sets of scores do you have?

Many of the commonly used tests compare just two sets of scores. If you have three or more, you need a test which deals with that situation. The parametric test which allows you to compare three or more sets of scores is the analysis of variance. The basic principles are described in section 11.9.

1 Are you testing for a difference (go to 2) or a relationship (go to 3)?

2 Testing differences

    2.1 Will you use a nonparametric test (go to 2.2) or a parametric one (go to 2.5)?

    2.2 Nonparametric

    How many sets of data do you want to compare?

        Two – go to 2.3

        Three or more – go to 2.4

    2.3 Two sets of data

    Are the respondents in each group the same people?*

        Same – Wilcoxon test (Trend test: Page's *L*)

        Different – Mann–Whitney test (Trend test: Jonckheere's)

    2.4 Three or more sets of data

    Are the respondents in each group the same people?*

        Same – Friedman test

        Different – Kruskal–Wallis

    2.5 Parametric

    Are you comparing the means of sets of data (go to 2.6) or the mean of a sample with a standard (go to 2.9)?

    2.6 How many sets of data do you want to compare?

        Two – go to (2.7)

        Three or more – go to (2.8)

    2.7 Two sets of data

    Are the respondents in each group the same people?*

        Same – related *t*-test

        Different – independent *t*-test

    2.8 Three or more sets of data

    Is there one independent variable or more than one?**

        One – one-way analysis of variance

        More than one – two-way analysis of variance

    2.9 Comparing a mean with a standard – one-sample *t*

3 Testing relationships

    3.1 Will you use a nonparametric measure (go to 3.2) or parametric one (go to 3.5)?

    3.2 Nonparametric

    Do you have frequency data (go to 3.3) or ranked data (go to 3.4)?

    3.3 Frequency data

    Do you have one set of observed frequencies or more than one?

        One – one-sample chi-square

        More than one – chi-square

    3.4 Two sets of rank data – Spearman rank correlation

    3.5 Parametric

    Two sets of interval data – Pearson correlation

---

* If you have formed matched groups of respondents, you can assume you have the 'same' people in the groups, i.e. it is a within-subjects experiment.

** Be careful not to confuse the number of independent variables with the number of levels of one variable!

FIG. 11.6. *Deciding on the appropriate test of significance*

SAQ 11.6

1 Franks compared the ability of 16 respondents to recognize faces under two conditions – the faces were given names in condition A and not given names in condition B. All respondents took part in both conditions, and Franks hypothesized that condition A would yield higher scores than condition B. The scores were normally distributed, and so a parametric test was applied. Which statistical test would Franks use?

2 Larkins tested the hypothesis that facial recognition differs according to age, testing separate groups of children aged 4, 6 and 8 on a facial memory task. There were five participants in each age group, and Larkins obtained scores showing the number of faces recognized by each respondent. The test produced skewed data. Which test would be appropriate to test the hypothesis?

3 Myers also compared facial recognition across ages, using 15 children aged five and 14 aged ten. The hypothesis was that there would be a difference between the age groups, and was tested using a parametric test. Which test should be used?

4 Oliver had a group of nine respondents, and compared them on their ability to remember words using a within-subjects experimental design. One condition showed the words in a random order, one in an alphabetical order, and the third had the words organized according to meaning. The respondents' scores were not normally distributed, so a nonparametric test was used. Oliver predicted that the three conditions led to differences in recall. Which statistical test would she use?

5 Ross tested the hypothesis that alcohol affects driving. He recruited 50 male drivers, and gave half of them a dose of alcohol, while the other respondents were given a non-alcoholic drink. Ross reported that 20 of the alcohol group made more than eight driving errors in a 15-minute test drive, while 5 did not. In the non-alcohol group, 7 made more than eight errors, 18 did not. Which test would be used to test the hypothesis?

6 Evans asked an observer to rate the aggressiveness of each of a group of 20 children before and then again after the children had seen a violent film. Evans wanted to see whether there was a relationship between the ratings of aggression shown on the two occasions, using a parametric test. Which statistical test would Evans use?

7 Young asked 15 observers to rate the aggressiveness of a group of children before and then again after the children had seen a violent film. Young predicted an increase in the ratings of aggression shown on the two occasions, and tested this using a parametric test. Which statistical test would Young use?

With three or more sets of scores, you may be interested in seeing whether there is a particular trend. For example, suppose you have tested people's fear of spiders before they had treatment for their spider phobia, immediately after the treatment and then three months later. You may have predicted that pre-treatment scores would be highest, the immediate post-treatment scores lowest, and the three-month later scores in between. A trend test allows you to test whether the group scores fall in this predicted order. If you have used a within-subjects design, you use the Page's L test; if you have a between-subjects design, use the Jonckheere test.

If you wish to compare the mean of a single sample with the mean of a population (μ), you can use the one-sample t-test. It is used to answer this type of question: we measure the breadth of hands of a group of 25 male farmers and find the mean is 92.1 mm (s.d. = 3.6); is the farmers' mean significantly greater than the British men's mean, where the average hand width is 85 mm (s.d. = 5)?

(5) Same or different respondents?

If you are testing for differences between sets of scores, you need to know whether there were different respondents in the various conditions or whether the same people were used in the different conditions. If you have used a matched-group method, you can use the tests for within-subjects comparisons although some authors (e.g. Harris, 1986) believe it is safer to use between-subjects tests even when you have a matched-group experiment.

When you have answered these questions, Fig. 11.6 will help you decide which test to use. To check your understanding, try SAQ 11.6.

11.8 Using tables to determine whether an outcome is statistically significant

When you have calculated a test of statistical significance, you have to find whether the outcome demonstrates a statistically significant result. In almost all cases, you calculate a particular statistic, and then compare the calculated value with the value shown in a table.

There are different tables for different tests. Decide before you start calculating whether you have a directional or nondirectional hypothesis and the significance level you will use (usually 0.05, 5%). When you have calculated the statistic, locate the appropriate table in Appendix 3. Find the column for the appropriate probability level (0.05) for the appropriate hypothesis (nondirectional or directional). For most tests you calculate the degrees of freedom and will need to locate the row in the table appropriate to the degrees of freedom. The intersection of the column and row gives you the critical value for the statistic. In some tests, the result is significant at that probability level if your calculated value is equal to or larger than the critical value. In others, the calculated value must be less than the critical value for it to be significant. The relevant rule is shown in the table headings. An example of using the table for the t statistic is given in Box 11.1. Check that you can use the t-table correctly by completing SAQ 11.7.

You may find that the table does not contain a row for the particular number of degrees of freedom you have. When this happens, use the row with the smaller degrees of freedom closest to the actual degrees of freedom. For example, if d.f. = 44, and the table has rows for d.f. of 40 and 45, use the row for d.f. = 40.

Box 11.1 Example of using the table of *t* to decide whether a calculated value is statistically significant

The *t*-test is one of the most commonly used tests of statistical significance. Comparing the data for the two groups shown in Table 11.1, $t = 2.94$, and the degrees of freedom, d.f., = 18. To see whether this is statistically significant, check whether the hypothesis is directional or nondirectional. In this example, it is nondirectional: it states that the two groups will differ, but does not say which will have the higher mean. Find the table for *t* in Appendix 3. An excerpt from the table is shown here.

The result is significant at the relevant probability level if your calculated value is equal to or larger than the critical value.
Level of significance for one-tailed test

	0.05	0.025	0.01	0.005	0.0005

Level of significance for two-tailed test

d.f.	0.10	0.05	0.02	0.01	0.001
18	1.734	2.101	2.552	2.878	3.922

Find the row corresponding to the degrees of freedom. (The excerpt above shows only this row.) Using the conventional 0.05 significance level, find the column appropriate to a two-tailed test and a significance level of 0.05. The value shown at the intersection of the appropriate row and column is 2.101. Since the calculated *t* is 2.94, which is greater than 2.101, you can conclude the difference is statistically significant: there is a smaller than 5% probablility that the difference was due to chance, so you conclude it was not due to chance. This would be written as $t = 2.94$, d.f. = 18, $p < 0.05$.

If you look along the row, you can see that the calculated value of *t* is larger than the tabled critical value for a significance level of 0.01 for a two-tailed test, but it is not larger than the critical value for a significance level of 0.001. So you could say that the result is significant at the 0.01 level ($p < 0.01$). It is not significant at the 0.001 level, as 2.94 is less than 3.992.

SAQ 11.7
Each row shows the *n* and *t*-values for an experiment with a two-tailed hypothesis. Using the 0.05 significance level, fill in the d.f. and *p* values (NS for nonsignificant or $p < 0.05$) for each row.

	n_1	n_2	*t*	d.f.	*p*
a Between-subjects design	8	8	2.86		
b Between-subjects design	50	52	1.15		
c Between-subjects design	17	8	4.09		
d Within-subjects design	9	9	1.51		
e Within-subjects design	11	11	2.51		

11.9 Comparing three or more sets of scores from different respondents: analysis of variance (anova)

Analysis of variance is the parametric method for testing the hypothesis that the scores of three or more groups differ. As the name implies, it examines the variance within the whole sets of scores. Imagine we have sets of data from three separate groups of respondents, each group being tested on the number of problems they could solve. Group A carried out the task in noise, group B had background music, and group C had a silent background, as in Table 11.2. We want to know whether there is a difference between the three groups: did type of background affect number of problems solved? For this situation, comparing three or more sets of scores with one independent variable, you can use the one-way analysis of variance.

If there is no difference between the groups (the null hypothesis is true), the data would all come from the same population, and the three sets of data would all have similar means and variances. The variance of each group would be an estimate of the population variance, the variance due to random fluctuations between respondents, known as error variance because it arises through chance. The best estimate of the population variance is given by calculating the mean of the variances of the three groups.

If the null hypothesis is true, the means of the three groups will also be very similar (any differences being the result of random, error variance), and the variance of the means (i.e. how much the means differ from each other) will be very small. (It would be the same as the population variance.) The variance of the means of the three groups is known as the treatment variance. So if the null hypothesis is true, and the three groups do not differ from each other, the variance between the means (the treatment variance) will equal the error variance; if we divided the treatment variance by the error variance, the answer will be 1.00.

But if the null hypothesis is not true, there is a difference between the three groups, and the variance of the means will be larger than the population variance. If we divide the variance of the means (the treatment variance) by the error variance, we shall get a number bigger than 1.00. In the analysis of variance, the treatment variance is divided by the error variance to test the hypothesis that there is a significant difference between the means.

The way the results of a one-way analysis of variance are reported is shown in Table 11.5. The column headed 'Source' shows the meaning of each row. In

TABLE 11.5. *Example of the outcome of an analysis of variance*

Source	SS	d.f.	MS	F
Treatment	114.00	2	57.00	6.16
Error	222.00	24	9.25	
Total	336.00	26		

Table 11.5, one row (Treatment) refers to the results of comparing the different treatment groups and the other shows the effects of the random variance in the complete set of data, the error variance. The columns headed SS and d.f. show the sum of squares and degrees of freedom for each source; the values are obtained when you calculate the analysis. The values in the column headed MS (standing for mean square) are found by dividing the SS for each row by its d.f. The value of F is given by dividing the treatment MS by the error MS: in Table 11.5, $F = 6.16 = 57.00/9.25$.

One attraction of the analysis of variance is that it can be extended to complex experiments in which there are two or more independent variables. It can also be applied to within-subjects designs and to situations where the number of scores in each group differs, but the calculations are more difficult.

If you find that F is significant, you can conclude that there is a significant difference between the means of the three or more groups. But you do not know where this difference lies. For example, the means of the groups shown in Table C9 in Appendix 1, on calculating statistical tests, are 8.33, 5.33 and 3.33. As the F value is significant at the 0.05 level, there is a difference between these means. But we do not know whether the mean for group A is significantly larger than that for group B, whether B is larger than C or whether A is larger than C. It could be that A is significantly larger than B and C, but B and C do not differ from each other. To find out which means differ from each other, you have to apply other tests, such as the Scheffé.

To compare sets of scores from different respondents with two independent variables, you use the two-way anova for independent groups. Imagine you were investigating people's ability to solve problems with or without background noise, as in the previous example, but with just two levels of background: silence and speech. You also varied the speed (fast or slow) at which the problems were presented, giving a 2×2 experiment. The analysis of variance allows you to see whether there is an effect of background, whether there is an effect of presentation rate, and whether there is a significant interaction between the two variables. If you need a reminder about the meaning of interaction, refer back to Chapter 3.

As with the one-way analysis of variance, the F test can tell you that there are significant differences – whether each independent variable had a significant effect on the data. But it does not show where particular differences lie: is the mean for respondents who had variable A at level 1 and variable B at level 1 significantly different from those who had A at level 1 but variable B at level 2? To answer questions such as these, you need to apply further tests, such as the Scheffé test.

11.10 Chi-square

The chi-square test is used with nominal (frequency) data, where respondents are assigned to categories. The one-sample chi-square test can be used to compare an observed distribution of frequency scores with an expected one. For example,

TABLE 11.6 *Hypothetical responses to survey question on showing uncut films on TV*

Response	Respondents' age 18–40	41–60	Over 60	Total
No	35	22	34	91
Yes	54	49	6	109
Total	89	71	40	200

does the number of fatal road accidents for the four three-month periods of the year show that they differ from what one would expect if they were evenly distributed across the year?

The more common use of chi-square is when respondents are categorized along two dimensions and you have a cross-tabulation. For example, a recent survey asked adults whether they thought 'adult' films should be shown uncut on TV. Data were reported for different age groups. Hypothetical results are shown in Table 11.6. The cell entries show the number of respondents of that age giving the response indicated in each row. The chi-square test is concerned with answering the question: is there a relationship between the variable that distinguishes the columns (age, in Table 11.6) and the variable that distinguishes the rows (response 'no' or 'yes')?

The test can be used only when the data are independent, meaning that no respondent can appear in more than one of the cells of the table. It has traditionally been argued that no more than 20% of the *expected* frequencies in the table can be less than 5. Note that this restriction applies not to the observed frequencies, the numbers actually collected, but the expected frequencies. The contemporary view is that this rule is not as important as once thought (Howell, 1992, p. 141). If you do apply the rule and your data fail to meet the criterion, you have to collect more data so that the requirement is met or change the table by merging groups together if it makes sense to do so. In Table 11.6 you might collapse two of the age groups, so you had ages 18–40 and 41 and over.

11.11 Correlation and regression

11.11.1 Correlation

A correlation expresses the extent to which two variables vary together. At least one of the variables is measured on a rank or interval scale, and in most cases they are both rank or interval data. A scattergram shows the correlation between two variables. If one of the variables is a dependent variable, it is represented on the vertical axis. The two scores for each respondent are plotted at the intersection of their locations on the horizontal and vertical axes. For example, Fig. 11.7a is

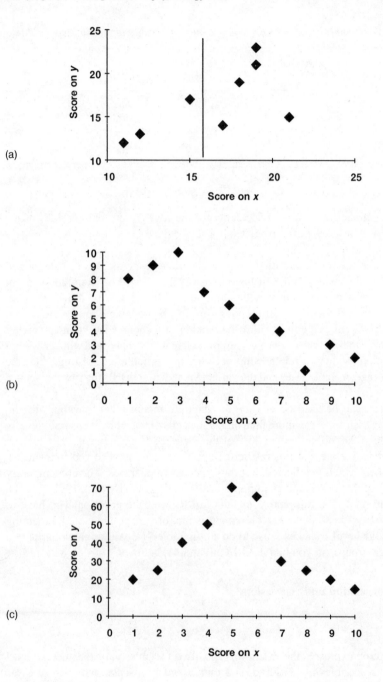

Fig. 11.7. *(a–c) Illustrations of scattergrams for positive, negative and curvilinear correlations*

a scattergram showing a positive correlation: as one variable increases, so does the other. A negative correlation, shown in Fig. 11.7b, is when one variable increases as the other decreases.

Correlations vary between -1.00 and +1.00; a correlation of 0.00 means there is no relationship between the two variables. The Spearman rank correlation is used when the data are on an ordinal scale, such as rank orders. When both variables have been measured on an interval scale the Pearson product moment correlation is used.

The Spearman and the Pearson express the relationship between two variables. If you have more than two sets of rank scores and want to assess the degree of agreement between them, you can use the coefficient of concordance, which is described in Howell (1992) and Siegel and Castellan (1988) . An example is where you have three or more judges ranking a set of items (such as quality of different beers) and wish to discover how far they agree with each other.

It is always wise to plot a scattergram of your data to see whether the variables might be related by a nonlinear function. Spearman and Pearson correlation coefficients only assess the extent to which two variables have a linear relationship. If there is a curvilinear relationship, as illustrated in Fig. 11.7c, the correlation coefficient can be highly misleading and suggest no relationship between the scores. The graph indicates that there is a strong relationship, but not a linear one.

The linear correlation between two variables is dependent on a number of factors, notably the range of scores one takes. In Fig. 11.7a, for example, if you draw a vertical line at a value of 16 on the horizontal (x) axis and calculate the correlation between x and y just for the scores greater than 16 on x, the correlation between x and y falls dramatically.

The correlation coefficient squared (r^2) indicates how much of the variance in y is explained by x. So if x correlates with y +0.6, then 0.36 (36%) of the variance in y is explained by the variance in x.

11.11.2 Regression and prediction

When two variables are correlated, you can predict the level of individuals on variable y from their standing on variable x (or vice versa: you can predict height from foot size or you can predict foot size from height). When you have a scattergram, it is possible to draw in the best-fitting straight line (known as the least-squares regression line) that represents the linear relationship between x and y. (If you have access to a computer package for analysing data, you will probably find that it can plot the regression lines for you.) A regression line can be expressed as an equation like this:

$$x = a + by$$

where 'a' is the intercept (the point at which the regression line crosses the axis of the graph) and 'b' is the slope of the line (how steeply it rises). To predict

163

scores on y from scores on x, you use the regression equation: if $y = 1.5 + (0.5)x$, and you know that the score on x was 60, then you predict y to be 31.5.

Multiple regression is when you use more than one variable to predict a dependent variable. For example, job satisfaction is correlated with pay and with level of occupation: you can predict someone's job satisfaction from their pay and from their level of occupation. But you get a better prediction if you use them both together as predictors, giving a multiple-regression equation of the form:

job satisfaction = a + pay multiplied by b + level of job multiplied by c

The calculation of multiple regression is not something done by hand, but is a frequently used technique in some areas of psychology (such as the study of job satisfaction). You will find it explained in textbooks such as Howell (1992) and Kerlinger (1986).

Data from qualitative research

12.0 Introduction

It is important to remember one fundamental principle that guides the process of interpretation in qualitative studies before you try to make sense of the material you have collected: the 'data' are produced by you in the course of the research rather than simply gathered fresh from the real world. Qualitative researchers would not want to speak about their activity as 'data collection' (Harre, 1982), for they do not believe that there is such a thing as uninterpreted 'raw' data that the psychologist then interprets. This injunction should also apply, of course, to quantitative studies, for the gathering of numerical 'data' also requires a good deal of interpretative work. This is not the place for another polemic against quantification in research (see Irvine *et al.*, 1979) but it must be emphasized that your interpretation of qualitative data will lose its way if you forget that you have already created something new, something that is yours when you gather your piles of interview and account transcripts and other selections of texts, as well as diaries and records of your observations. In this sense, the 'reflexive' character of qualitative research, discussed in Chapter 5, should become salient at the beginning of the analysis. How it then may appear in the written report is described in Chapter 14.

Other stipulations flow from this first principle. These include the two following points. Your analysis should focus on the data, with the guiding question being 'does this interpretation make sense in this context?' The plausibility of your interpretation can be assessed by a reader, to a greater degree than is the case in statistical summaries of behaviour, but only if you restrict your speculations to material that your reader also has access to. Second, your account is to be derived from material you have produced, and your responsibility for that creative activity should be marked by the use of the first person ('I', 'me') rather than hidden in third person phrases (such as 'the participants were selected from...' or 'it was discovered that...').

These points could be applied to quantitative research, but it is not at present accepted practice in school and undergraduate psychology courses to throw the empirical work of experimental psychologists into such disarray. The adherence to these starting reflexive points marks qualitative research as something different within the discipline this century. The analytic process in the interpretation of qualitative data is governed by the difficult task of bringing together two contradictory sets of assumptions, the guesses (or 'hypotheses') made by the researcher at the beginning of the study and the preoccupations which the material expresses during the study. You must be clear about what separates these two different agendas, about how your own expectations were formulated and why (which is your agenda), and then how those expectations were modified by the material itself (which is the agenda you did not expect).

We will describe the analytic process here in four stages. The first, which relates specifically to interviews, is where the interviewee is given a 'voice', and when this is the only stage of the analysis it may be because the aim of the research is to witness a story and empower a 'co-researcher'. The second is where the reading focuses on the generation of categories, and attempts to bring all selected parts of the text under relevant category headings. The third is a 'thematic analysis' of the material which aims to represent the meeting point of the competing sets of assumptions, these different agendas. The fourth stage is where we make connections between this text and other studies, where parts of the text are cited to exemplify particular conceptual points or to illustrate the presence of certain discourses. It is not necessary to move systematically through each stage to produce a full report, but you should be clear before you start why you want to stop at a particular stage.

12.1 Stage one: 'giving voice'

The task in this first stage applies specifically to interview data and may appear to be simple enough: it is to re-present clearly the story of the interviewees, or the story as they may wish it to be told. Simple selective quotation is insufficient here, and paraphrasing the interviewees' talk turn by turn is no better. It is helpful to approach the task of telling what has been told to you with what we may call a 'therapeutic' and a 'political' frame of mind. This does not mean that you are providing therapy to your interviewees (and you should not make any such claim) nor that you are planning to recruit them to some cause to liberate them (and it would not be helpful to try this in your research either).

Rather, the 'therapeutic' frame of mind will help you to work with the rapport that has been set up in the course of conducting the interviews, and to imagine yourself in the 'frame of reference' that holds together the various things your interviewees have said to you. You should go beyond sympathizing with your interviewees (though this is indeed is something you may want to do face to face in the interview) to empathizing with their view of the world, reconstructing what they say in the spirit in which it was told. This process could be considered as a 'reflection' back to the interviewees of their story. The 'political' frame of mind will help you to think about issues of power, and what it might mean for the interviewees' story to be told in conditions of their own choosing. The telling of the story will raise questions about what steps might be necessary to empower them, and you may also focus on how this empowerment is aided or abetted by your (powerful) role as a psychological investigator (Bhavnani, 1990).

The attempt to retell the story with an eye to empathy and empowerment makes the report very different from an account of a simple 'conversation', and you should leave some time at the end of your analysis to reflect on how your interviewees may have benefited from the experience. This question touches, of course, on 'ethical issues' in research, which we discussed in Chapter 2, but it also extends to what is 'discovered' in psychological research. It is possible, for example, for an interviewee to tell a story which reveals nothing of interest to academic psychology, but is valuable as a process in which a researcher learns how to 'witness' a story (and valuable to the interviewee whose story is 'witnessed' by another person).

SAQ 12.1

Imagine you are to carry out an interview study. You will need to consider the topic that you will focus upon, the people you would want to interview, and the types of questions you should ask. Now spend ten minutes listing the reasons why this study may be useful.

12.2 Stage two: 'grounded theory'

We are now considering the complete range of qualitative data that you may be faced with, ranging from interview transcripts to accounts, from diaries to media texts. This second stage of the analysis looks for the emergence of categories in the course of careful and repeated reading of the texts. The clearest rationale and description of this type of reading appears in the literature on 'grounded theory' (Glaser and Strauss, 1967; Strauss and Corbin, 1990). You may restrict yourself to this stage when you have carried out an unstructured interview, and it would also be possible (though less satisfactory, because some categories will already be represented in the interview format) using a semi-structured interview. (The difference between these two forms of interviews is discussed in Chapter 8; structured interviews do not lend themselves easily to qualitative analysis.) Accounts which have been gathered by way of interviews or semi-structured questionnaires or diaries completed by research participants or by researchers themselves can also be handled using grounded theory precepts.

This part of the analysis works from the base up, and systematically builds up conceptions of what issues seem to be important in the material, and what categories structure the text. The aim is not to build an account which is different from that used nor to uncover hidden motives or unconscious wishes or such like, but to make explicit what is implicit in the text. The final set of categories should represent as clearly as possible the picture of the world that the material has expressed. This does not mean that you are trying to capture the 'authentic' voice of your interviewee, of the person who has written the text or even of yourself when you filled in a diary, and some writers would argue that it is just not possible to do that (Silverman, 1993). Rather, you should think of your text as laying out bits of the picture, and as you fit these bits together you solve puzzles as to how contradictory images work alongside each other.

The skills of the researcher in reading the material include being able to identify different concepts under category headings, linking concepts that fit together, and organizing the sets so that the categories show good 'fit' with the data. The first step of 'coding' is where a number of categories which seem to sum up the key underlying ideas of the text are generated. It is best to start this process on about half a page of the text, and to work with that portion to keep the analysis in check before moving up to the complete text. Working again on one specific portion of the text, the next step is to 'saturate' the categories by dividing the text in such a way as to include all of it under your chosen category headings. You should keep track of the different quotes from your text, and each category label should operate as a 'good descriptor' of each of the instances you include. You will want to bring some headings together in the course of your coding (because they seem to cover the same ground), to drop some headings (because you have so few instances), or to split some headings (because different issues are addressed). The links between the different headings and the contrasts between headings will operate as connections to organize the material so that it can be presented in the analysis section of the report.

Grounded theory has had some attention in psychology in recent years (Henwood and Pidgeon, 1992). One advantage of this framework for psychologists is that it attends very closely to the data, it is 'grounded' in the interview text, for example. If you stop at this stage, you will then, in the discussion section of your report, have to address the 'fit' between your research question(s) and the saturated categories you describe in the analysis section. You may, however, want to move on to look at that 'fit' as part of your analysis. We turn to this work in the third stage of the analysis.

SAQ 12.2
Imagine you are preparing to interview someone for a piece of qualitative research. Would you choose to use a 'structured', 'semi-structured' or 'unstructured' interview format?

12.3 Stage three: 'thematic analysis'

The analysis requires a transcription of the material obtained; conventions for making a transcription are given in Box 12.1. The coordination of the researcher's and research participant's agendas is most clearly at issue when the interview is semi-structured. Although the interviewer's agenda is less apparent in the text of an unstructured interview, it can be reconstructed in the course of the analysis and taken alongside the research questions, which should have been made explicit before the investigation proceeds and will appear at the end of the introduction

Box 12.1 Transcription conventions

A detailed description of transcription conventions used in conversation analysis, which is one of the approaches that examines the details of language, is presented in Atkinson and Heritage (1984). The following elements are those used in discourse analytic research, and will be sufficient for the studies carried out using thematic analysis and in the other qualitative traditions described in this book. They are abstracted from Parker (1992).

(1) When there are doubts about the accuracy of material, put it in round brackets (like this).

(2) When the material has been omitted from the transcript, signal it by putting a pair of empty square brackets, [ ].

(3) When you need to clarify something, put the explanation in square brackets, like this: [to help the reader].

(4) When there are noises, words of assent, and so on, put this in slashes like this: /hmm/, /yes/.

(5) Indicate the absence of a gap between one speaker and another with = marks at the end of one and the beginning of the next utterance.

(6) Indicate pauses in the speech with seconds in round brackets, e.g. (2) for two seconds, and a full stop for pauses lasting less than a second: (.).

(7) Indicate an extended sound with colon marks: ye::s.

(8) Indicate emphases in speech by underlining those parts of the text.

(9) Indicate an intake of breath before a word by putting a full stop before it: .aah.

Box 12.2 Getting too personal constructs

The repertory grid is a powerful way of drawing out the constructs that a person uses to organize perceptions of self and others. Other methods are also used within the personal construct tradition in psychology that can flesh out the meanings of the various different bipolar dimensions. One such method is 'self-characterization', in which research participants are asked to provide a simple description, around a page, of how, for example, they see themselves. They could then be asked to provide a simple description of how they were once, or how they would like to be. The different self-characterizations can be analysed in terms of the constructs that structure each account. A related method, which takes us further into the participant's personal world, is 'laddering', in which the opposite poles of each construct are divided into a new set of overarching ('superordinate') constructs. This research process can

— Continued —

— — *Continued* — — — — — — — — — — — — — — — — — — —

then be used therapeutically, and there is a tradition of 'personal construct therapy', which uses these techniques in a qualitative way to assist change.

There is a case example of personal construct therapy in Fransella's (1984a) discussion of work with a woman whom she calls 'Hilda'. Hilda has a problem with weight. She does lose weight, but every time she succeeds, she quickly puts it on again, and she is confused and unhappy about this. There seems to be an opposition at work, a bipolar personal construct dimension of 'slim' versus 'overweight'. A self-characterization of herself as 'slim' outlines the way in which she sees that person as attractive but not very confident. The self-characteriz-ation of herself as overweight includes descriptions of a person who is more in control and quite giggly. Part of the therapy involved trying to 'loosen' these contructs, and to explore 'superordinate' constructs.

Examples of Hilda's constructs included the following: 'expect people to come to them versus vivacious; lazy versus motivate them-selves to do things; indecisive versus decisive and adventurous versus close-minded. The laddering of this last construct led to learn about life versus sit at home and do nothing, then on to take opportunities as they come along versus do not do so' (Fransella, 1984a, p. 147).

Being fat solved a problem, which was that she would not have to suffer the attention of men and would be in control, but the slim Hilda was a person who was more adventurous at the cost of being out of control. The therapy was then able to focus on the ways in which a slim Hilda could be in control rather than see herself at the prey of men. By looking at the ways in which the different constructs were locked together to produce a self-defeating and self-destructive set of experiences, Hilda was able to explore different ways of understanding herself and others.

In this example, personal constructs appear to be firmly rooted in the mind of the individual, in Hilda, and personal construct theory could be seen as a very individualist approach. Elsewhere, however, Fransella (1984b) has taken pains to point out that the constructs are often shared across a community, and an individual draws upon these social 'constructs' to make sense of his or her own experience. The account that Hilda developed to make sense of her body and relation-ships with men, for example, focuses on the personal constructs she uses, but these ideas are derived from a particular culture which portrays women and their weight in destructive ways and Hilda will be structuring her experience in a way that many other women will resonate with. Fransella's (1984b) argument that personal constructs are really very social parallels Curt's (1994) argument that Q sorts, which we describe in Chapter 8, pick up social meanings that then operate at a personal level. These arguments reflect a shift in psychol-ogy towards more social explanations of individual experience, a change that qualitative research assists.

part of the report. A similar principle operates in the case of material gathered as accounts from people. In the case of a diary study, the agenda of the person who is writing the diary changes, whether that person is the researcher or not.

It is useful at this point to list the sets of assumptions that underlay the research, and put these side by side with the categories that have emerged in the course of the second stage, 'grounded theory' part of the analysis. These research 'themes' may already have been explicated before the material was produced, but it is highly probable that additional assumptions will be evident in the course of the research. As notes for the Introduction section of the report are being collected, it is necessary, in the case of interviews, to code the interviewer interventions, and to set these alongside the stated aims of the research, and the range of different ideas that were discounted. In the case of accounts, diaries and other texts, a clear record should be kept of the assumptions made before the study commenced and of how these changed as the study proceeded. As a general point here, and one which becomes even more important in this type of analysis, much of the literature review and writing of drafts of the report introduction should be carried out before the study takes place.

Certain categories will have appeared that are perfectly consistent with your predictions, but you should in each case look for disconfirming instances. Each part of the text which could contradict the categories which underpin the researcher's starting viewpoint should be coded. The 'themes', which form the basis for the analysis section of the report, will then be an accommodation of the text's version to the issues that the investigation set out to address. 'Accommodation' involves a change in a category as it absorbs and contains new material, as against 'assimilation', in which the new information is simply squashed into a rigid, preset schema. Accommodation is the production of something new. This is taken a step further when we move on to look at how the language used in the material may be constructed as something new out of existing linguistic resources. These linguistic resources are one instance of cultural patterns that have been termed 'discourses' (Parker, 1992). As well as looking to shared cultural patterns, it is also possible to explore the ways in which these resources are distinctive to the person. Personal construct theory, which we described in Chapter 8, has made an important contribution to this endeavour, and has been helpful therapeutically too (see Box 12.2).

12.4 Stage four: 'discourse analysis'

Discourse analysis is the study of how language changes, how it is put together, and how it works. The assumptions that guide the selection of material, and, in the case of interviews, the description of the research that encourages participants to take part in the investigation, are important, and a semi-structured interview format will represent those first assumptions more explicitly than an unstructured interview. In any case, the discourse analytic study of the text should include the interventions made by the interviewer, and the investigator should step back from the text at this stage of the analysis to look at her or his own questions as part of the material. We have described in Chapter 5 how discourse analysis emerged in psychology as an approach which focused on variability, construction and function (Potter and Wetherell, 1987). These three aspects of the research can usefully structure a discourse analytic reading.

Variability is often deliberately obscured in psychological research because the aim of the investigation is to arrive at some underlying consistent picture. The first stage of the analysis that we have described, where you look for the story presented in the material, shares this tendency. The second stage looked to break the text into categories that could then be pieced together, and third stage focused on the ways in which categories imposed by the researcher collide with those employed in the text. Discourse analysis stays with this decomposition of the text into categories, and is particularly concerned with those categories that present different, contradictory pictures of the world. The aim is not to 'catch someone out', but to reveal how the text is organized by a number of competing themes.

The analysis builds on much of the work carried out in the second stage, 'grounded theory' analysis, by looking at how the different statements in the text form the basis for and are also constructed around the category headings, and also at how the statements draw on contrasting headings. Different functions can be identified by asking, at each point that a specific category is used, 'what is being done here?'. It is particularly useful to focus on the ways different turns of phrase might have different effects at different points in the text. A study of themes that underlie different accounts can also help us to understand the ways in which the accounts function as part of the wider social interaction between different groups. This is something we describe in Box 12.3.

When the different categories are linked to produce different pictures of the world, the analysis is moving from the level of themes (which are relevant, for analytic purposes, only to this text) to the level of discourses. Discourses are 'sets of statements which construct an object' (Parker, 1992); 'object' here means any category of thing or person that is spoken about by an interviewee (or which you will then read about when you work through the text), or which is found in your own account as you wrote a diary during the course of your research.

All text analysis is, in some sense, 'discourse analysis', and the selection of particular portions of the text may be used to illustrate different types of relationship. The interaction between the interviewer and the interviewee, for example, may be the focus of the analysis, and here the investigator may be interested in picking up, in the forms of language which structure the interview, the issues of power that we mentioned above, under stage one. All interviews are also, in some sense, 'accounts'. Much other material gathered in the course of psychological investigation is also someone's account, and it is one of the virtues of qualitative research that it can attend to this when the study is being written up.

This then addresses, as a matter of course, the moral position of the researcher, something that is usually set apart in traditional psychology as a peculiar optional extra (Shotter, 1975). An ethics checklist is sometimes added to the research

Box 12.3 Riots and representations

Qualitative interviewing approaches can add a great deal to our understanding of social processes, and can illuminate events that appear, at first site, to be incomprehensible. A series of street disturbances in Britain in the early 1980s, for example, raised the spectre of 'mob rule', and the idea that people who get together in crowds are overtaken by a 'group mind'. There is a close similarity here between the ways in which the popular tabloid press portrayed the disturbances and theories of the crowd in social psychology going back to the end of the last century. In both cases the perspective adopted is that of an 'outsider' who focuses attention on the crowd as a kind of mass irrational force. This is also an example, then, of how bad psychology can chime in with mistaken 'common sense'.

Journalists tend to see people in crowds, particularly when they attack the police, as if they were animals who have been stripped of the veneer of civilization that usually holds them in check. Social psychologists who have been influenced by the theories of the French writer Gustave Le Bon have been just as negative. Le Bon (1947, but first published in 1895) argued that the behaviour of people in crowds fell several rungs down the evolutionary ladder, to the level of 'beings belonging to inferior forms of evolution...women, savages, and children, for instance' (Le Bon, 1947, p. 36). These ideas take on a quite nasty political flavour when they are used to describe 'riots' by black people in inner-city areas, and the task of the psychologist should be to look at how popular images work, and how people in the crowd understand their actions. Qualitative interviewing can move to an 'insider' perspective on these events, and so assist this task.

One of the first 'riots' in the 1980s, in the St Pauls area of Bristol, was studied by Reicher (1984), a social psychologist whose training had been in the experimental tradition. Reicher was carrying out research on social identity at Bristol University when the April 1980 'riot' broke out, and he was able to interview participants. Their accounts did not correspond either with standard social psychological or journalistic images of people who had lost their minds, and the 'inside' story was of a community trying to defend itself against the police. One of the striking aspects of the insider accounts was that both black and white people who were in the crowd refused to accept the outsider claims that this was a racial disturbance. Private homes and shops within the community were left untouched, whereas the banks and the unemployment office were seen as legitimate targets. The stories collected in these qualitative interviews did also correspond with the descriptions of the damage given by the authorities. An examination of the accounts of outsiders and insiders by Reicher and Potter (1985) went on to illustrate the ways in which traditional 'scientific' explanations of crowd behaviour fail to account for the insider perspective, which in the case of St Pauls, stressed the meaningfulness of crowd action, and the feelings of solidarity and emotional warmth that came with defence of the community.

plan as if it were something to be considered after the study had been designed. Now, rather than researchers permitting themselves the luxury of qualms of conscience in an idle moment as if ethical issues arise only as minor technical hitches, their subjective involvement should be treated as part of the material under study as a moral question from the start. Many qualitative researchers would argue that because language is the stuff of human experience, and that subjectivity is, in large measure, constituted in language, empiricist and positivist assumptions lead us away from psychological reality. Qualitative research that takes subjectivity and interpretation seriously, then, also requires a new language, a different discourse and different kinds of rules and roles for the psychological investigator to play by and adopt.

One of the characteristics of qualitative research is that it focuses on contradiction, and this means that it would be out of keeping with this research endeavour to be too precise, or to close things up and pretend there was only one sure way of doing it. This is a debate, a discursive matter, not a matter of scientific 'truth'. So, perhaps a good way of providing a definition is to present it from three slightly different angles: 'Qualitative research is: (i) An attempt to capture the sense that lies within, and which structures what we say about what we do; (ii) An exploration, elaboration and systematisation of the significance of an identified phenomenon; (iii) The illuminative re-presentation of the meaning of a delimited issue or problem' (Banister *et al.*, 1994, p. 3).

When the discipline defines what 'science' is in a restricted way which pretends to model itself on the natural sciences, it also defines what desires we permit ourselves to express as we interpret qualitative data, and, as a consequence, we can easily forget what led many of us into psychology in the first place. The interpretation of qualitative data is a moral (and political) enterprise, and so it brings ethics from the margins to the centre of psychological investigation.

Using computers

13.0 Introduction

Computers have had a massive theoretical and practical impact on psychology over the last 20 years. The theoretical impact has come through the use of computer modelling and simulation, the relationship between psychology and artificial intelligence, and the development of cognitive science. The practical impact has been through the use of computers to perform tasks which previously required specialized apparatus or skills. As a psychology student, you will almost immediately find you are using computers in some part of your work, for clerical tasks, statistical calculation, or for presenting experiments or questionnaires. You may have some of your examination presented on computer and possibly some of your teaching too. In this chapter we describe these uses, which have taken some time to take root but are likely to become much more prominent in the future, especially as the number of students expands but the resources for teaching do not. The hardware and the software develop so rapidly that what we write will be out of date by the time this book is published, let alone by the time you read it. But it is important that you should be aware of the different ways in which computers are used in psychology, and we have suggested where to look to find out about current developments.

There has been an explosive growth of computing in the home (and psychology laboratory), and many people now have on their desk more computing power than a whole university department of even ten years ago. This development, which initially took place in the United States, started with Apple computers, and the Apple Macintosh (Mac) is the most common machine in university departments of psychology in the United Kingdom. But Apple did not acquire the overwhelmingly dominant position in Britain that they had in the USA. British higher education went through a period of using a limited range of computers, such as the BBC micro, which were supported by government funding. At that period, students were taught how to write programs in a language such as BASIC, but this stage has now passed. Many students have their own machine, which is very often a PC rather than a Mac, and most departments of psychology have PCs as well as Macs. Students are rarely taught how to write programs unless they are specializing in artificial intelligence, cognitive science or psychology and computing: the emphasis is on using pre-existing packages and programs rather than writing your own. Some of these packages, such as spreadsheets, are 'general purpose', but can be very useful for a psychology student. Others have been developed specially by and for psychologists.

13.1 Word processing, spreadsheets, databases

Three main types of computer program have revolutionized administrative office tasks throughout industry and commerce and most computer users will be familiar with them. One is the word processor, which allows you to edit and format text, keep disk copies and print as many copies as you require. You are almost certainly going to use a word processor to prepare your reports, even if you do not already do so. There are many different word-processing packages, each with its own particular conventions for invoking commands to move parts of the text, apply different typefaces and paragraph formats, etc. We can do no more than recommend that you make every effort to have a word-processing package available, and learn to use it with confidence.

Programs which provide desk-top publishing (DTP) are similar to word processors, and indeed as word processors have become more and more sophisticated the distinction between the two types of package has become blurred. DTP packages are intended to let you lay out pamphlets and books; they allow you to apply more complex forms of formatting than a word processor and they have more facilities for dealing with pictures, tables and graphs. They operate rather differently from a word processor, in that you design the layout of a page by drawing frames on it and then insert the text into these frames. The frames can be moved and their size altered. Using frames, you can arrange the text in a number of columns on each page, have a number of stories starting on the first page and then continued on later pages, position illustrations exactly where you want them. You can enter text directly into the frames of a DTP program, but this is usually a slow process. The usual way of using DTP is to prepare the text in a word processor first, and then import it into the DTP package, where minor final editing can be done. Modern word processors have many of the facilities of a DTP package, and for preparing your practical reports a word processor will be adequate.

Spreadsheets are one of the types of program which demonstrate the value of computers, since they provide facilities not readily obtained in any other way. A spreadsheet consists of a table, where the columns are labelled A, B C and so on and the rows are labelled numerically. So the top left cell of a table is A1, the one below it is A2, the one at the top of the second column is B1, and so on. You can insert values into these cells, and then tell the program to perform arithmetic operations on whatever numbers are in the cell. So if you have put 6 into cell A1 and 8 into cell B1, you can ask for it to add the content of these two cells and put the result into cell D1 by entering a formula such as +(A1..B1) into cell D1. This may seem very simple, but it is surprising how much a spreadsheet allows you to do. As a simple example, you could have a spreadsheet which calculated statistical significance tests for you. You would then simply have to enter the data into the

TABLE 13.1. *Using a spreadsheet to calculate t for related groups*

	A	B	C	D
1	$x1$	$y1$	+(a1-b1)	+(c1^2)
2	$x2$	$y2$	+(a2-b2)	+(c2^2)
3	$x3$	$y3$	+(a3-b3)	+(c3^2)
4	$x4$	$y4$	+(a4-b4)	+(c4^2)
5	$x5$	$y5$	+(a5-b5)	+(c5^2)
:	:			
:	:			
11	SUM(a1..a10)	SUM(b1..b10)	SUM(c1..c10)	SUM(d1..d10)
12				
13	COUNT(a1..a10)		+(c11^2)	
14	+(a11/a13)	+(b11/a13)	+(c11/a13)	
15			+(c13/a13)	
16				
17			+(d11-c15)	
18			+(c17/(a13*a13-1))	
19			SQR(c18)	
20			+(c14/c19)	

The data for each respondent are entered into columns A and B. The spreadsheet calculates the difference (d) between the scores for each respondent and puts the result into column C. The square of the d values are calculated and inserted into column D. The total of each set of scores is given in cells a11 and b11, the number of pairs of data (n) is in a13, the means of each set in a14 and b14. The sum of the difference scores, Σd, is in c11 and the sum of the squared difference scores, Σd^2 in d11. The square of Σd, $(\Sigma d)^2$, is in c13, the mean of d in c14, $(\Sigma d)^2/n$ in c15. Parts of the formula for the related t are calculated in cells c17 and c18, and the square root is taken in c19. The value of t occurs in cell c20.

spreadsheet and it would automatically calculate the statistic you wanted. An example of how a spreadsheet could be used to calculate the related *t*-test for up to ten pairs of numbers is shown in Table 13.1. The precise way the formulae are written will depend on the particular spreadsheet you are using, but you should be able to see how you can develop sheets to simplify the task of calculating statistical tests.

Databases are the third type of program in common use which you are likely to find useful. Unlike spreadsheets, which are mainly concerned with numerical material, databases are for storing alphabetical information. They are particularly valuable for storing references, since once you have created a database of references you can then search through your collection by author, by date, or by journal title. You can have the program search through the titles and look for particular words, and you can combine these searches so that if you know you have a reference to research on pain which was published in 1994 but you cannot remember the author, the program can search its records and find any that meet the criteria you have specified. You can then make up separate lists of subsets of your total collection of references, print them out, and append them to your essays or practical reports. Creating a database is rather time consuming, as you have to enter the material in the first place, but once you have it, you are likely to find it invaluable and well worth the effort of creating it and adding to it throughout your career.

A database contains a series of records, which might be a journal reference. The reference contains a number of parts: author, date, title, journal title, volume number, page numbers. Each of these is stored in a field, so one record is made up of a number of fields. You can search through the database and sort it by any of the fields you want; you might initially have it sorted by alphabetical order of authors but when you want to see all the references you have dating from 1993 you can sort it according to date, and then put it back into the original order. There are numerous different database programs. They all have a similar structure, but the exact instructions to achieve the same aim vary from one to the other. Again we urge you to learn how to use the one that is available to you. Also remember the use of databases such as the CD-ROM-based PsycLit, which we described in section 10.2. Entries can be down-loaded on to your own floppy disk and added to your own personal references database, but you must remember the copyright restrictions and the need to be selective. This is another area where computer technology gives you an easy opportunity to get totally overloaded with material.

When computing really started to become popular, word processors, spreadsheets and databases were separately developed; different companies specialized in one type and some made their fortune on the basis of one product. Now they tend to be integrated into a single application, often with Works or Office in the title. The advantage is that you then have all three types of program in one package, and can readily move from one to another. So you can prepare a table in the spreadsheet and then import it into your word-processing document, or readily bring into the word processor the information you have typed into your database. As the integrated package has been developed by one software company, all the modules use the same conventions; you use the same keys to change the typeface, for example. The integrated package often has a simpler version of each application than a stand-alone word processor, spreadsheet and database. But it is likely to have what you need, and be cheaper than buying three different programs. The ability to move between applications rather than have to close one, open another and transfer information between them makes them easy to use. If you are thinking about buying software, they are definitely worth serious consideration.

13.2 Quantitative analysis

As mentioned above, a spreadsheet program can be used to carry out statistical calculations, but there are many programs specifically for statistical computation.

There are two major types, the relatively simple (and cheap) ones and the highly complex and expensive, such as SPSS, Minitab and STATISTICA. Many students have access to one of the professional packages at college, but need something simpler for their personal needs. You will find some packages available as shareware, which means that you can buy them very cheaply (through advertisements in computer magazines) and try them out; if they fit your needs, you then register with the author for a small fee.

The cost of the large professional statistical packages means that they are out of reach of the single home user. They provide a huge range of facilities, including all those you need and many more, such as factor analysis, LISREL, log-linear analysis as well as graph drawing procedures. They will cope with huge amounts of data, such as the responses of hundreds of people to a questionnaire containing dozens of questions. The various packages have their supporters and detractors: some require a lot of learning before they can be used with confidence. The professional packages are undergoing continual development, with new techniques being added and simpler interfaces being provided. You will almost certainly need to become familiar with whichever package is used by your college. It is likely that your course will include tuition in using the package, either as a separate module or integrated into the teaching of statistics. The manuals to the packages are not always appropriate for the beginner, and copies may be in short supply. But you will find that there are books which explain how to use the package to obtain the kinds of analysis you want: Monk (1991) describes the use of Minitab, Foster (1993) and Kinnear and Gray (1994) cover SPSS.

The statistical package itself consists of a program or set of programs; how these are written and where they are stored are matters with which you can remain unfamiliar. But there are four fundamental things you need to know to use the package effectively. First, how do you prepare the data and submit them to the package? You may be able to write the data into a word processor, save them as a text file, and then import them into the package. For example, SPSS for Windows will read a data file which has been created in Windows Write and saved in text form. Once the data have been read into SPSS, they can be saved as a data file in the special SPSS format. This means you can do the data preparation privately when you do not have access to the SPSS package itself. Second, you must be able to control the package – instruct it to perform the analyses you want on the relevant set of data. What instructions are required and how do you give the order to carry out the instructions? In SPSS/PC+, for example, it is necessary to write a list of commands and then tell the package to run them by pressing key F10 on the keyboard. With SPSS for Windows this is not necessary: you select from a series of on-screen menus the analysis you want and can then merely click on a button marked 'OK'. If you are likely to want to run the instructions again, however, you can save them in a separate file which can be saved, printed out, and edited. Third, you need to be confident that you can save the data and the output on your own floppy disk so you can take them away with you and keep them. Fourth, you need to know how to edit the output file: can you simply import it into a word processor and treat it as a normal document? If so, you can extract relevant sections of the output and use them in your practical reports without having to retype.

The main danger with sophisticated statistical packages is that it is easy to obtain analyses that you do not understand; this is almost certainly a route to disaster. A few simple key presses can yield mountains of output and this can be quite counterproductive if you do not know what the program has done or why you asked it to do it. As a general rule, you should know *before* you approach the computer, before even you obtain the data, how you want them analysed.

Another danger is that you get the machine to carry out a test that you do understand, but you then fail to interpret the print-out properly. It is crucial that you understand the output. In SPSS, for example, the output for analysis of variance shows the F value and gives the probability of having obtained that value by chance. Students are familiar with the convention of $p<0.05$, $p<0.001$, and can get confused when SPSS gives the probability as 0.0000. This actually means the result is significant beyond the 0.0001 level. Similarly, the output may mention statistics which you have not come across and which are not mentioned in introductory statistics books, such as lambda or eigenvalue. Purists might argue that you should not be using procedures if you do not know what all the terms in its output mean, but our view is less extreme: you must be able to identify the figures you do understand from the output. When the package has done its stuff and computed chi-square, you should know which numbers are chi-square, which are the degrees of freedom, and which show the statistical significance level.

Statistical packages include facilities for drawing graphs and preparing diagrams such as stem-and-leaf plots. As the programs are revised and updated, these facilities become ever more sophisticated, allowing three-dimensional effects, multicoloured displays, exploded charts. Obtaining the precise display you want can be rather complicated, especially if you do not want the format that the package offers to you by default. As with the statistical analysis, it is wise to have decided beforehand which form of graphic display you require, although you will undoubtedly want to explore the alternatives... part of computer use which many people enjoy!

13.3 Qualitative analysis

Programs for carrying out qualitative analysis of data are not so common as those for quantitative analysis, partly because qualitative analysis has fewer definite rules about how to proceed. There are programs for analysing qualitative data, such as NU*DIST or TEXTBASE ALPHA, which, after the data have been typed in, assist the user in allocating segments to categories. The programs store which items have been put into the categories, and can count them, and tabulate them.

There are a number of programs for analysing repertory grids, such as INGRID, CIRCUMGRID and REPRID 2.0. Programs which are interactive in presenting, analysing and feeding back the analysis can be particularly useful in helping the user gain most insight from the technique.

13.4 Programs for administering experiments: experiment generators

Computers were welcomed by psychology not only because they could do the statistical work but also because they could administer experiments, replacing equipment such as the memory drum and the tachistoscope, which had previously been used to present stimuli for specified periods of time, and record the responses. An early development was authors putting familiar experiments and simulations on to disk for demonstration and teaching purposes. The drawbacks to these programs are that they tend to be inflexible: you have to use the materials and display specifications laid down by the creator. They were not intended for full-scale research purposes, and may not deal with the problems involved in using a computer to present displays for fractions of a second or measure response times accurately.

The alternative is a type of program which allows you specify the material you want to display, the way it is shown on the screen, and the time for which it is shown, and which records response times and aggregates them in a usable manner. Such a program is known as an experiment generator, and there are a number on the market, including Melab for the Macintosh and ERTS for the PC. These are sophisticated programs which do require some learning before they can be used, but allow you to use your computer as a research tool.

13.5 Programs for administering tests and questionnaires

Computer presentation of many standardized psychological tests is now available, and research has been conducted to demonstrate whether people score differently when responding to a screen presentation rather than a paper version. Many of these test programs include report generators, so that the computer also provides a commentary on the responses given by the test taker. Most of these tests are available only to those who have undergone recognized training.

If you are carrying out a study in which people are completing questionnaires, considerable time can be saved if you present the questionnaire by computer. This is not usually feasible, as you generally need a large number of respondents who are geographically distributed, so you have to rely on sending questionnaires out by post in paper form. But if you are asking a number of people one after the other and have access to a portable computer or if you can get your respondents to come to your computer installation, presenting the questionnaire via the machine does mean that it can automatically do the scoring for you and keep a record of the person's responses. There are a number of programs which will present questionnaires, some written by individual academics, others (such as QUESTION MARK) published by commercial software houses.

13.6 Computer-assisted learning (CAL) and testing

Since their early days, computers seemed to provide the means for teaching large numbers of students. Here is a machine that is tireless and flexible (unlike the 'teaching machines' of the 1950s): it looked perfect for presenting students with information, testing them to check they had understood it, presenting it again or explaining it further if they had not grasped the content. The actual implementation of CAL in Great Britain has been much less and much slower than its supporters had hoped. This is partly because it takes a considerable investment of time and effort to write CAL material, and university staff are rewarded more for research than for teaching, and partly because a number of psychology teachers do not accept that CAL can substitute for personal teaching and are suspicious of what it might lead to. But there is an increasing quantity of high-quality CAL modules available, and they are likely to prove valuable for those who have to teach large numbers of students with minimal resources.

The use of CAL has been greater in the USA, which is why much of the CAL for psychology originates in America. Its usefulness in the British context is open to question, as it concentrates on topics popular in American courses, uses American sources and references, and assumes the American model of education. But there are government-funded schemes to promote the use of CAL in British universities, and it is possible that these will lead to the production of high-quality CAL packages and stimulate their use.

Using computers to test students is very familiar in the USA, where the multiple-choice test is common and the British style of essay examination rare. Although the principles underlying multiple-choice tests have been discussed for many years, this type of assessment has only recently become common in the United Kingdom. It is particularly suitable for computer presentation as the machine presents the questions, records the answers and can perform an item analysis, showing how many students gave each alternative answer to each question. This lets the teacher refine the test, deleting those which are too easy or too hard. There are a number of commercially available packages, such as QUESTION MARK, for presenting multiple-choice tests.

13.7 Where to find out about computer use in psychology teaching

Developments in hardware and software are so rapid that we have given only a very broad picture of the ways computers are used in psychology. You will want an up-to-date list of what is available under the various headings. There are three main sources of information. *The Psychologist*, the monthly journal of The British Psychological Society, reviews software, as does *Psychology Teaching Review*, published by the BPS's Special Group for the Teaching of Psychology. In Britain there are 'Computers in Teaching Initiative' (CTI) centres for over 20 academic disciplines, each based in a university department. The CTI for psychology is based at the University of York and it publishes the *Psychology Software News*, which regularly reviews software. All psychology departments in United Kingdom universities have a link with the CTI and are provided with a copy of the newsletter. There are also journals such as *Computers in Education* which deal with broader topics. Developments in the main commercial word-processing, spreadsheet and database packages are discussed in the computer magazines available at any newsagent.

Chapter 14

Producing the report

14.0 General introduction

To see a model of a psychology report, read a paper in a journal, such as the *British Journal of Psychology*. As a beginner you are obviously not expected to reach journal standard from the outset, but you should be able to appreciate the way the report is structured in a series of sections, how material is allocated to the various sections, the way it provides an account of a study such that the reader can say 'I don't believe it – I'm going to repeat this study and see if I get the same results!'

There are certain conventions which are used in writing reports which may seem rather constraining, but do mean that they share a common structure, and therefore it is possible to scan a report and locate particular parts of it speedily – a benefit you will appreciate as you read more of them. The conventional structure is most appropriate for reports on experimental work, less so for case studies and qualitative work. We have found that the most successful teaching method is to ask students to learn the conventional format at the outset. Unless it is mastered first, students have difficulty using the conventions when they need to. So we give the conventional format first, and then look at the reporting of nonexperimental and qualitative research, where the conventions are less strict. When you have read through our recommendations, you will find a checklist at the end of the chapter in Box 14.6, which should help you to implement them.

14.1 Writing the report of an experiment

14.1.1 Sections of the report: title

The title should be brief, but informative so the reader is immediately aware of the topic being reported, as in: 'Do people avoid sitting next to someone who is facially disfigured?' (Houston and Bull, 1994). It is helpful if the title indicates the method as well as the topic; so 'an experimental study' or 'a survey' or whatever was appropriate could be added. A title such as 'Memory for faces' is inadequate for an account of a particular study, as it implies a paper which reviews a body of research.

14.1.2 Sections of the report: author

Do not forget it!

Box 14.1 Example of a poor and a better abstract

Note that the report used in the examples in Boxes 14.1 to 14.5 concerns an experiment planned and carried out by a group of students. The means are those they found, but other figures have been added purely to illustrate how results should be presented. This should not be taken as a serious research finding. The examples of poor report sections have been taken from real student work, modified to demonstrate some of the errors you should avoid. The appendices mentioned are not reproduced here, but you should be able to see what they would contain.

An Experiment to Investigate Whether Concrete Words Are Easier to Remember than Abstract Words

Abstract

This experiment is to investigate whether abstract words are harder to remember than concrete words. In order for this to be carried out, there were two groups of 15 subjects for abstract and two groups of 15 subjects for concrete words. Subjects read 20 words, and were then asked to recall as many as possible immediately afterwards or after a 5-minute delay.

This fails to describe the procedure adequately and makes no mention of the outcome of the study. Compare it with this, which provides these details rather more fully than would be acceptable to a journal but which would be suitable for a student report:

Abstract

A between-groups experiment was conducted to test the hypotheses that respondents find it easier to remember a list of concrete words than a list of abstract words (1) with immediate recall and (2) with delayed recall. Four groups of first-year students ($n = 15$) were formed. Each respondent was given 1 minute to study a list of 20 abstract or 20 concrete words. Free recall was tested after 0 or 5 minutes. There was no significant difference between the number of abstract and concrete words recalled with immediate recall, but with delayed recall the difference was significant. The results are interpreted as providing some support for the notion that it is more difficult to rehearse lists of abstract words.

14.1.3 Sections of the report: abstract

The abstract is usually placed before the report itself, but is actually written last. It should be four or five sentences, summarizing (1) the topic of the study; (2) the participants and procedure; (3) the outcome (results), and (4) some mention of the interpretation put on the results. Box 14.1 includes examples of a poor and a better abstract. Writing the abstract in its final form should be done after the paper has been written, although it is often helpful to write a draft abstract before you begin, simply as a guide to how you expect the final report to look.

14.1.4 Sections of the report: introduction

The introduction and discussion sections are the longest components of the report. In the introduction you introduce the study by (1) summarizing relevant background literature, and (2) demonstrating how the study you are reporting has developed from it.

Initially, you have little familiarity with the background to the study you are reporting, and so have to rely on information given in the handout which usually accompanies a practical. You then have to write the introduction as though you had more knowledge than you actually do. Even when you are mainly rewriting the information given to you, do rewrite it and not merely transcribe it. The introduction should be your own work, a distillation of the handout information and the reading you have done. If it is too similar to the handout, you are likely to be penalized.

Handouts often contain far more information than would be expected in a report's introduction. They summarize relevant literature and provide references, but also cover material which, while not directly relevant to the study, shows how it relates to other areas of research. This latter type of material is not usually needed in the report's introduction.

The handout will contain a number of references, so you should be able to locate at least one or two of them. If you are (for good reason) unable to read any of them, you should look up the topic in your basic textbook, and use that material. You are expected to demonstrate in the introduction that you have done some background reading.

How long should the introduction be? It is impossible to be precise, since it depends on how much background material there is for the particular practical, but about 900 words is usually expected. An introduction that is too short is likely to provide an inadequate summary of the background, while one that is too long is likely to contain irrelevant material.

One of the most difficult aspects of writing the introduction is structuring it so that the aim of the study develops out of the background survey, appearing to be a sensible extension of the preceding material. Ideally you should be able to conclude your introduction with some phrase like this: 'The aim of the present study was to extend this line of investigation by testing Bloggs' (1988) claim that ...' and completing the sentence appropriately.

Box 14.2 Examples of a poor and a better introduction

Introduction
Why is that people remember some things but not others? Why is it
that people remember some words but forget some? The field of
memory is widely studied by many psychologists. It has been said that
words have three distinct encoding systems: (1) orthographic – the
pattern of letters; (2) phonological – sound of the word; (3) semantic –
the meaning of the word.

Conrad ('64) carried out a study on whether people could remember
confusable sequences of letters (e.g. CTVG) or non-confusable (e.g.
XVSL). Conrad found that it was more difficult to remember confusable letters.

Baddeley (1964) extended Conrad's experiment and showed that
this only occurred when subjects had to repeat back immediately
sequences of similar sounding words. For instance, mad, map, man as
compared with pen, sky, dog. But it was also not difficult to remember
semantic words, such as huge, great, big.

Armstrong carried out a study where students were given these
instructions: 'Think of some definite object – suppose it is your
breakfast table as you sat down to it this morning – and consider
carefully the picture that rises before your mind's eye'. The students
then had to answer questions such as 'Is the image clear? Are the
colours of the china quite distinct?' Armstrong came up with a number
of conclusions about the nature of images.

The study of imagery has been revived by Paivio, who claimed to
show that imagery could be studied in an experimental manner. In
1969 Paivio used paired-associate learning to investigate imagery in
verbal learning. He studied how subjects could learn associations when
the stimuli were concrete or abstract words. Paivio came to the
conclusion that it was easier to learn associate pairs related to concrete
words rather than abstract ones.

Paivio believes that imagery is separate from verbal knowledge. He
put forward the theory of the 'dual coding hypothesis', arguing that
everyone has two systems. One is a nonverbal imagery system, which
processes things about objects and events. The other is a verbal
system, designed for speech and writing.

Hypothesis
Concrete words are easier to remember than abstract words.

*This example demonstrates many flaws in both its overall structure
and in particular details. First, you can see that it begins with simple-
minded questions and then makes a totally unrelated point ("It has*

— Continued — — — — — — — — — — — — — — — — — — —

— — *Continued* — — — — — — — — — — — — — — — — —

been said...") *which is not relevant and really needs a substantiating reference. The experiments mentioned by Conrad and Baddeley are not described adequately: at least a one-sentence summary of their procedure is needed. But they are not really relevant to this topic at all. The introduction should be very clearly related to the study being reported. The work of Armstrong is not given a date, and the conclusions he came to are not stated so one cannot judge whether they are relevant or not. (They very probably are not. Also, the work described was carried out by Galton, not Armstrong.)*

The work of Paivio is mentioned, and this is what the introduction should concentrate on, as his research has been dominant in this area. But the description of his study gives no account of the procedure he used. There have been many studies of this topic since 1969, and the introduction should certainly refer to more recent work.

According to the abstract, the experiment included obtaining recalls at different intervals after the initial presentation of the items, but this variable is not mentioned at all in this introduction. All independent variables should be mentioned and some relevant previous research summarized.

The introduction should lead up to the aims and hypothesis. The hypothesis stated in the example is not a hypothesis, because it does not make a precise prediction. Also, it does not develop naturally from the preceding material.

Below is an example of an introduction to this experiment. In order to make it a realistic model for a beginner, we have not used journal papers but only the Eysenck and Keane (1990) and Baddeley (1976) texts. You should, of course, use journal papers if you have access to them.

Introduction

The study of imagery has been revived in recent years, largely as a result of the work of Paivio (surveyed in Paivio, 1986). He developed the dual-coding theory, which is summarized by Eysenck and Keane (1990, p. 210) in these words: 'the essence of the dual-coding theory is that there are two distinct systems for the representation and processing of information. A verbal system deals with linguistic information and stores it in an appropriate verbal form. A separate nonverbal system carries out image-based processing'.

The theory suggests that when respondents are required to memorize a set of items, they will perform better if the items are processed by both systems rather than only one of them. When people are asked to remember pictures of common objects, the pictures will suggest their names and so the pictures will be encoded both as visual images and as a set of verbal names. Consequently, people will be able to

— — *Continued* — — — — — — — — — — — — — — — — —

— — Continued —

remember pictures of common objects better than words, which will be encoded only by the verbal system. This prediction has been supported (Paivio, 1971).

This difference in memory ability according to item type has also been found for different classes of word. Lists of concrete words are remembered better than lists of abstract words (Paivio *et al.*, 1968), and this may be because concrete words readily stimulate a visual image and therefore are encoded by both systems, whereas abstract words are encoded only by the verbal system. Baddeley (1976, p. 226) states that this finding is not restricted to lists of unconnected items: 'Sentences that comprise concrete or imageable words are also easier to remember than abstract sentences'.

Memory has been one of the most popular areas of investigation by cognitive psychologists, and has generated a vast literature. This has suggested that memory systems can be distinguished by their duration, so one has sensory stores, a short-term memory system and a long-term memory. Eysenck and Keane comment on this multi-store theory, and point out that it emphasizes the role of rehearsal: 'The .theory assumes that the major way in which information is stored in long-term memory is via rehearsal in the short-term store' (p. 142). Although not mentioned by Eysenck and Keane, if one accepts Paivio's dual-coding model one might expect that lists of abstract words are more difficult to rehearse than lists of concrete words, owing to their being held in only one system rather than two. If this were the case, memory for abstract words would decline more rapidly than memory for concrete words and with delayed recall there would be a larger difference between memory for abstract and concrete words. One would expect there to be a difference between recall for the two item types with delayed recall.

The aim of the present study was to test this prediction, by comparing memory for concrete and abstract words after different retention intervals. A subsidiary aim was to replicate the finding that with immediate recall, concrete words are remembered better than abstract ones.

Hypotheses
(1) With immediate free recall, respondents will remember more items from a 20-item list of concrete words than from a 20-item list of abstract words.

(2) With recall after a 5-minute retention interval, respondents will remember more items from a 20-item list of concrete words than from a 20-item list of abstract words.

— — Continued —

--- *Continued* —

> *Note that the argument developed here suggests that the difference between memory for concrete and abstract words will be greater with delayed recall. To test this prediction one needs to compare recall for the two types of word with immediate and delayed recall, and see whether there is an interaction. The students who did the experiment were not trained in the analysis of variance needed to test for an interaction, and so had to design a study within their level of statistical competence. This is why they simply predicted that there would be an effect at both retention intervals.*

The aim should not be confused with the hypothesis or hypotheses. The aim is more general – e.g. 'The aim of this study was to examine gender-related differences in memory performance'. Hypotheses are precise statements about the outcome of the study, stating what you predict will happen. For example, '(1) Women will recall a shopping list better than men'. The hypotheses are either the final part of the introduction, or are put in a separate section which follows immediately after the introduction. They lead into the method section, which describes how the hypotheses were tested. It is not usual to state the null hypothesis explicitly. Box 14.2 gives an example of a poor introduction and a better version.

14.1.5 Sections of the report: method

The method should summarize the design of the study, list the apparatus and materials used, describe the people who took part, the manner in which the independent variable was manipulated, the way the dependent variable was measured.

You have to balance the need to provide sufficient information with the need to avoid trivialities. You do not, for example, need to say that pencils and blank paper were used; on the other hand you would be criticized if you did not describe the materials that were used in a test of memory. The make of tape-recorder in an interview study is not important, but it is worth stating whether a tape-recorder with external microphones was used. Some apparatus is more intrusive than others, and it is useful for the reader to know how equipment was used, so that the study can be replicated.

Design
Give a simple summary of the design. For example, you might write: 'The study was a 2 × 2 mixed-design experiment, with age (20–25 years old or 40–45 years old) being a between-subjects variable and presentation mode (visual or oral) being within-subjects variable.'

Respondents

There is always a query over how far one can generalize from the particular participants to other kinds of people, so it is important that the reader should be able to see a description of the people you tested.

At a minimum, you need to state the number of respondents, their age group (preferably with a mean age, although this is more important when the age is a critical aspect of the study), the number of males and females, and whether the group had any particular characteristics relevant to the study. For example, if you were investigating the skills of left-handed people you would mention how many left- and right-handed subjects you had. But for many studies handedness is not relevant, so you would not give this information. It is also usual to explain how any specific disabilities were dealt with; for example, in studies of reading, you would say whether people who normally wear glasses did so. You should indicate how the respondents were recruited: did you ask people in the coffee-bar, passers-by in the street, colleagues at work? If you gave them some reward or payment, this also should be mentioned.

If the study involved allocating respondents to different groups, then the way the allocation was achieved must be described. A major source of confounding arises when respondents are allocated to groups in a potentially biasing manner, so you need to make clear how this confounding was avoided.

Apparatus/materials

This subsection should describe any equipment, such as a tachistoscope, tape recorder, etc., that was used. Many studies now use computers to present the stimuli, so an indication of the hardware and software is required. In some research, the apparatus needs to be described very accurately, since the exact conditions under which stimuli were presented is crucial. But at student, 'beginner' level, this is rarely the case. So you do not need to specify the model of computer used, just its type (Mac or PC), the size of the screen and whether it was a colour display. Write this part in complete sentences, not just as a list of apparatus.

The conditions under which stimuli are presented need describing; in a study where subjects are looking at a computer screen, you should give an indication of the screen size, the distance from which it is being viewed, and the size of the stimuli presented. This should really be expressed in terms of visual angle, but if that is not feasible, just state the size in mm or cm.

If auditory stimuli are used, you should specify how they were presented (speakers or headphones?) and give some indication of the loudness, either using physical measurements (dB) or subjective ones (e.g. 'In preliminary trials, the loudness of the recording was adjusted until the respondents reported that it was at their preferred loudness level').

Describe the material which was presented, such as the items used in a memory experiment and list the complete set in an appendix. So, for example, this section might say: 'Twenty five-letter words were used, randomly allocated to list A or B. The words were selected from ... [indicate where they were selected from, or

191

at least indicate how you came to select these words and not others], and all began with the letter K. The complete list of words is given in Appendix 3.'

If you used a published questionnaire or psychological test, simply say so: e.g. 'Job satisfaction was assessed using the Occupational Stress Indicator reproduced in Arnold *et al.* (1991, p. 145)'. A reader can then find out about the test or questionnaire from published sources. But if your study involves a questionnaire that is not published, perhaps one that you devised yourself, then it will need to be described – what was the content, and what is the evidence that it is reliable and valid? You should describe the questionnaire in this subsection, and reproduce the whole thing in an appendix.

Box 14.3 includes a poor and a better methods and procedure section.

14.1.6 Sections of the report: pilot study

If you performed a pilot study, include a brief account indicating how many respondents were used, the procedure that was followed, and the outcome. It is particularly important to tell the reader what changes were made to the procedure as a result of the pilot study. If the pilot indicated that the original procedure was satisfactory, this too needs emphasizing, as it shows that you have some rationale for using it in the main study.

14.1.7 Sections of the report: procedure

This is a narrative account of what the experimenter and the respondent did, what the respondent was asked to do (instructions), how the stimuli were presented, whether people were tested singly or in groups, the nature of the responses and how they were recorded, what debriefing occurred, and how subjective reports were collected. The description should be sufficiently detailed that readers could repeat the study for themselves, but on the other hand the section must not get out of control: include the important, omit the trivial... and expect to learn which is which as you become more experienced. Reading journal papers will give you a guide, and examples are shown in Box 14.3.

One important aspect is the order in which tasks were presented to respondents. Order effects are an important feature of experimental design, and if they are not dealt with they render the results useless. If the same subjects are doing more than one task, you have to control order effects and describe how you did so. For example: 'The 20 participants were randomly divided into two groups of 10. The first group had the tasks in the order A,B and the second group had them in the order B,A.' Here, as throughout your report, you must be truthful: you should claim to have formed the groups using random allocation only if you did actually do so. If you used some nonrandom method, be honest and admit it.

If you have a single task presented to different groups of respondents, you probably have to run the different groups at different times, so it is sensible to state how you avoided time of day biasing the results: 'Group B was tested immediately after group A', or 'It was necessary to test the groups on separate days. All tests sessions were run between 2 and 3 p.m.'

Remember that the order in which the groups are tested can be important: the experimenter may become more competent or less enthusiastic as the study proceeds. You should organize the testing so that any effects of this kind are balanced out. For example: 'The two groups, A and B, were each subdivided into equal-sized subgroups. The first subgroup of group A was tested first, then the two subgroups of group B. Finally, the second subgroup of group A was tested.'

14.1.8 Sections of the report: results

There are two fundamental points to bear in mind before presenting your results: (1) know what you are trying to communicate, and (2) select the most clear and appropriate ways to do so. These recommendations are so clearly common sense that you may think they are hardly worth saying and so general as to be remarkably unhelpful. In fact, they are worth saying to yourself again and again as you construct your results section. Box 14.4 is an attempt to demonstrate the points mentioned below.

Before you ever start to gather your data you should have specified the aim of the study, stated a hypothesis, and decided which form of statistical analysis you will use. You should also, before gathering any data, have decided what the data tables in your report will look like, by drawing them up advance. You should know from the outset what are the most important aspects of the results; the presentation should make these aspects the most prominent parts of the display.

The results section of a report may have up to six components. The first essential is a statement of the major finding. For example: 'The data from the two groups of respondents are shown in Table 1, which indicates that the mean score for group 1 was 5.82 (s.d. = 1.74) and for group 2 was 8.71 (s.d. = 2.03)'.

The second component is the table of results, which should be labelled 'Table 1' (assuming it is the first table in the report), and have a title that indicates what the contents are. A title that reads 'Scores of the two groups' is not sufficient, since it does not explain what the figures in the table represent: write an informative title which tells the reader what the table includes, for example 'Table 1. Number of items correctly recalled for groups with oral and visual presentation'. Guidance on the way tables should be laid out is given in Chapter 15.

Try to present the results that are pertinent to the aim of the study, and to leave out unnecessary detail. If you look at journal papers, you will see that the results section usually presents tables of averages and measures of dispersion, rather than data on individual respondents. You should follow this model, but with one proviso: tabulate the full set of results you obtained in an appendix. This is so that the person marking your work can check your calculations and graphs against the original data. The appendix should have a title briefly explaining its contents, such as 'Appendix 1. Reaction times for groups with and without distraction'. The appendices are put at the very end of the report, but you should

Box 14.3 Example of poor and better methods and procedures sections

Method
Subjects
Two experimenters each recruited 30 subjects who were randomly picked but all students aged between 18 and 24.

Apparatus
Twenty words were printed in black ink white paper. Two lists were created: one had 20 abstract words and the other had 20 concrete words.

Design
The experiment had word type as the independent variable.

Procedure
Each subject was shown one of the lists for 60 seconds. The list was then removed and the subject asked to write down as many as they could remember. For half the subjects, there was a 5-minute delay before they were asked to write down the words they could remember.

This fails to describe the materials or the procedure adequately. Remember that this section should give enough description of what you did for readers to be able to repeat the study themselves. A better example is this:

Method
Design
There were two independent variables, item type and retention interval. A 2 × 2 between-subjects experimental design was used.

Respondents
Sixty students were recruited by asking people in the student coffee-bar to take part in a short experiment. There were 39 females and 21 males, ranging in age from 18 to 29, the mean age being 21.

Participants were randomly allocated to the four conditions of concrete or abstract words and immediate or delayed recall with the proviso that there should be 15 in each group. From random-number tables, a random ordering of the numbers 01 to 60 was obtained. The first 15 numbers of the random ordering were assigned to the abstract words/immediate recall condition, the second 15 to concrete/immediate recall, the third 15 to abstract/delayed recall, and the final 15 to concrete/delayed recall. All participants were numbered in sequence as

— — Continued — — — — — — — — — — — — — — — — —

— — Continued —

they entered the laboratory, and by referring to the random-order list it was found which condition they were in.

Apparatus and materials
Two lists of 20 items were created. One consisted of abstract words and the other of concrete words. The words were selected by entering a dictionary at a page according to a three-digit number obtained from random-number tables and finding the first five nouns on that page which were not more than six letters long. This was repeated 20 times to give a list of 100 words. One of the investigators went through this list rating each word according to its abstractness on a scale of 1 to 5, and the 20 with the highest and the 20 with the lowest ratings were used as the materials. Copies of the lists used are reproduced in Appendix 1.

Each list was printed in 12-point type on a Laserjet printer.

Procedure
The experiment took place in a departmental cubicle and each partici-pant was tested individually. All trials were conducted between 10 a.m. and 3 p.m.

When each participant entered and had been assigned to the abstract or concrete and immediate or delayed recall condition, the following instructions were read: 'You will be given a list of words to read for on minute,' and then either 'At the end of that time, we shall remove the list and ask you to write down as many of the words as you can remember in three minutes. Do you understand?' or 'At the end of that time, we shall remove the list and ask you to wait for five minutes, and then write down as many of the words as you can remember in three minutes. During the five-minute gap you should try to rehearse the items in your head. Do you understand?'

When the participants indicated they understood the instructions, the appropriate list of words was presented. The experimenter checked the time using a digital watch, and after one minute the list was removed. Participants were asked to write the words they could recall using paper and pen provided. When they had indicated they had finished or when three minutes was up, their recall record was rem-oved. For those having delayed recall, during the five-minute gap the experimenters remained silent in order to allow the participants to rehearse their memory for the items.

After the recall attempt, participants were told the aim of the study and asked not to discuss it with anyone else. Those in the delayed recall conditions were asked how they had tried to remember the items and rehearse them during the retention interval.

refer to them in the main report's results section, so that the reader knows they exist. To do this, it is often sufficient to put 'The full set of data is shown in Appendix 1' as the second sentence of the results.

The third, optional component is a graphical display of the results: a graph, histogram, pie chart, etc. Advice on when to use which is given in section 15.2, but whichever one you use, ensure it is labelled 'Fig. 1' (assuming it is the first figure in your report) and has an explanatory title much as the table of results. Bear in mind that a graphical display is not always appropriate, particularly if you are comparing just two sets of scores. Although a graph may look impressive to you, it is justified only if it communicates the major features of the data more effectively than a simple statement. As a rule of thumb, assume that the difference between two sets of scores is adequately communicated textually; if you have more than two sets of scores, then a graphical display is likely to be worthwhile. Editors of journals do not usually allow authors to show the same data in a table and a graph, since this repetition is wasteful of space; but in a student report you may be permitted to display the same data in two ways since it tests your skill at choosing the appropriate type of graph for the tabulated data.

The fourth component of the results is a statement of the statistical analysis which was performed and the outcome of that analysis. For example: 'The scores of the two groups were compared using the independent t-test, and it was found that there was no significant difference between the two sets of scores ($t = 1.58$; d.f. $= 19; p > 0.05$).' Observe that this sentence specifies which test was employed, the calculated statistic that was obtained ($t = 1.58$), the degrees of freedom and whether or not the outcome was significant ($p > 0.05$). Remember to be clear in your own mind, and use appropriately the $<$ and $>$ signs. If $p < 0.05$, then the result is statistically significant at the 5% level; $p > 0.05$ indicates the result was not statistically significant at the 5% level.

The details of the calculations for the statistical analysis are not usually included in journal papers, but they are needed in student reports. Nowadays, students are soon taught how to use a computer program to analyse their data, and after the first few reports you will probably not be doing calculations 'by hand' (which now means 'by calculator'!). If you are doing 'hand' calculations, a neat summary of the various steps should be given in an appendix so that the marker can check your accuracy. It is very difficult to help someone whose statistical analysis is incorrect, if you have only the answer, with no indication of how it was obtained.

Once you are using computer analysis, the appendix should contain the printout of the analysis, with an explanation of what it signifies. Some programs give an output where parts of the table are labelled variable A, variable B, etc., which is remarkably uninformative to the reader, who has to work out what variables A and B are. Provide a key explaining what the labels denote.

You might have additional, informal observations on how the participants reacted to the situation. These can give valuable information about the procedure and the validity of the study. So you might include something like this: 'The performance of respondents in group A was disrupted because many of them

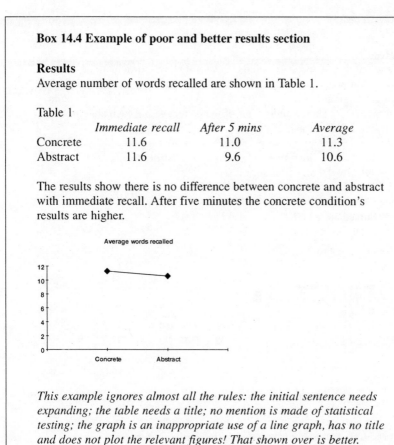

Box 14.4 Example of poor and better results section

Results
Average number of words recalled are shown in Table 1.

Table 1

	Immediate recall	*After 5 mins*	*Average*
Concrete	11.6	11.0	11.3
Abstract	11.6	9.6	10.6

The results show there is no difference between concrete and abstract with immediate recall. After five minutes the concrete condition's results are higher.

This example ignores almost all the rules: the initial sentence needs expanding; the table needs a title; no mention is made of statistical testing; the graph is an inappropriate use of a line graph, has no title and does not plot the relevant figures! That shown over is better.

broke out into laughter during the task'. You would then comment on the implications of this for the validity of the results in the discussion section.

You may have collected subjective reports during the experiment, and these should also be included in the results, forming the sixth component. Summarize the comments your respondents made, quoting their remarks to support your points.

14.1.9 Sections of the report: discussion

There are a number of components to a discussion, and Box 14.5 illustrates how not to do it and how it should be done. First you should state whether results and statistical analysis support or do not support the hypotheses which you stated at the end of the introduction. You should point out any peculiarities of the results,

— — Continued — — — — — — — — — — — — — — — — — —

Results

The number of words recalled correctly for each participant on each occasion was recorded. No deduction was made if a word not included in the original list was 'recalled'. The complete set of data is given in Appendix 2. The mean number of words recalled in each condition is shown in Table 1 and displayed graphically in Fig. 1.

TABLE 1. *Mean number of concrete or abstract words recalled after a delay of 0 and 5 minutes*

	Concrete		Abstract	
	mean	*s.d.*	*mean*	*s.d.*
Immediate recall	11.63	1.47	11.64	1.84
After 5 min	11.02	1.91	9.62	1.88

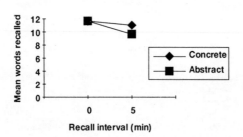

FIG. 1. *Mean words recalled by interval and item type*

Independent *t*-tests were used to compare the means for item types at each retention interval. (Analysis of variance is the appropriate procedure, but the experimenters have not been taught this technique.)

One *t*-test was used to compare the concrete and abstract means with immediate recall. It was found that the difference between the means is not statistically significant ($t = 0.41$; d.f. $= 28$; $p > 0.05$). After the five-minute delay, the difference between the means is significant ($t = 2.04$; d.f. $= 28$; $p < 0.05$). Details of the calculations will be found in Appendix 3.

The subjective reports of the delayed-recall participants indicated that all had tried to rehearse the items during the five-minute gap. Three of the concrete group, but none of the abstract group, reported that they had created composite images of the items such as 'a horse sitting on a chair holding an apple'.

Box 14.5 Example of poor and better discussion section

Discussion
On average, the subjects remembered more concrete words than
abstract ones. This proves the hypothesis. There are a number of
reasons why it is easier to remember concrete words. They are definite
objects that people can see, people have had more practice at learning
concrete words, they suggest images, they are more common words.

The subjects were all students, which may have had an effect. They
might be better at remembering abstract words than ordinary people.

It would be interesting to see whether children remember concrete
words better than abstract words, more than adults do. This would need
another experiment.

*This is totally inadequate, as you will appreciate if you compare it with
the advice given in section 14.2.9. The summary of the outcome is
misleading, and you never 'prove' the hypothesis. There is no consideration of the inadequacies of the study, how it relates to previous
work, or its theoretical implications. The suggestion for further work
raises an issue not previously mentioned: the possible effect of age
differences. The 'suggestions' section should not suddenly introduce a
new topic, but build on those previously mentioned, in the introduction
or discussion.*

*The example over is shorter than is usually expected, but will give
you an idea of what a discussion should look like.*

— — *Continued* — — — — — — — — — — — — — — — — — — —

such as one group having scored very differently from the other, or some
respondents having yielded unusual data.

In psychology practicals, the experiment often does not produce the 'expected'
outcome – many psychological phenomena are unstable (i.e. are not easy to
replicate). Failing to produce the 'expected' result is not necessarily a sign that
you have done something wrong; and obtaining the expected result does not
mean that it was a 'good' experiment. (Indeed, you should never describe an
experiment as good or bad on the basis of whether it supported the hypothesis or
not. A good experiment is one that is properly designed and performed; a bad
one is poorly designed or carried out in a sloppy fashion so that extraneous
variables were not controlled.) However, failing to obtain the predicted effect
may be due to faults in the way the experiment was conducted, and these should

┌ — *Continued* — — — — — — — — — — — — — — — — — — — ┐

Discussion

The first hypothesis, that there would be a difference in recall of abstract and concrete words with immediate recall, was not supported. This fails to replicate the finding of Paivio *et al.* (1986) as stated by Eysenck and Keane (p. 210). As it was not possible to refer to Paivio *et al.*'s original paper, it is not possible to comment in detail on the differences between their procedure and materials and those used here. Assuming their finding referred to immediate recall, it would be worth repeating the study with Paivio *et al.*'s words and procedure to confirm that their effect is replicable with a short retention interval.

The second hypothesis was supported: the concrete items were remembered better than the abstract ones when recall occurred after five minutes. This does replicate the abstract/concrete word memory effect and supports the prediction derived from applying to it the concept of rehearsal.

Before considering the implications of this finding, it is necessary to consider the validity of the experiment. As mentioned above, there are doubts about how far the words used were distinctively concrete and abstract. It would have been better to have more than one judge rate the initial pool of words, and to use judges unconnected with the experiment, so that there would have been less likelihood of any bias operating. Were the study to be repeated, we would recommend this modification to the procedure.

The argument developed in the introduction predicts that there would be an interaction between the two independent variables. It would have been better to use analysis of variance rather than *t*-tests for the analysis.

The support for the second hypothesis favours the argument that it is more difficult to rehearse abstract words. Presumably this has an increasing effect, and so one would expect the concrete/abstract effect to increase with longer retention intervals. Further experiments could be done to see how the magnitude of the effect changes with retention intervals longer than those used here.

be revealed in your report, even if you did not intend to reveal them, or had not realized they were there!

Consider any flaws in the study – equipment failing or respondents apparently not understanding what they were supposed to do (experimenters not understanding what they were supposed to do!) should be admitted. You may also realize at a late stage that your study had some major design fault – perhaps you had failed to take account of order effects, confounded variables, or discovered that the task was too easy or too difficult, that the instructions were ambiguous or some other disaster. As a learner, major mistakes like these are more likely to happen to you than to an expert. When your work is being assessed, such blunders in the early months of your career will be forgiven if you acknowledge them, point out where you went wrong, and explain how, if you repeated the study, you would avoid making the same mistake again. There is some truth in the aphorism that 'we learn by our mistakes', and making mistakes is part of being a beginner; but do ensure you learn from them! If you have made some major blunder of the type described above and fail to notice it, fail to comment on it, and fail to explain how it could and should have been corrected, then you are likely to be penalized.

Another section of the discussion compares your results with previous studies mentioned in the introduction. Do your findings correspond to those of previous researchers? If they do, and you have confirmed the hypothesis that you deduced from previous work, well and good. If, however, the results are not as predicted, you need to suggest why. There are always any number of dissimilarities between the study you conducted and that of previous experts, but try to identify what seem to be most crucial. For example, was your sample of respondents smaller, were the people of a different type (in age, ability, sex, personality, motivation), were your materials different, the instructions different, the procedure different? This is a part of the discussion where you need to think about what you have done, read closely the study upon which yours was based, and try to identify where the important contrasts lie.

A further subsection of the discussion is where you draw out the theoretical implications of your study. As a beginner, this may be impossible, as you are likely to have relatively little knowledge about the theory underlying the topic you have studied. But as your knowledge develops, you should try to include this aspect. If your findings confirmed the hypothesis, how does the hypothesis fit into the theory: does it suggest some extension or limitations? If you failed to confirm the hypothesis, is it a 'valid' outcome? Assuming the failure to fulfil the prediction is not due to some procedural error, does this indicate that the theory does not apply to the type of respondents you used, that the independent variable was not altered sufficiently, that the way in which the dependent variable was measured is open to query?

The final part of the discussion is 'suggestions for further research', where you should make sensible recommendations about how the topic you have studied could be developed further. Students often have difficulty with this, making suggestions that are unrelated to what has gone before. Box 14.5 provides an example. Sensible suggestions can include the following: recommending extending the study to a different sample of people where there is good reason from earlier work to expect that they will react differently; recommending that you should confirm that a similar or greater effect is obtained if you use more extreme levels of the independent variable; recommending an alternative method of measuring performance. This 'suggestions' section concludes the discussion, and ends the main report with a forward-looking tone.

14.1.10 Sections of the report: references

In journal papers, the references are a crucial component of the report, citing examples of similar work on the topic, and giving precedents for using particular techniques of varying the independent variable or measuring performance.

It is generally accepted that when a reference is listed in the report, the authors are asserting that they have read it. As a beginner, you will not have read all the papers to which you might want to refer. To keep to the conventions, and retain your honesty, it is proper to acknowledge that you are listing references that have not been read. This can be done by adding 'cited in handout' after the reference or following the details of the reference with a phrase such as 'as cited in Eysenck and Keane, 1993'. Note that this implies that the authors have read Eysenck and Keane.

The organization of the references needs some attention. They should be in alphabetical order of first author (surname followed by initials), and if there are a number of papers by the same author, they should be in date order. Where the same author has two or more papers of the same date, the convention is to refer to them as, for example, Jones (1990a) and Jones (1990b). The 'a' is given to the first one that is mentioned in the report, 'b' to the second, and so on.

Most references contain the following information: author, date, title of paper, journal in which it was published, volume of journal, and page numbers. There are different conventions, but the most widely used format is illustrated in the reference section at the end of this book, which includes examples of how to refer to items in books as opposed to journals.

14.1.11 Sections of the report: appendices

You are likely to have at least two appendices, one containing the raw, complete data, and the other the details of your statistical calculations. Each should have an informative title. In addition, you may use appendices for the verbatim instructions, to provide details of a computer program used to present the stimuli, to illustrate the materials (such as lists of words or drawings of pictures), and anything else that you feel is necessary to provide a full description of the study.

14.2 Writing the report of a quantitative but nonexperimental study

Reports on surveys, correlational studies, and case studies share the same basic structure as reports on experiments, with introduction, method, procedure, results and discussion. But you must adapt the conventions so that they fit the study you are reporting. In a survey or a correlational study, you do not have dependent and independent variables, so it is a mistake to describe the study in those terms. Similarly, they do not use one of the experimental designs explained in Chapter 3, so do not describe them as though they did.

Do avoid the mistake of asserting that every study is an experiment. It is sensible to state the type of study you are reporting in the title, so that you and the reader are clear about the style of research you have done.

14.3 Reporting qualitative studies

The presentation of qualitative research should follow the same general format as for quantitative work. The abstract should clearly specify the focus of the study, what was done to explore it further, what happened, and what conclusions were drawn.

14.3.1 Introduction

The introduction should discuss the background to the topic and other research that has been carried out in that area. In many cases it will be relevant to refer to previous research which used quantitative approaches, and the questions you want to explore may be prompted by the drawbacks in the methods used before. Because qualitative approaches are fairly new in psychology, you will not necessarily be able to refer to a background of work on the issue you want to focus upon. Your task will then be to identify an absence, and to offer some suggestions as to why that may be the case. Take care though. It is not good enough to claim there is an absence when you have not taken the trouble to look! Another possibility is to look across the borders of the discipline to neighbouring areas, such as sociology or health-care studies. There may be little on health visitors' accounts of stress in cognitive psychology, but a lot in work on community medicine.

The survey of previous research should comprise roughly two-thirds of the introduction. The other third should be taken up with a review of the appropriate methodology: the general and then specific reasons why a particular qualitative approach is appropriate. An overview of methodology in the introduction section of a qualitative report is a bit longer than in quantitative studies, for a number of reasons. First, qualitative approaches are still fairly new and need to be justified against the mainstream methods. Second, there may be a suspicion that the researcher is taking an easy option and has not thought through the reasons why quantification is not appropriate. Third, reflection upon methodology is a crucial part of the qualitative tradition, and how we do our research is seen as central to the sense we make.

14.3.2 Method

The method section of the report should be as straightforward as in a quantitative report. You need to specify enough information for a reader to replicate your study. Qualitative researchers do not believe that they could obtain the same 'results', but they still want to know that they could do the same as you and use that experience to learn something more. The number of interviewees in an interview study needs to be specified, for example, together with ages and other relevant information, such as whether they are men or women.

14.3.3 Analysis

In qualitative reports, the sections describing the results is better labelled 'Analysis'. Qualitative research is concerned with the process by which sense is made, and the simple presentation of 'results' as if they could be just harvested from the data is anathema to this alternative tradition of work. The 'analysis' of the material, however, is a deliberate and self-consciously artful creation by the researcher, and must be constructed to persuade the reader of the plausibility of an argument.

In the case of an interview, media or account study or diary study, it is not sufficient to present lists of quotes under headings as if they could stand alone as self-evident truths that had been 'discovered'. The analysis section should start with an account of the process by which the quotes were selected. Examples include exhaustive coding of categories initially obtained from prior research literature or generation of themes through repeated reading of key sections of the transcripts and discussion with colleagues. The analysis should carry the quotes along on a narrative, with some interpretation of each quote, some justification as to why it was chosen, some brief summary at the end of each subsection drawing together the points made in the quote and warranting the identification of a theme or discourse that underlies them. Do not, at this point, bring in direct reference to the established research literature. That connection should be left to the discussion.

14.3.4 Discussion

The discussion section should serve the same sort of function as in a quantitative study. Two main tasks should be carried out. First, the material should be connected to that presented in the introduction. If the analysis differs from the previous literature, say so and offer some suggestions as to why that may be the case. The second task concerns methodology. You should include some reflection upon the process you engaged in to produce this report. Often, a good way of doing this is in a separate subsection called 'Reflexive analysis'. There are different practices in different psychology departments at present, and this reflexive analysis may be placed either at the end of the analysis section or in the discussion. A reflexive analysis in the analysis section can be a useful way of showing how the position of the researcher played a part in the production of the analytic categories (themes, discourses). A reflexive analysis in the discussion can be helpful in identifying absences in the study that would need to be addressed in later research.

14.3.5 Language and report writing

Qualitative research is centrally concerned with language, and the language of the report should be compatible with the research approach adopted. It is not right, for example, to refer to research participants as 'subjects', or to claim that you were able to put your interviewees at ease so you could 'extract more information' from them. You should be sensitive to the perceptions of the participants in your study, and some qualitative workers would prefer to enrol their 'subjects' as 'co-researchers'. One way of keeping this in mind is to write your report as if those you had studied will read it. Research always affects all those involved in some way, and the role of good psychology should be to ensure that it has positive consequences. In this sense 'action' is already built into this research, and is part of 'real life'.

14.4 Presentation of the report

If you have the facilities and the skills, we cannot urge you too strongly to use a word processor. Markers do get annoyed when reports have to be deciphered, and in extreme cases have been known to refuse to struggle with illegible material.

Ensure the section headings (Introduction, Method, Results, etc.) are clearly differentiated from the running text. Markers find it helpful if you use one side of the paper only.

Demonstrate that you can use English in a grammatically correct manner, and can spell the words you use. Poor grammar or spelling will produce uncomplimentary comments on your reports, and may reduce the marks. Word processing your work means that you can use a spell-checking program. Learning to use a spell-checker takes no more than a few minutes. Remember that a spell-checker is mindless, and does not understand English: it will not find the mistakes in this sentence: 'The task was to hard for the ate subjects in group won', since all three errors are words correctly spelt.

If you do not have access to a word processor, typing is the next best alternative, if your typing is of a reasonable standard. A report that is typed with numerous typing mistakes is better than a hand-written one with numerous mistakes, but no mistakes is best!

Ensure the pages are numbered, and are in the correct order. To prevent the pages coming out of order, a staple or tag is better than a paper clip, which can easily fall off.

A final word of advice: keep a copy of your report! It is not unknown for them to go astray, or for there to be heavy delays in them being marked and returned to you. Unless you have a copy, it is just hard luck if this happens. So if at all possible, make a back-up... which is of course far easier if the report is on a word processor, another argument in favour of using one if you possibly can.

14.5 Plagiarism (copying)

In some instances you may be allowed to work in groups and submit one report on behalf of all members of the group. But usually you will be expected to write your own report, and it is important that this should be your own work.

The increasing use of word processors does make it much easier to plagiarize, that is, copy somebody else's work and submit it as your own. This is an extremely serious misdemeanour: the basis for any assessment must be the assumption that what is being assessed is your work.

When people have worked together on the study, it is easy for them to also work together on writing the report and end up with similar reports, using the same basic references ... and the similarity between their reports is likely to be questioned. Unless you know that it is acceptable for all members of a group to submit the same report, it is wise for group members to complete the study and data analysis, and then go off and write their own reports without collaborating over the write-up at all.

This is not to say that you should not discuss your work with your colleagues; of course you should, and you may well find that this is an important component of your learning process. But you are strongly advised not to show them copies of your reports or essays until after everyone has handed their work in.

Plagiarism covers not only copying the work of another student, but also unacknowledged copying from books and other sources. Of course you should use the journals and text books – that is how you will learn. But you should use the material you read to help you produce your own essay or report, not copy it out. You can quote sections directly, but this should form only a small part of your own work, and quotations must be acknowledged, with wording such as: 'Stanhope and Cohen (1993, p. 59) conclude that "information about occupation interferes with memory for the name"'. Or you can simply quote material within quotation marks and then put the source at the end: '"information about occupation interferes with memory for the name" Stanhope and Cohen (1993, p. 59)'. When using quotations, it is expected that you will show the page number.

With so many thousands of journal papers and books available, you may be tempted to think that a few unacknowledged quotes will not be spotted; and certainly your markers have not read everything that has been published, even in the areas of their particular expertise. But they are likely to have read the sources you are most likely to come across, and they are familiar with the standard of reporting and writing which students usually attain. So the unacknowledged quote is often spotted because the style, the number of references quoted, and the level of exposition are simply far better than a normal student can produce.

Direct plagiarism is one thing, and you know it is dishonest. But there is a problem when you are tempted to summarize an authoritative source: some students have plagiarized by selective copying and editing a source, stringing together sentences that in the original were separated by a few paragraphs, so that their version was not a direct transcription of the original. This is still plagiarism if the original source is not acknowledged. If you have any doubt at all, ensure that the source of all quotations is given. If you have rewritten a source, admit to it, using such phrasing as: 'This issue is discussed by Stanhope and Cohen (1993). Their argument may be paraphrased like this:...' or 'Stanhope and Cohen (1993, p. 59) make the following points:...'.

Remember, above all, do not give any grounds for allowing anyone to suspect you of plagiarism!

Box 14.6 Checklist when writing the report

If you check all these points, you will avoid many of the commoner mistakes that students make.

(1) Title: does it provide a concise, clear statement of the study?
(2) Is the author indicated?
(3) Does the abstract cover the aim, participants, procedure, findings, and interpretation? It should not usually exceed 5 sentences.

Introduction
(4) Does it provide a clear summary of an acceptable amount of previous work on the topic?
(5) Does it include up-to-date references?
(6) Have you ensured you have omitted irrelevant material?
(7) Does the aim of the study develop naturally from the previous work mentioned?
(8) For quantitative studies, have you stated a hypothesis in terms of a precise prediction?

Method
(9) Have you described the participants and, if relevant to the type of study you are reporting, the order of conditions and testing, and the materials used?

Procedure
(10) Have you given an account of what happened so that a reader could repeat the study? Have you checked that it does not include trivialities?

Results
(11) Does this section start with a sentence?
(12) Have you labelled (Table 1, Fig. 1) and given an informative title to all tables and any figures?
(13) Have you checked the formatting of tables and graphs against Box 15.1 (p. 218)?
(14) Is the statistical analysis summarized correctly?
(15) Are details of calculations in an appendix and clearly labelled?

Discussion
(16) Have you summarized the outcome?
(17) Have you mentioned any flaws in the procedure which would lessen the study's validity?
(18) Have you referred to the previous work you mentioned in the introduction and compared the outcome with it?
(19) Have you tried to indicate the theoretical implications of your findings?
(20) Have you made some suggestions about further research which would be a natural development of what you have found?

— *Continued* — — — — — — — — — — — — — — — — — —

─ ─ *Continued* ─ ─ ─ ─ ─ ─ ─ ─ ─ ─ ─ ─ ─ ─ ─ ─ ─ ─ ─

References
(21) Have you checked that all references are listed?
(22) Are references in the proper order?
(23) Are all references complete, with journal title, page numbers, etc.?
(24) Have you acknowledged which references you have not read yourself?

Appendices
(25) Have you listed the materials you used?
(26) Have you recorded the full set of data?
(27) Are all appendices provided with an informative title?

Generally
(28) Have you ensured you do not say you have 'proved' a hypothesis or a theory?
(29) Have you made sure that if you describe the study as an experiment, it is an experiment?
(30) Have you checked for spelling and grammatical errors?
(31) Have you numbered the pages and put them in the correct sequence?
(32) Have you made a copy of the report?

Chapter 15

Presenting quantitative results

15.0 Introduction

Ensure that you understand the difference between independent and dependent variables, and the distinction between variables and levels of a variable. The principles for preparing tables are: aim for clarity; do not try to tabulate the results of more than three or four variables within a single table; ensure the columns and rows are clearly labelled; and make sure all your tables and figures are numbered ('Table 1', 'Fig. 1') and have an informative title. When you have read this chapter, use Box 15.1 to help you implement our recommendations.

15.1 Tables of results

Tables can become complicated when you have carried out a study where there are many conditions or subgroups of respondents. As a rule of thumb, two factors across and two factors down is the upper limit to use. If there are more than this, the table becomes very difficult to read, and a series of tables is to be preferred.

15.1.1 Frequency tables

Frequency tables are used to show the number of cases occurring in specified categories and subcategories. They are the normal way of reporting the results of surveys in which respondents give categorical responses. They are usually analysed to discover any relationship between variables, using the chi-square

TABLE 15.1. *Example of a frequency table (hypothetical data on church attendance and attitude towards women priests; n = 284)*

	Church attenders		Nonattenders	
	Young	*Old*	*Young*	*Old*
Positive attitude	50	69	35	20
Negative attitude	25	30	30	25
n	75	99	65	45

TABLE 15.2. *Example of results table with three sets of data*

	Condition		
	A	B	C
n	12	16	14
Mean	28.92	35.67	39.18
s.d.	2.17	1.96	2.03

test. Suppose, for example, you have assessed the attitude of young and old church attenders and nonattenders towards women priests, and divided the respondents according to whether they show a negative attitude or a positive attitude. Your table of results would resemble Table 15.1, where the figures show the number of people in each category. The columns are used to separate the different types and subtypes of respondent, and the rows distinguish between the different levels of the dependent variable.

15.1.2 Comparing two sets of scores

The simplest type of study is one that compares two sets of scores. The crucial statistics will be the measure of central tendency (mean or median) and the index of variability (standard deviation or interquartile range), but with only two sets of scores a table is often unnecessary.

15.1.3 Comparing more than two sets of scores

One factor, more than two levels
If you have scores for three or more conditions, the table will resemble Table 15.2, with a separate column for each condition.

Two factors: between-subjects designs or within-subjects designs
In a two-factor study, you have two independent variables. For example, suppose you have measured the attitude towards women priests of church attenders and nonattenders in the 18–25 and 48–55 age groups. A two-dimensional matrix allows the clear presentation of the data: use the columns to separate the levels of one of the factors and the rows to separate the levels of the other, as in Table 15.3.

Two factors: mixed designs
A mixed-factor design is where one or more of the factors is within-subjects and at least one is between-subjects. For example, suppose you have investigated the speed with which respondents can solve problems presented in an abstract or a

TABLE 15.3. *Mean scores on attitude to women priests scale by age and church attendance (hypothetical data)*

| | Church attendance | | | | | |
| | Yes | | | No | | |
Age group	Mean	s.d.	n	Mean	s.d.	n
18–25	25.12	2.41	25	11.04	2.06	48
48–55	32.74	2.82	32	15.04	1.82	58
Overall	28.93	2.56	57	13.04	1.97	106

realistic form, as a function of the respondents' age. You used a mixed design in which there are three age groups of respondents (a between-subjects factor with three levels), but everyone does problems in both abstract and realistic forms (the within-subjects factor with two levels). With such a design it is sensible to use the columns to separate the levels of the between-subjects factor, and the rows to separate the levels of the within-subjects factor, as shown in Table 15.4.

More than two factors
The data table for a study which has three or more factors should follow the conventions for the simpler designs described above: use column divisions and subdivisions to separate between-respondent factors and levels of factors, and use rows to subdivide within-respondent factors and levels. An example is illustrated in Table 15.5. The cells at the foot of the columns and the end of the rows make it simple to include the overall means for the various subcategories of condition. This helps demonstrate which factors seem to be having most effect on the scores. In Table 15.5, for example, comparing the data in the last row indicates that the age of respondent seems to have little influence. Comparing the overall means for the two presentation conditions in the final column, one can see immediately that presentation mode seems to have had a large effect.

In Table 15.5, the penultimate row shows the overall means for the separate sexes at each age while the final row gives the overall means for each age group.

TABLE 15.4. *Format for the results table of a two-factor mixed-design experiment*

| | Age group (years) | | |
	15–25	35–45	55–65
n			
Presentation mode			
Abstract			
Realistic			
Overall			

If you wanted to emphasize the overall means for each sex disregarding age group, you would use sex rather than age as the first variable for distinguishing the columns, as in Table 15.6.

TABLE 15.5. *Format for the results table of a three-factor mixed-design experiment (the numbers are merely illustrative)*

Age group	16–25		26–35		36–45		
Sex	Male	Female	Male	Female	Male	Female	
n	10	12	18	22	21	30	Overall
Presentation							
Visual							
mean	8.24	9.36	7.47	9.22	7.81	8.04	8.36
s.d.	1.24	1.31	1.68	2.01	1.41	0.92	1.81
Oral							
mean	6.16	7.82	5.13	7.38	7.04	6.22	6.63
s.d.	0.87	1.11	0.92	1.03	1.23	0.88	1.18
Overall, by age and sex							
mean	7.20	8.59	6.30	8.30	7.43	7.13	
s.d.	1.02	1.22	1.34	1.67	1.32	0.90	
Overall, by age							
mean	7.90		7.30		7.56		
s.d.	1.18		1.46		1.22		

TABLE 15.6. *Alternative layout of Table 15.5*

	Sex						
	Male			Female			
Age group	16–25	26–35	36–45	16–25	26–35	36–45	Overall
n	10	18	21	12	22	30	
Presentation							
Visual							
Oral							
Overall means							
by sex and age							
s.d.							
by sex							
s.d.							

15.2 Graphical displays

The most common techniques for displaying quantitative data graphically are line graphs, barcharts, histograms, pie charts, and scattergrams. Box plots and stem-and-leaf plots have become more popular with the growth of interest in exploratory data analysis (EDA). Lovie and Lovie (1991) suggest that EDA 'promotes risky inductions because it draws attention to the novel and surprising aspects of the data' (p. 19). EDA uses graphic displays to reveal the 'surprising aspects of the data', and box plots are one way of doing this. It is, however, always important to use the appropriate format, the one that is suitable for the data you want to display and which will bring out clearly the trends you wish to emphasize.

Line graphs, barcharts and histograms should always be drawn so that the dependent variable (the aspect of behaviour that you measured) is on the vertical axis, with the independent variable represented along the horizontal.

15.2.1 Line graphs and barcharts

A line graph is used to show how the scores on the dependent variable change as the independent variable on the horizontal axis alters. As a general rule, a line graph should not be used when the horizontal axis represents a categorical or nominal variable. But it must be admitted that this rule is very often broken. A definite error which is often made is illustrated in Fig. 15.1, where the horizontal axis represents the different respondents. It is misleading to use a line graph because the distance along the axis does not represent any increasing quantity. The respondents' numbers are only a nominal scale, and there is no reason why the respondents are plotted in this order. They could just as easily be in the opposite sequence. A line graph would be appropriate only if the respondents' numbers represented some quantity, such as rank order on a test. Always check that this is the case before you plot a line graph with respondents on the horizontal.

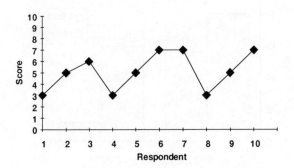

Fig. 15.1. *A misuse of the line graph (subjects along horizontal). Do* not *do this!*

Should the data shown Fig. 15.1 be plotted at all? Is there any reason to show the data for individual respondents? In most cases the answer is 'no': the individuals' responses are not of particular interest. Usually you need to plot just the mean of each condition in a barchart such as Fig. 15.2, where the horizontal axis represents discrete categories and the bars are drawn with gaps between them to illustrate this fact. A bar chart is also used if the categories are in an ordinal sequence ('young', 'middle', 'old' age groups, for example).

When the horizontal represents a categorical variable, do not connect the bars with lines. If you find it difficult to decide which type of variable you are plotting, draw a rough line graph, and take a point along the line between the plotted data points. Drop a vertical from this point to the horizontal, and ask yourself 'what does this point on the horizontal axis represent?' In Fig. 15.1, it would represent a value between two of the respondents. This is absurd, so it is nonsensical to join the data points with a line.

Another issue about line graphs is the use of lines when there are only two data points. It is always possible to join two points with a straight line, but the relationship may be nonlinear. You will find many examples of a straight line being used to join just two points, but should always be aware that the implication of a simple relationship may be false.

15.2.2 Barcharts and histograms

Barcharts and histograms represent quantity by the height of a rectangle, as in Fig. 15.2. If the horizontal represents a nominal, categorical variable such as the 'slow' and 'fast' groups in Fig. 15.2, you have a barchart. When the horizontal represents a quantitative variable, you have a histogram, and the bars have no gaps between them. Histograms are often used to show the frequency with which scores are obtained.

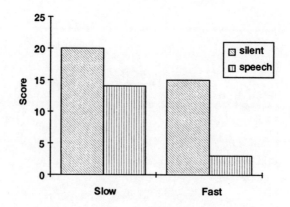

FIG. 15.2. *Barchart displaying two independent variables*

A barchart can be used to show the average results for different groups and subgroups, as in Fig. 15.2, but avoid the temptation to make the diagram too complicated.

Complex types of barchart or histogram with divided bars or three-dimensional effects are readily obtained with some computer programs. Although they create a visual impact, they suffer from a drawback: the lines representing quantity do not all share a common horizontal baseline, and therefore it is harder to compare their relative lengths accurately.

15.2.3 Box plots

Box plots, such as Fig. 15.3, show the median as the centre of a box which has the 75th percentile as its upper limit and the 25th percentile as its lower limit. Lines, referred to as whiskers, are extended from the box to show the largest and smallest values which are not outliers, where outliers are defined as values which are more than 1.5 box lengths from the 75th and 25th percentiles.

Box plots are more complex than barcharts, but they show the central tendency (the median) and the length of the box indicates the spread of the scores. If the median is not in the centre of the box, the data are skewed. They can be a useful way of comparing the scores of different groups of respondents.

15.2.4 Stem-and-leaf plots

Stem-and-leaf plots are like histograms in that the lengths of lines are used to represent the frequency of scores. The lines are made up of the numerical values of the actual scores. A score of 28 is split into 20 and 8: the first (leading) digit

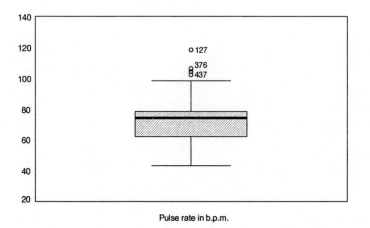

Pulse rate in b.p.m.

FIG 15.3. *Example of a boxplot (the cases shown individually are outliers)*

forms the stem and the trailing digit forms the leaf. So 28 is shown as 2 8. Another score of 29 becomes 2 9 and the two scores together are represented like this:

2 89

The 2 (representing 20) is the stem, and the 8 and 9 are the leaves. Fig. 15.4 shows a stem-and-leaf plot for a set of 23 scores. A stem-and-leaf plot includes more information than a simple histogram, since it shows every score.

15.2.5 Plotting interactions

Graphical displays are especially useful when you have two (or more) factor designs, and want to understand and portray the interactions. Interaction is explained in section 3.4.5 and Box 3.8. The concept is straightforward, but the statistical analysis of interactions often produces major confusion. If you have a complex study, with interactions, the easiest way of starting to get to grips with it is to plot a line graph of the data, like Fig. 3.6 (see p. 40). Note that this is a rough plot, simply intended to help the researcher understand the data, so the rules about the use of line graphs versus barcharts can be ignored.

15.2.6 Pie charts

These show the way a total quantity is subdivided between subgroups (see Fig. 15.5). They can be helpful for displaying frequency data, such as the outcomes of a survey.

Frequency	Stem	Leaf
2.00	2 .	89
6.00	3 .	036899
7.00	4 .	0123688
1.00	5 .	8
2.00	6 .	08
4.00	7 .	1269
1.00	8 .	3

Stem width: 10
Each leaf: 1 case

FIG. 15.4. *Example of a stem-and-leaf plot*

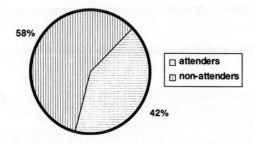

FIG. 15.5. *Example of a pie-chart*

15.2.7 Scattergrams

These are used to illustrate a correlation between two variables. When you have carried out a correlational study you should always plot a scattergram to see whether the relationship appears to be linear or not. How to plot a scattergram is explained in section11.11.1. Many computer programs will give you the best-fitting straight lines (the least-squares regression lines).

15.2.8 Presentation of graphs

If you are preparing graphs by hand, use graph paper and a ruler to draw the axes. Label the axes neatly and accurately, put the heading and title at the top of the page (e.g. 'Fig. 1: Graph showing the mean scores of students from different disciplines on the Conservatism scale'). Do not spend time colouring in your barcharts: the result looks less rather than more professional.

If you have access to a computer, you may be able to have it generate graphs for you, in which case you should use these print-outs rather than hand-drawn graphs. But remember that the program is mindless: it is up to you to ensure that the graph is meaningful. The computer will readily supply graphs that illustrate nothing of any interest except that the people requesting the graph do not understand what the program is doing.

Box 15.1 Checklist on presenting tables and graphs

Tables
(1) Make sure the table shows the data in a way which is relevant to the hypothesis or aim of the study.
(2) With just two means, you may not need a table.
(3) With a mixed-design study, use columns for separate levels of between-subjects variables and rows for within-subjects variables.
(4) Avoid creating tables which are too complicated. Two or three may communicate the information better than one.
(5) Include in the table the measure of central tendency (mean, median), the measure of dispersion and, if it varies between the various conditions, the number of participants for each condition.
(6) Check that the table is labelled ('Table 1') and has a title.

Graphs
(1) Know what you want to communicate before you draw the graphs.
(2) Check which type of display is appropriate for the data.
(3) If preparing it by hand, draw the graph neatly on graph paper and use a ruler.
(4) Do not plot respondents along the horizontal axis unless there is very good reason for doing so, and never do this in a line graph.
(5) If you have carried out a correlational study, always plot a scatter-gram.
(6) Make sure all axes and lines are clearly labelled.
(7) Check that the graph is labelled ('Fig. 1'), has a title and that there is a legend explaining what the different lines, bars or areas represent.

Postscript: after the practical class

In this book we have provided a guide for the beginning student to the methods and techniques psychologists use in carrying out their investigations. As we have noted at various points, psychology has historically modelled itself on an image of the natural sciences, with a powerful belief in the value of the experimental method as the 'best' way of making progress in developing an understanding of human behaviour. This belief has been severely challenged, both by researchers within this tradition and by psychologists working in areas where the traditional 'scientific' method has seemed of less relevance. In the UK, the discipline's response has been a gradual acceptance that there may be some justification to the criticisms, and a willingness at least to try the 'new paradigm' methods.

Those who accept the traditional approaches, who believe in the use of the conventional scientific method, have always realized that they cannot readily be applied when psychologists are asked to venture from the laboratory into the 'real' world. The relationship between 'pure' and 'applied' psychology has long been the subject of discussion, with some arguing that dealing with real-life problems means carrying out research in the real world, and others arguing that the way to solve real-life problems is to deduce likely solutions from pure, laboratory work. But even when this strategy is adopted, it is usually necessary to confirm that the deductions do actually apply, and therefore real-world research is needed. Furthermore, some areas, such as industrial and clinical psychology, have always been 'applied', dealing with real-life issues such as the sources of job satisfaction or the creation of treatment regimes. These areas have made less use of the traditional laboratory approach.

It has long been appreciated that real-life research cannot apply the strict conditions recommended in the textbooks on research methodology. True experiments, with controlled conditions and random allocation of participants to conditions, are simply not feasible and so the researcher faced with a client demanding a solution to a psychological problem has to compromise and attempt to match the demands of the scientific approach with the practicalities of the real-world problem and its context. This leads to the use of quasi-experiments, correlational studies, case studies, etc., where the lack of full control over extraneous variables reduces the strength of any claim that one factor causes alterations in another. This does not mean that psychological research can make no useful contribution to dealing with 'real-life' issues. Bull observed some time ago (1982) that 'perfect solutions to applied problems do not exist' (p. 340), and made the point that 'The ultimate question... is not whether psychologists can answer perfectly questions about human behaviour, but whether anyone else can produce better answers' (p. 344–5). Unsurprisingly, he thought not: with all their limitations, the psychological methods offer the most hopeful way of increasing our understanding of ourselves.

Some issues, often those which seem most important, do not lend themselves to fully 'scientific' investigation. An example that regularly generates a lot of interest is the effect of sex and violence on television on viewers: do they learn to copy the behaviours shown or do the TV portrayals act as a catharsis and make people less likely to indulge in antisocial practices such as rape and physical attack? There have been numerous investigations of this question (Parliamentary Office of Science and Technology, 1993), using a variety of methods, and in many cases the outcome has been inconclusive: the null hypothesis has not been rejected or the study has been correlational so that there are no firm grounds for establishing causation. The conclusion that there is no firm evidence that the portrayal produces antisocial behaviour has sometimes been met with derision, and taken to show that the research is faulty. In other words, it is assumed that the answer is known, and that if the research fails to support it then the research is in error.

The range of topics to which psychology is rightly expected to be able to contribute is so vast that it is impossible to offer detailed guidance on how methodological purity should be diluted to allow any particular topic to be investigated. (Indeed, there are increasing numbers of psychologists who reject the validity of the 'pure' approach, as we have acknowledged.)

When presented with a 'real-life' problem, you will have to decide on the appropriate method or methods to use; we hope that you will have seen the potential of using a range, not just one. Using experiments to investigate a real-world situation may be unrealistic; on the other hand, study of the real-life situation using a nonexperimental method may suggest experiments worth doing to see whether one factor can be shown to be influential. Robson (1993), in discussing this issue, notes that case studies are particularly valuable for exploratory research, surveys for descriptive studies, and experiments for explanatory studies. We concur with other points he makes: each strategy has strengths and weaknesses, alternative strategies are possible for many research topics, and consider combined strategies: the multi-method approach may produce additional illumination and fertilization of ideas.

This book was designed as a guide to the beginning student, based on our experience of the problems students have in learning the skills involved in the conventional practical/laboratory course of an education in psychology. Such courses embrace a range of research methods, but have traditionally been concerned with the quantitative approach and used experiments, surveys and correlational studies. We have deliberately extended the content to include the 'new paradigm', qualitative approach, which is growing increasingly prominent in the discipline. Although we have different preferences ourselves, we hope that you will have appreciated the need to adopt an open mind in deciding on the appropriate methods for any issue, and have picked up some of the skills needed for whichever approach you prefer.

Calculating statistical tests

C1 Nonparametric tests of differences between sets of scores

C1.1 Comparing two sets of scores from the same respondents: Wilcoxon test

TABLE C1. *Calculating the Wilcoxon test*

Respondent	Score 1	Score 2	Difference	Rank of difference	Rank with signs added
1	45	36	+9	9	+9
2	41	40	+1	1.5	+1.5
3	39	40	-1	1.5	-1.5
4	42	38	+4	6	+6
5	48	42	+6	7.5	+7.5
6	47	47	0		
7	41	35	+6	7.5	+7.5
8	46	48	-2	4	-4
9	44	42	+2	4	+4
10	43	41	+2	4	+4

(1) Calculate the differences between the scores for each respondent.

(2) Where the difference score for any respondent is 0, that person is dropped from the analysis.

(3) Rank the difference scores for the remaining respondents, giving rank 1 to the smallest difference etc., but *ignore the sign*, i.e. rank on the absolute value of the difference score. (See the column headed 'Difference' in Table C1.)

Where a number of respondents have the same difference scores (again, ignoring sign), they each get the average rank. For example, in Table C1 respondents 2 and 3 both have a difference score of 1, so they each get the rank of $(1 + 2)/2 = 1.5$. Similarly, respondents 8, 9 and 10 all have a difference score of 2, so they each get the rank of $(3 + 4 + 5)/3 = 4$.

(4) Transfer the + or - signs of the difference scores to the ranks: see the final column of Table C1.

(5) Count up the number of cases where the difference score was not 0. This is N.

(6) If $N < 50$, calculate the sums of the rank values for the + ranks and then for the - ranks. In Table C1 the sum of the + ranks is 39.5 and the sum of the - ranks is 5.5. Take the smaller of these two sums, which is W. In Table C1 $W = 5.5$.

(7) To find out whether the result is significant, look up the critical value of W in Table A2 in Appendix 3 for the appropriate value of N. The difference between the two sets of scores is significant if the calculated value of W is equal to or *less* than the critical value shown in the table. In Table C1, $N = 9$; the probability level is 0.05 and we have a two-tailed hypothesis since we have predicted a difference between the scores but not said which one will be greater. The critical value in Table A2 is 6. The calculated value, 5.5, is less than the critical value, so we can conclude there is a significant difference between the two sets of scores.

If $N > 50$, calculate z, where:

$$z = \frac{W - \dfrac{(N(N+1))}{4}}{\sqrt{\dfrac{N(N+1)(2N+1)}{24}}}$$

To find whether the result is significant, look up the value of z in the first column of Table A1 (the z table). The entry in the column headed 'Smaller portion' gives the one-tailed probability of z occurring by chance, so the two-tailed probability is found by doubling that value. If this doubled value is less than 0.05, you can conclude there is a significant difference between the sets of scores.

C1.2 Comparing two sets of scores from different respondents: Mann–Whitney

TABLE C2. *Calculating the Mann–Whitney test*

Respondent	Score	Rank	Respondent	Score	Rank
1	45	15	11	36	2
2	41	8	12	40	5.5
3	39	4	13	40	5.5
4	42	11	14	38	3
5	48	19.5	15	42	11
6	47	17.5	16	47	17.5
7	41	8	17	35	1
8	46	16	18	48	19.5
9	44	14	19	42	11
10	43	13	20	41	8
		Sum = R_1 = 126			Sum = R_2 = 84

(1) Rank the scores, taking the whole collection of scores as one set, as shown in Table C2. The lowest score of the whole set has a rank of 1, the next lowest score a rank of 2 and so on. Where a number of respondents have the same scores, they each get the average rank. For example, in Table C2 respondents 12 and 13 both have a score of 40, equivalent to ranks of 5 and 6. So each is given the average of these two ranks $(5 + 6)/2 = 5.5$

(2) Calculate the sum of the ranks (R_1, R_2) for each group. In Table C2 $R_1 = 126$ and $R_2 = 84$.

(3) Calculate

$$U = n_1 n_2 + \left[\frac{(n_1(n_1 + 1))}{2} \right] - R_1$$

and

$$U' = n_1 n_2 + \left[\frac{(n_2(n_2 + 1))}{2} \right] - R_2$$

In Table C2,

$$U = 10 \times 10 + \left[\frac{((10)11)}{2} \right] - 126 = 29$$

and

$$U' = 10 \times 10 + \left[\frac{((10)11)}{2} \right] - 84 = 71$$

(4) Take the smaller of U or U'.

(5) To find out whether the result is significant, if n for the larger group < 21, locate that part of Table A3 in Appendix 3 appropriate for whether you have a one- or two-tailed hypothesis. Find the column corresponding to n_1 and the row corresponding to n_2; the critical value of U is shown where they intersect. If the calculated U is equal to or *less* than the critical value, there is a significant difference between the two sets of scores.

If n for the larger group > 20, take the smaller of U or U' and calculate

$$z = \frac{U - \frac{(n_1 n_2)}{2}}{\sqrt{\frac{(n_1)(n_2)(n_1 + n_2 + 1)}{12}}}$$

You can look up the critical value in the normal curve (z) table (Table A1). If you are testing a two-tailed hypothesis, the result is significant at the 0.05 level if $z \geq 1.96$. If it is a one-tailed hypothesis, the result is significant at 0.05 if $z \geq 1.65$.

In Table C2, $U = 29$ and the largest n is 10. So referring to Table A3 for $n_1 = 10$ and $n_2 = 10$, the critical value is seen to be 23. The calculated U is 29, and as this is larger than the critical value, there is not a significant difference between the two sets of scores.

C1.3 Comparing three or more sets of scores from different respondents: the Kruskal–Wallis test

Wilson compared the fear of spiders of three groups, one consisting of people who had enrolled on a course of treatment to help them overcome a fear of spiders, one of people who had completed the course of treatment, and a control

TABLE C3. *Calculating the Kruskal–Wallis test with hypothetical data on fear of spiders*

Pre-treatment Respondent	Score	Rank	Post-treatment Respondent	Score	Rank	Control Respondent	Score	Rank
1	10	11	6	8	9.5	11	6	6
2	11	12	7	4	2.5	12	8	9.5
3	12	13	8	6	6	13	6	6
4	14	14.5	9	4	2.5	14	4	2.5
5	14	14.5	10	7	8	15	4	2.5

ΣR_1: 65
$(\Sigma R_1)^2$: 4225
$(\Sigma R_1)^2/n$: 845

ΣR_2: 28.5
$(\Sigma R_2)^2$: 812.25
$(\Sigma R_2)^2/n$: 162.45

ΣR_3: 26.5
$(\Sigma R_3)^2$: 702.25
$(\Sigma R_3)^2/n$: 140.45

$\Sigma((\Sigma R)^2/n) = 845 + 162.45 + 140.45 = 1147.9$

group of people randomly sampled from the general public. Scores are shown in Table C3.

(1) Rank the scores, taking the whole collection of scores as one set. The lowest score of the whole set has a rank of 1, the next lowest score a rank of 2, and so on. Where a number of respondents have the same scores, they each get the average rank. For example, in Table C3 respondents 7, 9, 14 and 15 all have a score of 4, equivalent to ranks of 1, 2, 3 and 4. So each is given the average of these appropriate ranks: $(1 + 2 + 3 + 4)/4 = 2.5$.

(2) Calculate the sum of ranks (ΣR) for each group. Square each of the ΣR values and divide by its n to get $(\Sigma R)^2/n$. Add up the $(\Sigma R)^2/n$ values to get $\Sigma((\Sigma R)^2/n)$. These values are shown at the bottom of Table C3.

(3) Calculate U:

$$U = \frac{12}{N(N+1)} \sum \frac{(\Sigma R^2)}{n} - 3(N+1)$$

Calculate the degrees of freedom, d.f. $= c - 1$, where c is the number of groups and N is the total number of scores. In Table C3, $U = [12/(15(16))]1147.9 - 3(16) = 9.4$, and d.f. $= 3 - 1 = 2$.

(4) To find whether the result is significant, use Table A4 in Appendix 3. U = chi-square, and the degrees of freedom $= c - 1$. Find the row corresponding to the d.f. and the column with the heading of the probability level you are using (usually 0.05). The intersection gives the critical value of chi-square. The result is significant if the calculated value of U is equal to or greater than the tabled value.

In Table C3, $U = 9.4$ and d.f. $= 2$. The critical value of chi-square with d.f. $= 2$ and a 0.05 level of significance is 5.99; as the calculated value is greater than this, you can conclude there is a significant difference between the groups.

C1.4 Comparing three or more sets of scores from the same or matched respondents: the Friedman test

Young investigated the effects of a programme intended to help people overcome a fear of spiders. She had five respondents and tested this same group on three occasions. She measured their attitude to spiders before the treatment, at the end of the treatment, and three months later. Results are shown in Table C4.

TABLE C4. *Calculating the Friedman test*

Respondent	Pre-treatment Score	Rank	Post-treatment Score	Rank	Three months later Score	Rank
1	10	3	8	1	9	2
2	11	3	4	1	8	2
3	12	3	4	1	5	2
4	14	3	6	1.5	6	1.5
5	14	3	7	2	6	1

Sum, T_a: 15   Sum, T_b: 6.5   Sum, T_c: 8.5

T_a^2: 225 T_b^2: 42.25 T_c^2: 72.25

$\Sigma T^2 = 339.5$

(1) Create a table where each row is the data for one respondent and rank the data *within each row* as shown in Table C4. If two scores in a row are the same, they have the mean of the appropriate rank values (see row 4 in Table C4).

(2) Calculate the sum of ranks (T) for each column. Square each of the T values and add them up to obtain ΣT^2. These values are shown at the bottom of Table C4.

(3) Count the number of conditions, c, and the number of respondents, N. In Table C4, $c = 3$ and $N = 5$. Remember that N is the number of respondents, not the number of scores in the table.

(4) Calculate

$$\chi_r^2 = \left[\frac{12}{Nc(c+1)} \times (\Sigma T^2) \right] - 3N(c+1)$$

and d.f. $= c - 1$.

In Table C4

$$\chi_r^2 = \left[\frac{12}{(5)(3)(4)} \times (339.5) \right] - [(3)(5)(4)] = 7.9$$

d.f. $= 3 - 1 = 2$.

(5) To find whether the result is significant, use Table A4. χ_r^2 = chi-square and the degrees of freedom = $c-1$. Find the row corresponding to the d.f. and the column with the heading of the probability level you are using (usually 0.05). The intersection gives the critical value of chi-square. The result is significant if the calculated χ_r^2 is equal to or greater than the tabled value.

In Table C4, $\chi_r^2 = 7.9$, d.f. = 2. The critical value of chi-square with d.f. = 2 and a 0.05 significance level is 5.99; as the calculated value is greater than this, you can conclude there is a significant difference between the groups.

C2 Nonparametric tests for trend

C2.1 Page's L (for a within-subjects study)

We shall test the hypothesis that the data in Table C4 indicate that in this within-subjects study fear of spiders is greatest for the pre-treatment condition, lowest at the post-treatment state, with the delayed condition (three months later) having an intermediate position.

TABLE C5. *Calculating Page's L*

Respondent	Post-treatment		Three months later		Pre-treatment	
	Score	Rank	Score	Rank	Score	Rank
1	8	1	9	2	10	3
2	4	1	8	2	11	3
3	4	1	5	2	12	3
4	6	1.5	6	1.5	14	3
5	7	2	6	1	14	3
	T_1: 6.5		T_2: 8.5		T_3: 15	
	$(T)c = (6.5)1$		$(T)c = (8.5)2$		$(T)c = (15)3$	

$\Sigma((T)c) = L = 68.5$

(1) Rearrange the table so that the condition for the predicted lowest score is in column 1, the condition for the next lowest score is in column 2, and so on. Table C4 has been recast in this way as Table C5.

(2) Rank the data across each row. If two scores in a row are the same, they have the mean of the appropriate rank values (see respondent 4 in Table C5).

(3) Calculate the sum of ranks for each column.

(4) Calculate L where $L = \Sigma(T \times c)$. T is the sum of ranks for the column and c is the numerical order of the column. For the left most column $c = 1$, for the second column $c = 2$, etc.

The values of T, $((T)c)$ and $(\Sigma(T)c)$ are shown at the bottom of Table C5.

(5) To find whether the result is significant use Table A5 in Appendix 3.

The number of conditions (columns) = c. The number of respondents = N. If $N < 12$ and $c < 6$, look up the critical value of L in Table A5. If the calculated value is equal to or larger than the table value, the results are in the predicted direction.

C2.2 Jonckheere's test (for a between-subjects study)

The various conditions must have an equal number of respondents. If you have unequal groups, select respondents at random from any group with an excess number and delete them from the table. Use the test if you have 10 or fewer respondents in each condition.

TABLE C6. *Calculating Jonckheere's test*

Post-treatment score	n+	Control score	n+	Pre-treatment score
8	5	6	5	10
4	8	8	5	11
6	6	6	5	12
4	8	4	5	14
7	6	4	5	14
Sum: 33		Sum: 25		
$n = 5$	$c = 3$	Total $n+ = A = 58$		

(1) Rearrange the table of results so that the columns are in the order predicted by your hypothesis. For example, with the data from Table C6, we are predicting the order will be post-treatment group having the lowest scores, followed by the control group and the pre-treatment group having the highest scores.

(2) For each score in the left-hand column count up the number of larger scores in each of the columns to the right. Repeat this for all the scores in every column except of course the right-most one. See Table C6; for the first score of 8 in the left-most column, 5 is the $n+$ figure because in the two columns to the right there are 5 scores larger than 8.

(3) Add up the $n+$ numbers to give A. The number of conditions (columns) is c; n is the number of respondents in each condition. These values are shown at the bottom of Table C6.

(4) Calculate B where $B = [((c(c-1))/2) \ n^2]$. In Table C6, $B = [((3(2))/2)(25)] = 75$

(5) Calculate $S = 2A - B$. In Table C6, $S = 2(58) - 75 = 41$.

(6) To find whether the result is significant, use Table A6 in Appendix 3, if $c < 7$ and $n < 11$. Look up the critical value of S for the appropriate values of c and n. If the calculated value of S is equal to or greater than the critical value, the groups are in the predicted order.

C3 Parametric tests of differences between scores

C3.1 Comparing two sets of scores from different respondents (between subjects design): the independent t-test

The *t*-test is used to compare two sets of scores. The formula for *t* is:

$$t = \frac{\bar{x}_A - \bar{x}_B}{\sqrt{\left[\dfrac{\left[\Sigma x_A^2 - \dfrac{(\Sigma x_A)^2}{n_A}\right] + \left[\Sigma x_B^2 - \dfrac{(\Sigma x_B)^2}{n_B}\right]}{(n_A - 1) + (n_B - 1)}\right]\left[\dfrac{1}{n_A} + \dfrac{1}{n_B}\right]}}$$

d.f. $= (n_A - 1) + (n_B - 1)$

TABLE C7. *Calculating t for independent groups*

	Group A		Group B	
x_A	x_A^2	x_B	x_B^2	
25	625	15	225	
21	441	17	289	
8	64	9	81	
20	400	12	144	
12	144	30	900	
30	900	19	361	
		14	196	
		18	324	
		16	256	
		10	100	
		5	25	
		13	169	
Σx_A: 116	Σx_A^2: 2574	Σx_B: 178	Σx_B^2: 3070	
	$(\Sigma x_A)^2$: 13456		$(\Sigma x_B)^2$: 31684	
	n_A: 6		n_B: 12	
	$\bar{x}_A$: 19.33		$\bar{x}_B$: 14.83	

(1) Calculate the sum (Σx), mean ($\bar{x}$) and sum of *x* squared (Σx^2) for each of the two groups. The sum of *x* squared is obtained by taking each score within the group, squaring it and then finding the total of these squared values. For each group, also calculate the square of the sums ($\Sigma x)^2$. Table C7 shows these values for each of the two groups.

(2) Calculate the difference between the means. In Table C7, the difference between the means is 19.33-14.83 = 4.50.

(3) Calculate *t*, using the formula shown above. Note that *t* can be negative, if you have taken the larger mean from the smaller one. In Table C7,

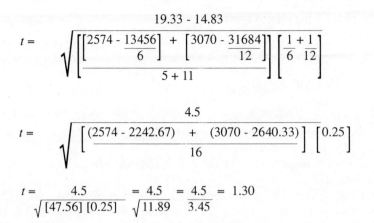

$$t = \frac{19.33 - 14.83}{\sqrt{\left[\dfrac{\left[2574 - \dfrac{13456}{6}\right] + \left[3070 - \dfrac{31684}{12}\right]}{5 + 11}\right]\left[\dfrac{1}{6} + \dfrac{1}{12}\right]}}$$

$$t = \frac{4.5}{\sqrt{\left[\dfrac{(2574 - 2242.67) + (3070 - 2640.33)}{16}\right]\left[0.25\right]}}$$

$$t = \frac{4.5}{\sqrt{[47.56][0.25]}} = \frac{4.5}{\sqrt{11.89}} = \frac{4.5}{3.45} = 1.30$$

(4) Calculate the degrees of freedom, d.f. $= n_A + n_B - 2$. In Table C7, d.f. $= 6 + 12 - 2 = 16$.

(5) To find whether the result is significant, take the absolute (positive) value of t. Find the critical value of t in Table A7 in Appendix 3 by locating the entry corresponding to the d.f. and the probability level for your hypothesis (nondirectional or directional). If your calculated value is greater than the critical value shown in the table, the difference between the two means is significant at the probability level you are using.

The critical value of t with d.f. $= 16$ at the 5% level for a two-tailed hypothesis is 2.120. In Table C7, the calculated $t = 1.30 < 2.120$, so we conclude there is not a significant difference between the two means, and summarize the outcome like this: $t = 1.30$, d.f. $= 16$, $p > 0.05$.

C3.2 Comparing two sets of scores from the same respondents (within subjects or repeated measures design): the related or paired t-test

TABLE C8. *Calculating t for related groups*

Respondent	x_1	x_2	d	d^2
1	5	3	2	4
2	2	4	-2	4
3	15	9	6	36
4	9	7	2	4
5	4	3	1	1
6	11	10	1	1
7	3	1	2	4
8	2	2	0	0

Σx_1: 51 $\quad$ Σx_2: 39 $\quad$ Σd: 12 $\quad$ Σd^2: 54
$\bar{x}_1$: 6.375 $\quad$ $\bar{x}_2$: 4.875 $\quad$ $\bar{d}$: 1.50

The formula for the related *t*-test is:

$$t = \frac{\bar{d}}{\sqrt{\dfrac{\Sigma d^2 - (\Sigma d)^2/N}{N(N-1)}}} \qquad \text{with d.f.} = N - 1$$

where *d* represents the difference between the scores the respondent obtained under the two conditions and *N* is the number of pairs of scores. Note that in totalling *d* you *do* take account of signs!

(1) For each respondent, calculate the difference between the two scores, keeping the signs.

(2) Find the sum of the *d* scores, taking account of the signs. Calculate the square of the sum of the *d* scores $(\Sigma d)^2$. In Table C8, $\Sigma d = 12$ and $(\Sigma d)^2 = 144$.

(3) Calculate the mean of the *d* scores. In Table C8, $\bar{d} = 1.50$.

(4) Square each of the *d* scores. Calculate the sum of the squared *d* scores, Σd^2. In Table C8, $\Sigma d^2 = 54$.

(5) Calculate *t* using the formula given above. In the Table,

$$t = \frac{1.5}{\sqrt{\dfrac{54 - (144/8)}{8(7)}}}$$

$$= 1.5/0.8 = 1.875$$

(6) Calculate the degrees of freedom, d.f. $= N$-1. In Table C8, d.f. $= 7$.

(7) To find whether the result is significant, take the absolute (positive) value of *t*. Find the critical value of *t* in Table A7 for the appropriate significance level and degrees of freedom. If your calculated value is greater than the critical value in the table, the difference between the two means is significance level you are using.

C3.3 Comparing the mean of a sample with the mean of a population: the one-sample t-test

The formula for the one-sample *t* is:

$$t = \frac{\bar{x} - \mu}{\sqrt{\dfrac{\Sigma x^2 - (\Sigma x)^2/N)}{N(N-1)}}} \qquad = \frac{\bar{x} - \mu}{(\text{s.d.}/\sqrt{N})} \qquad \text{with d.f.} = N\text{-1.}$$

Suppose we measure the breadth of hands of a group of 25 farmers and find the mean is 92.1 mm (s.d. $= 3.6$). We want to know whether their hands are broader than those of the population in general (a one-tailed hypothesis), where the average hand width of British men is 85 mm. Here the population mean is 85. The sample mean, $\bar{x} = 92.1$ with s.d. $= 3.6$ and number in sample, N, $= 25$. Using the formula with this data, $t = (92.1 - 85)/(3.6/\sqrt{25}) = 7.1/0.72 = 9.86$ and d.f. $= 24$.

To find whether the result is significant take the absolute (positive) value of t. Find the critical value of t in Table A7 in Appendix 3 for the appropriate significance level and degrees of freedom. If your calculated value is greater than the critical value shown in the table, the difference between the sample and population means is significant at the 5% level.

In our example, the critical value of t with d.f. = 24 at the 5% level for a one-tailed hypothesis is 1.711. The calculated $t = 9.86 > 1.711$, so we conclude there is a significant difference between the two means, and summarize the outcome like this: $t = 9.86$, d.f. = 24 , $p < 0.05$. The farmers do have larger hands on the average than the general population.

C3.4 Comparing three or more sets of scores from different respondents: analysis of variance (anova)

TABLE C9. *Calculating one-way independent analysis of variance*

Group A: silence		Group B: music		Group C: speech		
x_A	x_A^2	x_B	x_B^2	x_C	x_C^2	
5	25	5	25	0	0	
8	64	2	4	3	9	
11	121	8	64	6	36	
8	64	8	64	3	9	
5	25	2	4	0	0	
14	196	8	64	9	81	
8	64	5	25	3	9	
5	25	2	4	0	0	
11	121	8	64	6	36	
$n_A = 9$		$n_B = 9$		$n_C = 9$		$N = 27$
$\Sigma x_A = 75$		$\Sigma x_B = 48$		$\Sigma x_C = 30$		GT = 153
						$GT^2 = 23,409$
						$GT^2/N = 23409/27 = 867$
$\Sigma x_A^2 = 705$		$\Sigma x_B^2 = 318$		$\Sigma x_C^2 = 180$		$\Sigma x^2 = 1203$
$(\Sigma x_A)^2 = 5625$		$(\Sigma x_B)^2 = 2304$		$(\Sigma x_C)^2 = 900$		
$(\Sigma x_A)^2/n = 625$		$(\Sigma x_B)^2/n = 256$		$(\Sigma x_C)^2/n = 100$		
$\bar{x}_A = 8.33$		$\bar{x}_B = 5.33$		$\bar{x}_C = 3.33$		

Preliminary warning: if at any time you have a negative value, you have made a mistake!

(1) Calculate the correction term. Calculate the total of all the scores (GT), square it and divide by N. In Table C9, GT = 153, $GT^2 = 23409$, $GT^2/N = 23409/27 = 867$.

(2) Find the total sum of squares, SStot. Square every score and find the total of the squared values, Σx^2. Subtract the correction term to obtain SStot. In Table C9, $\Sigma x^2 = 1203$; SStot = 1203 - 867 = 336.

(3) Calculate SStreatments. For each group, take the total (Σx), square it to obtain ($\Sigma x)^2$, and divide by the number of scores in the group to get $(\Sigma x)^2/n$. Add up the results for all the groups to get $\Sigma(T^2/n)$ and then subtract the correction term. In Table C9, $(\Sigma x_A)^2/n = 625$, $(\Sigma x_B)^2/n = 256$, $(\Sigma x_C)^2/n = 100$; $\Sigma(T^2/n) = 981$. SStreatment $= \Sigma(T^2/n) - GT^2/N = 981 - 867 = 114$.

(4) Calculate SSerror. Subtract SStreatment from Sstot: SSerror = SStotal - Sstreatment. Here SSerror = SStotal - SStreatment = 336 - 114 = 222.

SSerror can be obtained by (1) summing the squared scores in each group and subtracting the group total squared divided by n; (2) adding up the result for all the groups: SSerror $= (\Sigma x_A^2 - (\Sigma x_A)^2/n_A) + (\Sigma x_B^2 - (\Sigma x_B)^2/n_B) + (\Sigma x_C^2 - (\Sigma x_C)^2/n_C)...$ But the subtraction method is easier!)

(5) Calculate the degrees of freedom. The total degrees of freedom is $N-1$, the degrees of freedom for treatments is the number of treatments $c-1$, and the degrees of freedom for error is the total d.f. - treatment d.f.

In Table C9, total d.f. $= 27-1 = 26$, treatment d.f. $= 3-1 = 2$, error d.f. $= 26-2 = 24$.

(6) Complete a summary table like Table C10. Put the SS and degrees of freedom values you have calculated in the columns of the appropriate rows. For each row, divide SS by d.f. to obtain MS (mean square) for that row. Divide the MS for treatments by the MS error to get F.

TABLE C10. *Example of the outcome of an analysis of variance*

Source	SS	d.f.	MS	F
Treatment	114.00	2	57.00	6.16
Error	222.00	24	9.25	
Total	336.00	26		

(7) To find whether the result is significant, decide on the significance level to be used, and locate the appropriate section of Table A8 in Appendix 3. To look up the critical value of F for the two values of degrees of freedom (d.f. treatment and d.f. error), find the column that has the d.f. for treatments, and then find the row that has d.f. for error; the critical value of F is at the intersection. Your value is significant at the level for which the table is relevant if it is equal to or larger than the critical value.

The critical value of F with d.f. $= 2$ and 24 at the 5% level for a two-tailed hypothesis is 3.40. In Table C10, the calculated $F = 6.16 > 3.40$, so we conclude there is a significant difference between the three means, and summarize the outcome like this: $F = 6.16$; d.f. $= 2,24$; $p < 0.05$.

C3.5 Testing differences between pairs of means: the Scheffé test

Table C9 shows the data from three groups in a single factor, three-level experiment, and the analysis of variance summary table on those data is Table

C10. The sums and means of the three groups are: 75 and 8.33 for group A, 48 and 5.33 for group B, and 30 and 3.33 for group C. Is group A significantly different from groups B and C? Is group B significantly different from group C? The Scheffé test answers these questions. It is assumed that, as here, the n of all groups is equal.

(1) Calculate the standard error of the difference among the means, using the mean square (MS) within groups, which is the MS error in the analysis of variance summary table:

standard error of means = $\sqrt{[((2)(MSwithin))/n]}$

For the example used here, standard error of means = $\sqrt{[(2(9.25))/9]}$ = 1.43

(2) Look up the value of F for the 5% level in Table A8, with the two degrees of freedom being the number of groups (c)-1 (= 3-1 in our example) and $c(n$-1). As n is the number of scores in each group, here $c(n$-1) = 3(9-1) = 24. With the probability level set at 5%, the F value with d.f. of 2 and 24 = 3.40.

(3) Multiply the value of F found at step 2 by c-1 and take the square root. Here F = 3.40, c-1 = 2, (3.40)2 = 6.80 and the square root = 2.61

(4) Multiply the result of step 3 by the result of step 1 to get the Critical Difference value. Here CDiff. = (2.61)(1.43) = 3.73.

(5) Take the means of each group and calculate the differences between each pair of means. In Table C9, the mean are for group A = 8.33, for group B = 5.33, and for group C = 3.33. So A-B = 3.00; B-C = 2.00; A-C = 5.00. Any difference is significant at the 5% level if the difference exceeds the value found at step 4. In this example, the difference between A and B is not significant, the difference between B and C is not significant, but the difference between A and C is.

C3.6 Comparing sets of scores from different respondents with two independent variables: the two-way anova for independent groups

This example only covers between-subjects experiments with equal n values. If you have a within-subjects variable or unequal groups and have to carry out calculations by hand, you will need a more advanced text, such as Howell (1992).

Imagine you used a between-subjects design to investigate people's ability to solve problems with or without background noise. Call this factor A, with two levels: A1 and A2. You also varied the speed (fast or slow) at which the problems were presented, and this is factor B, which also has two levels: B1 and B2. So there was a 2 × 2 experiment, with separate respondents in each of the four groups.

Preliminary warning: if at any time you have a negative value, you have made a mistake!

(1) Calculate the totals for each subgroup. In Table C11 they are 49, 27, 66, and 84.

(2) Calculate the correction term (CT). Take the total of all the scores, GT, square it and divide by N to obtain CT. Here it is $226^2/16$ = 3192.25.

(3) Calculate the sum of squares for factor A, SS_A.

(a) For all of the groups at level 1 of factor A, calculate the combined total, square it, and divide by the number of scores going to make up that total. In the

TABLE C11. *Calculating the two-way anova for independent groups*

| Factor B | Factor A | | |
	1	2	
			Total for level 1 of factor B
1	8	5	
	16	7	
	14	7	
	11	8	
Group sum	49	27	76
Mean	12.25	6.75	
			Total for level 2 of factor B
2	18	19	
	16	21	
	17	24	
	15	20	
Group sum	66	84	150
Mean	16.5	21	
Column totals:	115	111	Grand total, $GT = 226$
			$GT^2 = 51076$
			$GT^2/N = 51076/16 = 3192.25$

table, at level 1 of factor A, the sum is 115, so the sum squared and divided by the number of scores for that level (8) is $13225/8 = 1653.125$.

(b) For all the groups at level 2 of factor A, calculate the combined total, square it, and divide by the number of scores going to make up that total. In Table C11, at level 2 of factor A, the sum is 111, so the sum squared and divided by $n (= 8)$ is $12321/8 = 1540.125$.

(c) Add the results of steps 3(a) and 3(b) and subtract CT. In Table C11, $SS_A = 1653.125 + 1540.125 - 3192.25 = 1.00$

(4) Calculate the sum of squares for factor B, SS_B.

(a)For all the groups at level 1 of factor B, calculate the combined total, square it, and divide by the number of scores going to make up that total. In the table, at level 1 of factor B, the sum is 76, so the sum squared and divided by the number of scores for that level (8) is $5776/8 = 722$.

(b) For all the groups at level 2 of factor B, calculate the combined total, square it, and divide by the number of scores going to make up that total. In Table C11, at level 2 of factor B, the sum is 150, so the sum squared and divided by the number of scores for that level (8) is $22500/8 = 2812.5$.

(c) Add the results of steps 4(a) and 4(b) and subtract CT. Here, $SS_B = 722 + 2812.5 - 3192.25 = 342.25$

(5) Calculate the total sum of squares, SS_{tot}. $SS_{tot} = \Sigma x^2 - CT$. Square each score and sum the squares to find Σx^2; then subtract CT. In Table C11, $\Sigma x^2 = 8^2 + 16^2 + ... 20^2 = 3696$; $SS_{tot} = 3696 - 3192.25 = 503.75$

(6) Calculate the interaction sum of squares, $SS_{A \times B} = \Sigma((\Sigma x)^2/n) - SS_A - SS_B - CT$, where Σx refers to the total of each subgroup.

(a)Take the total of each subgroup, square it and divide by the number of scores in the subgroup. Add these values to obtain $\Sigma((\Sigma x)^2/n)$. In the table, $\Sigma((\Sigma x)^2/n) = 49^2/4 + 27^2/4 + 66^2/4 + 84^2/4 = 3635.5$.

(b) Subtract SS_A, SS_B, and CT. Here, $SS_{A \times B} = 3635.5 - 1.00 - 342.25 - 3192.25 = 100.00$.

(7) Calculate the sum of squares for the error term, $SS_{error} = SS_{tot} - SS_A - SS_B - SS_{A \times B}$. In the table, $SS_{error} = 503.75 - 1.00 - 342.25 - 100.00 = 60.5$

(8) Calculate the various degrees of freedom.

The total degrees of freedom (d.f.$_{tot}$) is N-1. The degrees of freedom for variable A (d.f.$_A$) is (number of levels of factor A) - 1. The degrees of freedom for variable B (d.f.$_B$) is (number of levels of factor B) - 1. The degrees of freedom for the A $\times$ B interaction is given by d.f.$_A$ $\times$ d.f.$_B$. Finally, the degrees of freedom for error is found by subtraction: d.f.$_{tot}$ - d.f.$_A$ - d.f.$_B$ - d.f.$_{A \times B}$. In Table C11, d.f.$_{tot} = 16 - 1 = 15$; d.f.$_A = 2 - 1 = 1$; d.f.$_B = 2 - 1 = 1$; d.f.$_{AxB} = 1 \times 1 = 1$; d.f.$_{error} = 15 - 1 - 1 - 1 = 12$

(9) Complete a summary table, like Table C12. Put the SS and degrees of freedom values you have calculated in the appropriate rows of the columns headed SS and d.f. For each row, divide SS by its d.f. to obtain MS (mean square) for that row. Divide each of the MS values for A, B and A $\times$ B by the MS for error to get F for each source of variance.

TABLE C12. *The outcome of the analysis of variance*

Source	SS	d.f.	MS	F
A	1.00	1	1.00	0.2
B	342.25	1	342.25	67.91
A × B	100.00	1	100.00	19.84
Error	60.5	12	5.04	
Total	503.75	15		

(10) To find whether the result is significant look up the significance of each F value, using the appropriate degrees of freedom. An explanation of how to do this is given in the section above dealing with the one-way anova. For Table C12, the critical value of F with d.f. of 1 and 12 is 4.75. So the F value for variable A is not significant, as it is smaller than the critical value, but the F values for variable B and the A $\times$ B interaction are significant.

Interpreting a significant F value

The nonsignificant F for variable A means that there is no difference between the overall mean scores for the two levels of this variable, which are 14.375 for level 1 and 13.875 for level 2. The significant F for variable B means that there is a significant difference between the means for the two levels of B: the mean for level 1 of variable B is 9.50, and for level 2 it is 18.75. The significant interaction can mean that the difference between the levels of variable B at one level of variable A is greater than the difference between the levels of variable B at the other level of variable A. It can also mean that there is a difference between the two levels of variable A when variable B is at one level but not at another.

The analysis of variance tells you that there are significant differences, but does not show where these differences lie: is the mean for respondents who had variable A at level 1 and variable B at level 1 significantly different from those who had A at level 1 but variable B at level 2? To answer questions such as these, you need to apply further tests, such as the Scheffé test described in section C3.5. To apply it to factorial experiments, the experiment is taken as involving separate conditions (4 in a 2 × 2 experiment, 6 in a 2 × 3, etc.), and the test run as though the experiment had been a one-way design.

C4 Tests of association with frequency data

C4.1 Chi-square for a contingency table

The chi-square test is used with nominal (frequency) data, where respondents are assigned to categories. A recent survey asked adults whether they thought 'adult' films should be shown uncut on TV. Data were reported for different age groups. Hypothetical results are shown in Table C13. The cell entries show the number of respondents of that age giving the response indicated in each row.

TABLE C13. *Hypothetical responses to survey question on showing uncut films on TV*

| Response | Respondents' age | | | |
	18–40	41–60	Over 60	Total
No	35	22	34	91
Yes	54	49	6	109
Total	89	71	40	200

The chi-square test is concerned with answering the question: is there a relationship between the variable that distinguishes the columns (age, in Table C13) and the variable that distinguishes the rows (response 'no' or 'yes')? The test compares the observed frequencies with the expected frequencies, which are calculated for each cell in the table by multiplying the appropriate row and column totals and dividing by N. The formula for chi-square is:

$$\chi^2 = \Sigma[(O - E)^2 / E]$$

To calculate chi-square, follow these steps. Note that this example uses the data from Table C13, a 3 × 2 table. With a 2 × 2 table, there is an easier formula (see following).

TABLE C14. *Expected frequencies for the data in Table C13*

Response	Respondents' age			Total
	18–40	*41–60*	*Over 60*	*Total*
No	40.50	32.31	18.20	91
Yes	48.51	38.70	21.80	109
Total	89	71	40	200

TABLE C15. *(Observed - Expected) frequencies for the data in Table C13*

Response	Respondents' age		
	18–40	*41–60*	*Over 60*
No	-5.50	-10.31	15.80
Yes	5.49	10.30	-15.80

TABLE C16. $(O - E)^2$ *values for the data in Table C9*

Response	Respondents' age		
	18–40	*41–60*	*Over 60*
No	30.25	106.30	249.64
Yes	30.14	106.09	249.64

TABLE C17. $(O - E)^2/E$ *values for the data in Table C13*

Response	Respondents' age		
	18–40	*41–60*	*Over 60*
No	0.75	3.29	13.72
Yes	0.62	2.74	11.45

(1) For each cell in the table, calculate the expected frequency by taking the total for its row and multiplying that by the total for its column, then dividing by N, the total number of respondents. In Table C13, the expected frequency for the top left-hand cell is $(91 \times 89)/200 = 40.50$. The other expected frequencies are included in Table C14.

(2) Calculate the difference between the observed (O) and expected (E) frequencies for each cell in the table, to give (O-E), as shown in Table C15.

(3) Square each of these values to obtain $(O-E)^2$, as in Table C16.

(4) For each cell, divide $(O-E)^2$ by the expected value for that cell to obtain $(O-E)^2/E$. From Tables C14 and C16, the $(O-E)^2/E$ value for the top left cell is: $30.25/40.50 = 0.75$. The values for all the cells are shown in Table C17.

(5) Add up all the $(O-E)^2/E$ values; this is chi-square. (Note that it cannot be a negative number.) For Table C17, chi-square $= 0.75 + 3.29... + 11.45 = 32.57$.

(6) Calculate the degrees of freedom (d.f.). For a two-way table, the d.f. equals the number of rows minus 1 multiplied by the number of columns minus 1: d.f. $= (r-1)(c-1)$. In Table C13, it is $1 \times 2 = 2$.

(7) To find out whether the result is significant, find the critical value of chi-square in Table A4 in Appendix 3 by finding the column for the probability level you are using (usually 0.05) and the row for the degrees of freedom you have calculated. The table entry at the intersection of this column and row is the critical value. If the calculated value is larger than the critical value, you can conclude chi-square is significant at the probability level you are using.

With d.f. $= 2$ and the 0.05 probability level for a two-tailed hypothesis, the critical value of chi-square is 5.99. The chi-square value for Table C13 is $32.57 > 5.99$, so there is a significant association between age and response: the figures suggest that people over 60 are much more likely to say 'no'.

Chi-square for a two-by-two table
When the frequency table is 2×2 (such as Table C18), a simpler formula for chi-square can be used:

$$\chi^2 = [N(AD - BC)^2]/[(A + B)(C + D)(A + C)(B + D)] \text{ with d.f.} = 1.$$

TABLE C18. *Example of a 2 × 2 frequency table*

			Total
	25 A	75 B	100 A + B
	90 C	10 D	100 C + D
Total	115 A + C	85 B + D	200 A + B + C + D

For the data in Table C18:

$$\chi^2 = [200((25)(10)-(75)(90))^2]/[(25 + 75)(90 + 10)(25 + 90)(75 + 10)] = 86.45$$

C4.2 The one-sample chi-square

The chi-square test can be used to compare an observed distribution of frequency scores with an expected one. For example, the number of fatal road accidents in

Manchester in 1989 for the four three-month periods of the year are shown in the 'Observed frequency' column of Table C19. Do these figures show that the number of fatal accidents differed from what one would expect if they were evenly distributed across the year?

TABLE C19. *Fatal road accidents by three-month period, 1989*

	Observed frequency	Expected frequency	$(O\text{-}E)$	$(O\text{-}E)^2$	$(O\text{-}E)^2/E$
January–March	43	46.25	-3.25	10.5625	0.2284
April–June	34	46.25	-12.25	150.0625	3.2446
July–September	46	46.25	-0.25	0.0625	0.0014
October–December	62	46.25	+ 15.75	248.0625	5.3625
Total	185	185			$\chi^2 = 8.8369$

(1) Calculate the total of the observed frequencies. Divide the total by the number of categories (four in this example) to get the frequencies expected if there were no difference between the categories.

(2) Carry out a chi-square on the table of observed and expected values, using the chi-square formula given earlier.

In Table C19, for the first period, $(O\text{-}E)$ is 43-46.25 = -3.25; $(O\text{-}E)^2 = 10.5625$ and $(O\text{-}E)^2/E = 10.5625/46.25 = 0.2284$. The values for the other periods are calculated in a similar fashion. Chi-square is the sum of the $(O\text{-}E)^2/E$ values.

(3) Calculate the degrees of freedom, c-1 (the number of data cells minus 1). Here it is 4-1 = 3.

(4) To find out whether the result is significant, find the critical value of chi-square in Table A4, as explained in step 7 of section C4.1.

With d.f. = 3 and a 0.05 probability level, the critical value is 7.82. As the calculated chi-square for Table C19 is greater than the critical value, there is a significant tendency for rate of fatal accidents to differ according to period of the year.

In this example, chi-squared was used to test whether the observed frequencies differed from those expected if accidents were equally distributed across the three-month periods. So the null hypothesis was that the probability for each category (three-month period) was the same. The test can also be used to compare the observed frequencies with expected frequencies when the null hypothesis is not that all probabilities are equal. You could, for example, test the observed frequencies against those expected if the null hypothesis was that 50% of accidents occur in January–March, and the remaining 50% are equally distributed across the other periods. With a total of 185 accidents, the expected frequency for the January–March period under this hypothesis is 50% of 185 = 92.5. The expected frequencies for each of the other three periods is (185 - 92.5)/3 = 30.83.

C5 Tests of association between variables with ranked (ordinal) or interval measurement

C5.1 Spearman rank correlation

This correlation is used when the data are on an ordinal scale, such as rank orders.

TABLE C20. *Calculating the Spearman rank correlation coefficient (rho)*

Respondent	Rank score on x	Rank score on y	d	d^2
1	1	3	-2	4
2	2	1	1	1
3	3	4	-1	1
4	4	6	-2	4
5	5	2	3	9
6	6	7	-1	1
7	7	5	2	4
8	8	8	0	0
9	9	10	-1	1
10	10	9	1	1
			Σd: 0	Σd^2: 26

(1) Rank the data for each set of scores.
(2) Calculate the difference (d) between each pair of ranks.
(3) Square these differences to obtain d^2.
(4) Calculate the sum of the squared differences, Σd^2.
(5) Calculate rho using the formula

$$rho = 1 - \left[\frac{6(\Sigma d^2)}{N(N^2 - 1)} \right]$$

In Table C20,

$$rho = 1 - \left[\frac{6(26)}{10(10^2 - 1)} \right] = 1 - \left[\frac{156}{990} \right] = 1 - 0.16 = 0.84$$

(6) To find whether the correlation is significantly different from zero, if $N \geq 10$, calculate

$$t = rho \left[\sqrt{\frac{(N - 2)}{1 - rho^2}} \right] \qquad \text{with d.f.} = N - 2.$$

Here,

$$t = 0.84 \left[\sqrt{\frac{10 - 2}{1 - 0.84^2}} \right] = 0.84 \left[\sqrt{\frac{8}{0.29}} \right] = 0.84(5.25) = 4.41$$

with d.f. = 10 - 2.

Look up the critical value of t in Table A7 for $p = 0.05$ on a two-tailed test and the appropriate degrees of freedom. If the calculated t is greater than the critical value, rho is statistically significantly different from zero. If $N < 10$, rho is significant on a two-tailed test at 0.05 if it exceeds the values shown in Table C21.

TABLE C21. *Critical values for rho for N = 5 to N = 9 on a two-tailed test at the 0.05 level of significance*

N	
5	1.000
6	0.886
7	0.786
8	0.738
9	0.700

C5.2 Pearson product–moment correlation

This is the parametric measure of correlation, which expresses the relationship between two variables which have both been measured on an interval scale.

TABLE C22. *Calculating the Pearson product–moment correlation*

Respondent	Score x	Score y	x^2	y^2	xy
1	15	17	225	289	255
2	12	13	144	169	156
3	19	23	361	529	437
4	19	21	361	441	399
5	11	12	121	144	132
6	18	19	324	361	342
7	17	14	289	196	238
8	21	15	441	225	315

Totals: Σx:132 Σy:134 Σx^2:2266 Σy^2:2354 Σxy:2274

$(\Sigma x)^2$:17424 $(\Sigma y)^2$:17956

$N = 8$

(1) Calculate xy for each pair of scores and sum these to obtain Σxy.

(2) Find the total of the x scores (Σx) and of the y scores (Σy); square each of these totals to obtain $(\Sigma x)^2$ and $(\Sigma y)^2$.

(3) Square the scores in each column to obtain x^2 and y^2. Add the x^2 values to obtain Σx^2 and then add up the y^2 values to obtain Σy^2.

(4) Calculate r using the formula:

$$r = \frac{N\,\Sigma xy - \Sigma x \Sigma y}{\sqrt{\;[(N\Sigma x^2 - (\Sigma x)^2)(N\Sigma y^2 - (\Sigma y)^2)]}}$$

In Table C22,

$$r = \frac{8(2274) - (132)(134)}{\sqrt{\;[(8(2266) - 132^2)(8(2354) - 134^2)]}}$$

$$= 504 / 785.31 = 0.64$$

(5) To find whether the correlation is significantly different from zero, if $N > 12$, calculate

$$t = r \left[\sqrt{\frac{(N-2)}{(1-r^2)}} \right]$$

with d.f. $= N$-2. Look up the critical value of t in Table A7 for $p = 0.05$ and the appropriate degrees of freedom. If the calculated t is greater than the critical value for a two-tailed hypothesis, r is statistically significantly different from 0. If $N \leq 12$, r is significant on a two-tailed test at the 0.05 level if it exceeds the values given in Table C23.

Table C23. *Critical values for product moment correlation for N = 8 to N = 12 on a two-tailed test at the 0.05 level of significance*

N	
8	0.7067
9	0.6664
10	0.6319
11	0.6021
12	0.5760

For Table C22, $r = 0.64$; $N = 8$. The critical value of r is 0.7067, and as the calculated r is less than this, you would conclude that there was not a significant correlation between the two sets of scores ($p > 0.05$).

Random number tables

TABLE N1. *Random digits*

8	9	2	6	1	8	8	1	4	1	8	9	7	7	3	0	7	4	0	1	5	1	8	2	8	8	6
1	6	2	3	7	0	5	1	6	9	9	3	3	9	3	2	2	3	1	2	8	6	8	8	4	1	6
3	3	1	9	0	9	0	5	3	2	3	4	6	3	7	6	9	0	2	9	3	3	6	1	4	0	7
3	3	0	5	2	8	2	9	7	3	2	1	2	6	8	8	8	5	1	3	0	4	7	9	1	7	8
1	4	6	9	2	3	7	3	6	3	3	4	9	5	2	0	7	1	5	1	4	4	2	0	0	5	2
5	4	2	4	6	4	4	6	0	9	8	8	8	7	5	4	6	0	2	0	0	6	8	3	1	5	1
5	0	1	5	0	3	6	5	2	2	6	2	5	1	3	2	2	5	2	1	0	6	5	1	3	4	4
2	0	8	8	4	2	8	5	6	6	1	4	5	3	7	4	2	9	3	4	4	8	4	4	8	6	5
1	4	6	7	4	7	4	2	5	0	2	5	8	9	4	0	8	5	4	9	7	4	6	8	8	2	1
0	0	1	5	9	1	3	3	0	0	6	3	3	6	0	4	4	8	2	6	5	4	2	6	2	3	9
5	1	9	4	6	5	4	0	5	2	3	1	6	5	0	9	1	7	0	9	5	4	5	5	2	7	0
0	6	2	7	2	4	3	7	7	8	9	8	3	2	0	7	9	5	6	5	4	5	4	9	6	0	5
8	5	0	6	2	8	3	5	5	9	9	3	2	1	5	3	1	1	5	0	5	4	2	5	8	3	0
4	4	2	3	0	7	6	4	6	9	8	0	0	0	3	5	5	9	5	3	6	6	2	4	3	9	5
4	3	8	0	5	6	9	8	3	1	4	7	5	9	4	4	2	2	2	4	8	3	8	6	8	8	3
2	5	9	2	7	2	1	9	4	4	7	7	7	4	1	2	0	1	4	2	0	5	2	6	0	2	4
4	0	3	1	5	8	5	0	6	3	7	0	6	3	8	1	5	8	6	0	9	9	9	1	9	7	9
6	7	5	9	9	8	8	3	3	4	0	6	2	1	3	0	0	1	2	9	1	4	9	9	6	3	7
0	8	1	6	4	1	5	5	9	4	5	4	4	6	0	0	7	4	7	3	8	8	7	1	8	5	6

TABLE N2. *Each row shows the digits 0–9 in a random order*

3	7	8	9	0	4	1	6	5	2
3	7	5	4	9	8	2	1	6	0
4	8	3	6	7	5	2	9	0	1
0	9	6	7	3	4	5	1	2	8
1	3	7	0	2	4	6	9	5	8
9	7	4	5	3	8	0	2	6	1
4	8	9	5	1	6	2	7	0	3
8	7	3	5	4	2	1	6	0	9
3	6	1	0	5	4	8	2	7	9
6	1	2	4	8	9	7	0	5	3
9	4	6	2	5	8	0	3	1	7
7	5	8	3	4	9	0	2	1	6
6	5	3	9	0	7	4	1	8	2
2	7	5	3	8	6	1	4	9	0

Tables for statistical tests

TABLE A1. *The normal curve*

The *Mean to z* column shows the proportion of the curve between the value of z and the mean. When z is not zero, an ordinate at z divides the distribution into two unequal parts. The size of the larger part, as a proportion of the whole area under the curve, is shown in the column headed *Larger portion*. The size of the smaller part, as a proportion of the whole area under the curve, is shown in the column headed *Smaller portion*. See Fig. 11.5 in Chapter 11 for a visual explanation.

z	Mean to z	Larger portion	Smaller portion	z	Mean to z	Larger portion	Smaller portion
0.00	0.0000	0.5000	0.5000				
0.01	0.0040	0.5040	0.4960	0.31	0.1217	0.6217	0.3783
0.02	0.0080	0.5080	0.4920	0.32	0.1255	0.6255	0.3745
0.03	0.0120	0.5120	0.4880	0.33	0.1293	0.6293	0.3707
0.04	0.0160	0.5160	0.4840	0.34	0.1331	0.6331	0.3669
0.05	0.0199	0.5199	0.4801	0.35	0.1368	0.6368	0.3632
0.06	0.0239	0.5239	0.4761	0.36	0.1406	0.6406	0.3594
0.07	0.0279	0.5279	0.4721	0.37	0.1443	0.6443	0.3557
0.08	0.0319	0.5319	0.4681	0.38	0.1480	0.6480	0.3520
0.09	0.0359	0.5359	0.4641	0.39	0.1517	0.6517	0.3483
0.10	0.0398	0.5398	0.4602	0.40	0.1554	0.6554	0.3446
0.11	0.0438	0.5438	0.4562	0.41	0.1591	0.6591	0.3409
0.12	0.0478	0.5478	0.4522	0.42	0.1628	0.6628	0.3372
0.13	0.0517	0.5517	0.4483	0.43	0.1664	0.6664	0.3336
0.14	0.0557	0.5557	0.4443	0.44	0.1700	0.6700	0.3300
0.15	0.0596	0.5596	0.4404	0.45	0.1736	0.6736	0.3264
0.16	0.0636	0.5636	0.4364	0.46	0.1772	0.6772	0.3228
0.17	0.0675	0.5675	0.4325	0.47	0.1808	0.6808	0.3192
0.18	0.0714	0.5714	0.4286	0.48	0.1844	0.6844	0.3156
0.19	0.0753	0.5753	0.4247	0.49	0.1879	0.6879	0.3121
0.20	0.0793	0.5793	0.4207	0.50	0.1915	0.6915	0.3085
0.21	0.0832	0.5832	0.4168	0.51	0.1950	0.6950	0.3050
0.22	0.0871	0.5871	0.4129	0.52	0.1985	0.6985	0.3015
0.23	0.0910	0.5910	0.4090	0.53	0.2019	0.7019	0.2981
0.24	0.0948	0.5948	0.4052	0.54	0.2054	0.7054	0.2946
0.25	0.0987	0.5987	0.4013	0.55	0.2088	0.7088	0.2912
0.26	0.1026	0.6026	0.3974	0.56	0.2123	0.7123	0.2877
0.27	0.1064	0.6064	0.3936	0.57	0.2157	0.7157	0.2843
0.28	0.1103	0.6103	0.3897	0.58	0.2190	0.7190	0.2810
0.29	0.1141	0.6141	0.3859	0.59	0.2224	0.7224	0.2776
0.30	0.1179	0.6179	0.3821	0.60	0.2257	0.7257	0.2743

z	Mean to z	Larger portion	Smaller portion	z	Mean to z	Larger portion	Smaller portion
0.61	0.2291	0.7291	0.2709	1.06	0.3554	0.8554	0.1446
0.62	0.2324	0.7324	0.2676	1.07	0.3577	0.8577	0.1423
0.63	0.2357	0.7357	0.2643	1.08	0.3599	0.8599	0.1401
0.64	0.2389	0.7389	0.2611	1.09	0.3621	0.8621	0.1379
0.65	0.2422	0.7422	0.2578	1.10	0.3643	0.8643	0.1357
0.66	0.2454	0.7454	0.2546	1.11	0.3665	0.8665	0.1335
0.67	0.2486	0.7486	0.2514	1.12	0.3686	0.8686	0.1314
0.68	0.2517	0.7517	0.2483	1.13	0.3708	0.8708	0.1292
0.69	0.2549	0.7549	0.2451	1.14	0.3729	0.8729	0.1271
0.70	0.2580	0.7580	0.2420	1.15	0.3749	0.8749	0.1251
0.71	0.2611	0.7611	0.2389	1.16	0.3770	0.8770	0.1230
0.72	0.2642	0.7642	0.2358	1.17	0.3790	0.8790	0.1210
0.73	0.2673	0.7673	0.2327	1.18	0.3810	0.8810	0.1190
0.74	0.2704	0.7704	0.2296	1.19	0.3830	0.8830	0.1170
0.75	0.2734	0.7734	0.2266	1.20	0.3849	0.8849	0.1151
0.76	0.2764	0.7764	0.2236	1.21	0.3869	0.8869	0.1131
0.77	0.2794	0.7794	0.2206	1.22	0.3888	0.8888	0.1112
0.78	0.2823	0.7823	0.2177	1.23	0.3907	0.8907	0.1093
0.79	0.2852	0.7852	0.2148	1.24	0.3925	0.8925	0.1075
0.80	0.2881	0.7881	0.2119	1.25	0.3944	0.8944	0.1056
0.81	0.2910	0.7910	0.2090	1.26	0.3962	0.8962	0.1038
0.82	0.2939	0.7939	0.2061	1.27	0.3980	0.8980	0.1020
0.83	0.2967	0.7967	0.2033	1.28	0.3997	0.8997	0.1003
0.84	0.2995	0.7995	0.2005	1.29	0.4015	0.9015	0.0985
0.85	0.3023	0.8023	0.1977	1.30	0.4032	0.9032	0.0968
0.86	0.3051	0.8051	0.1949	1.31	0.4049	0.9049	0.0951
0.87	0.3078	0.8078	0.1922	1.32	0.4066	0.9066	0.0934
0.88	0.3106	0.8106	0.1894	1.33	0.4082	0.9082	0.0918
0.89	0.3133	0.8133	0.1867	1.34	0.4099	0.9099	0.0901
0.90	0.3159	0.8159	0.1841	1.35	0.4115	0.9115	0.0885
0.91	0.3186	0.8186	0.1814	1.36	0.4131	0.9131	0.0869
0.92	0.3212	0.8212	0.1788	1.37	0.4147	0.9147	0.0853
0.93	0.3238	0.8238	0.1762	1.38	0.4162	0.9162	0.0838
0.94	0.3264	0.8264	0.1736	1.39	0.4177	0.9177	0.0823
0.95	0.3289	0.8289	0.1711	1.40	0.4192	0.9192	0.0808
0.96	0.3315	0.8315	0.1685	1.41	0.4207	0.9207	0.0793
0.97	0.3340	0.8340	0.1660	1.42	0.4222	0.9222	0.0778
0.98	0.3365	0.8365	0.1635	1.43	0.4236	0.9236	0.0764
0.99	0.3389	0.8389	0.1611	1.44	0.4251	0.9251	0.0749
1.00	0.3413	0.8413	0.1587	1.45	0.4265	0.9265	0.0735
1.01	0.3438	0.8438	0.1562	1.46	0.4279	0.9279	0.0721
1.02	0.3461	0.8461	0.1539	1.47	0.4292	0.9292	0.0708
1.03	0.3485	0.8485	0.1515	1.48	0.4306	0.9306	0.0694
1.04	0.3508	0.8508	0.1492	1.49	0.4319	0.9319	0.0681
1.05	0.3531	0.8531	0.1469	1.50	0.4332	0.9332	0.0668

z	Mean to z	Larger portion	Smaller portion	z	Mean to z	Larger portion	Smaller portion
1.51	0.4345	0.9345	0.0655	1.96	0.4750	0.9750	0.0250
1.52	0.4357	0.9357	0.0643	1.97	0.4756	0.9756	0.0244
1.53	0.4370	0.9370	0.0630	1.98	0.4761	0.9761	0.0239
1.54	0.4382	0.9382	0.0618	1.99	0.4767	0.9767	0.0233
1.55	0.4394	0.9394	0.0606	2.00	0.4772	0.9772	0.0228
1.56	0.4406	0.9406	0.0594	2.01	0.4778	0.9778	0.0222
1.57	0.4418	0.9418	0.0582	2.02	0.4783	0.9783	0.0217
1.58	0.4429	0.9429	0.0571	2.03	0.4788	0.9788	0.0212
1.59	0.4441	0.9441	0.0559	2.04	0.4793	0.9793	0.0207
1.60	0.4452	0.9452	0.0548	2.05	0.4798	0.9798	0.0202
1.61	0.4463	0.9463	0.0537	2.06	0.4803	0.9803	0.0197
1.62	0.4474	0.9474	0.0526	2.07	0.4808	0.9808	0.0192
1.63	0.4484	0.9484	0.0516	2.08	0.4812	0.9812	0.0188
1.64	0.4495	0.9495	0.0505	2.09	0.4817	0.9817	0.0183
1.65	0.4505	0.9505	0.0495	2.10	0.4821	0.9821	0.0179
1.66	0.4515	0.9515	0.0485	2.11	0.4826	0.9826	0.0174
1.67	0.4525	0.9525	0.0475	2.12	0.4830	0.9830	0.0170
1.68	0.4535	0.9535	0.0465	2.13	0.4834	0.9834	0.0166
1.69	0.4545	0.9545	0.0455	2.14	0.4838	0.9838	0.0162
1.70	0.4554	0.9554	0.0446	2.15	0.4842	0.9842	0.0158
1.71	0.4564	0.9564	0.0436	2.16	0.4846	0.9846	0.0154
1.72	0.4573	0.9573	0.0427	2.17	0.4850	0.9850	0.0150
1.73	0.4582	0.9582	0.0418	2.18	0.4854	0.9854	0.0146
1.74	0.4591	0.9591	0.0409	2.19	0.4857	0.9857	0.0143
1.75	0.4599	0.9599	0.0401	2.20	0.4861	0.9861	0.0139
1.76	0.4608	0.9608	0.0392	2.21	0.4864	0.9864	0.0136
1.77	0.4616	0.9616	0.0384	2.22	0.4868	0.9868	0.0132
1.78	0.4625	0.9625	0.0375	2.23	0.4871	0.9871	0.0129
1.79	0.4633	0.9633	0.0367	2.24	0.4875	0.9875	0.0125
1.80	0.4641	0.9641	0.0359	2.25	0.4878	0.9878	0.0122
1.81	0.4649	0.9649	0.0351	2.26	0.4881	0.9881	0.0119
1.82	0.4656	0.9656	0.0344	2.27	0.4884	0.9884	0.0116
1.83	0.4664	0.9664	0.0336	2.28	0.4887	0.9887	0.0113
1.84	0.4671	0.9671	0.0329	2.29	0.4890	0.9890	0.0110
1.85	0.4678	0.9678	0.0322	2.30	0.4893	0.9893	0.0107
1.86	0.4686	0.9686	0.0314	2.31	0.4896	0.9896	0.0104
1.87	0.4693	0.9693	0.0307	2.32	0.4898	0.9898	0.0102
1.88	0.4699	0.9699	0.0301	2.33	0.4901	0.9901	0.0099
1.89	0.4706	0.9706	0.0294	2.34	0.4904	0.9904	0.0096
1.90	0.4713	0.9713	0.0287	2.35	0.4906	0.9906	0.0094
1.91	0.4719	0.9719	0.0281	2.36	0.4909	0.9909	0.0091
1.92	0.4726	0.9726	0.0274	2.37	0.4911	0.9911	0.0089
1.93	0.4732	0.9732	0.0268	2.38	0.4913	0.9913	0.0087
1.94	0.4738	0.9738	0.0262	2.39	0.4916	0.9916	0.0084
1.95	0.4744	0.9744	0.0256	2.40	0.4918	0.9918	0.0082

z	Mean to z	Larger portion	Smaller portion	z	Mean to z	Larger portion	Smaller portion
2.41	0.4920	0.9920	0.0080	2.76	0.4971	0.9971	0.0029
2.42	0.4922	0.9922	0.0078	2.77	0.4972	0.9972	0.0028
2.43	0.4925	0.9925	0.0075	2.78	0.4973	0.9973	0.0027
2.44	0.4927	0.9927	0.0073	2.79	0.4974	0.9974	0.0026
2.45	0.4929	0.9929	0.0071	2.80	0.4974	0.9974	0.0026
2.46	0.4931	0.9931	0.0069	2.81	0.4975	0.9975	0.0025
2.47	0.4932	0.9932	0.0068	2.82	0.4976	0.9976	0.0024
2.48	0.4934	0.9934	0.0066	2.83	0.4977	0.9977	0.0023
2.49	0.4936	0.9936	0.0064	2.84	0.4977	0.9977	0.0023
2.50	0.4938	0.9938	0.0062	2.85	0.4978	0.9978	0.0022
2.51	0.4940	0.9940	0.0060	2.86	0.4979	0.9979	0.0021
2.52	0.4941	0.9941	0.0059	2.87	0.4979	0.9979	0.0021
2.53	0.4943	0.9943	0.0057	2.88	0.4980	0.9980	0.0020
2.54	0.4945	0.9945	0.0055	2.89	0.4981	0.9981	0.0019
2.55	0.4946	0.9946	0.0054	2.90	0.4981	0.9981	0.0019
2.56	0.4948	0.9948	0.0052	2.91	0.4982	0.9982	0.0018
2.57	0.4949	0.9949	0.0051	2.92	0.4982	0.9982	0.0018
2.58	0.4951	0.9951	0.0049	2.93	0.4983	0.9983	0.0017
2.59	0.4952	0.9952	0.0048	2.94	0.4984	0.9984	0.0016
2.60	0.4953	0.9953	0.0047	2.95	0.4984	0.9984	0.0016
2.61	0.4955	0.9955	0.0045	2.96	0.4985	0.9985	0.0015
2.62	0.4956	0.9956	0.0044	2.97	0.4985	0.9985	0.0015
2.63	0.4957	0.9957	0.0043	2.98	0.4986	0.9986	0.0014
2.64	0.4959	0.9959	0.0041	2.99	0.4986	0.9986	0.0014
2.65	0.4960	0.9960	0.0040	3.00	0.4987	0.9987	0.0013
2.66	0.4961	0.9961	0.0039	3.25	0.4994	0.9994	0.0006
2.67	0.4962	0.9962	0.0038	3.50	0.4998	0.9998	0.0002
2.68	0.4963	0.9963	0.0037	3.90	0.49995	0.99995	0.00005
2.69	0.4964	0.9964	0.0036				
2.70	0.4965	0.9965	0.0035				
2.71	0.4966	0.9966	0.0034				
2.72	0.4967	0.9967	0.0033				
2.73	0.4968	0.9968	0.0032				
2.74	0.4969	0.9969	0.0031				
2.75	0.4970	0.9970	0.0030				

TABLE A2. *Critical values for Wilcoxon signed ranks test*

To find the critical value of W, check whether you are using a one-tailed (directional) or a two-tailed (non-directional) test and select the column for the level of significance you are using (usually 0.05). Find the row corresponding to N. The critical value of W is shown at the intersection of the column and row. If the calculated value is equal or *less* than the critical value, you can conclude that the difference between the two sets of scores is significant at the probability level of that column.

A dash, –, in the table indicates that no decision can be made at that significance level.

Level of significance for one-tailed (directional) test			Level of significance for one-tailed (directional) test		
	0.05	0.025		0.05	0.025
Level of significance for two-tailed (nondirectional) test			Level of significance for two-tailed (nondirectional) test		
N	0.10	0.05	N	0.10	0.05
5	1	–	31	163	148
6	2	1	32	175	159
7	4	2	33	188	171
8	6	4	34	201	183
9	8	6	35	214	195
10	11	8			
			36	228	208
11	14	11	37	242	222
12	17	14	38	256	235
13	21	17	39	271	250
14	26	21	40	287	264
15	30	25			
			41	303	279
16	36	30	42	319	295
17	41	35	43	336	311
18	47	40	44	353	327
19	54	46	45	371	344
20	60	52			
			46	389	361
21	68	59	47	408	379
22	75	66	48	427	397
23	83	73	49	446	415
24	92	81	50	466	434
25	101	90			
26	110	98			
27	120	107			
28	130	117			
29	141	127			
30	152	137			

TABLE A3. *Critical values for the Mann–Whitney* U *test at the 0.05 level*

To find the critical value of U, check whether you are using a one-tailed (directional) or a two-tailed (nondirectional) test, and select the appropriate table. Find the column corresponding to n for one of the groups and the row corresponding to n for the second group. The critical value of U is shown at the intersection of the column and row. If the calculated value is equal to or *less* than the critical value, you can conclude that the difference between the groups is significant at the probability level of that table.

A dash, –, in the table indicates that no decision can be made at that significance level.

n_2	2	3	4	5	6	7	8	9	10	11	12	13	14	15	16	17	18	19	20
Two-tailed (non-directional) test, p = 0.05																			
2	–	–	–	–	–	–	0	0	0	0	1	1	1	1	1	2	2	2	2
3	–	–	–	0	1	1	2	2	3	3	4	4	5	5	6	6	7	7	8
4	–	–	0	1	2	3	4	4	5	6	7	8	9	10	11	11	12	13	13
5	–	0	1	2	3	5	6	7	8	9	11	12	13	14	15	17	18	19	20
6	–	1	2	3	5	6	8	10	11	13	14	16	17	19	21	22	24	25	27
7	–	1	3	5	6	8	10	12	14	16	18	20	22	24	26	28	30	32	34
8	0	2	4	6	8	10	13	15	17	19	22	24	26	29	31	34	36	38	41
9	0	2	4	7	10	12	15	17	20	23	26	28	31	34	37	39	42	45	48
10	0	3	5	8	11	14	17	20	23	26	29	33	36	39	42	45	48	52	55
11	0	3	6	9	13	16	19	23	26	30	33	37	40	44	47	51	55	58	62
12	1	4	7	11	14	18	22	26	29	33	37	41	45	49	53	57	61	65	69
13	1	4	8	12	16	20	24	28	33	37	41	45	50	54	59	63	67	72	76
14	1	5	9	13	17	22	26	31	36	40	45	50	55	59	64	67	74	78	83
15	1	5	10	14	19	24	29	34	39	44	49	54	59	64	70	75	80	85	90
16	1	6	11	15	21	26	31	37	42	47	53	59	64	70	75	81	86	92	98
17	2	6	11	17	22	28	34	39	45	51	57	63	67	75	81	87	93	99	105
18	2	7	12	18	24	30	36	42	48	55	61	67	74	80	86	93	99	106	112
19	2	7	13	19	25	32	38	45	52	58	65	72	78	85	92	99	106	113	119
20	2	8	13	20	27	34	41	48	55	62	69	76	83	90	98	105	112	119	127
One-tailed (directional) test, p = 0.05																			
2	–	–	–	0	0	0	1	1	1	1	2	2	2	3	3	3	4	4	4
3	–	0	0	1	2	2	3	3	4	5	5	6	7	7	8	9	9	10	11
4	–	0	1	2	3	4	5	6	7	8	9	10	11	12	14	15	16	17	18
5	0	1	2	4	5	6	8	9	11	12	13	15	16	18	19	20	22	23	25
6	0	2	3	5	7	8	10	12	14	16	17	19	21	23	25	26	28	30	32
7	0	2	4	6	8	11	13	15	17	19	21	24	26	28	30	33	35	37	39
8	1	3	5	8	10	13	15	18	20	23	26	28	31	33	36	39	41	44	47
9	1	3	6	9	12	15	18	21	24	27	30	33	36	39	42	45	48	51	54
10	1	4	7	11	14	17	20	24	27	31	34	37	41	44	48	51	55	58	62
11	1	5	8	12	16	19	23	27	31	34	38	42	46	50	54	57	61	65	69
12	2	5	9	13	17	21	26	30	34	38	42	47	51	55	60	64	68	72	77
13	2	6	10	15	19	24	28	33	37	42	47	51	56	61	65	70	75	80	84
14	2	7	11	16	21	26	31	36	41	46	51	56	61	66	71	77	82	87	92
15	3	7	12	18	23	28	33	39	44	50	55	61	66	72	77	83	88	94	100
16	3	8	14	19	25	30	36	42	48	54	60	65	71	77	83	89	95	101	107
17	3	9	15	20	26	33	39	45	51	57	64	70	77	83	89	96	102	109	115
18	4	9	16	22	28	35	41	48	55	61	68	75	82	88	95	102	109	116	123
19	4	10	17	23	30	37	44	51	58	65	72	80	87	94	101	109	116	123	130
20	4	11	18	25	32	39	47	54	62	69	77	84	92	100	107	115	123	130	138

TABLE A4. *Critical values for chi-square*

Find the column for the probability level you are using (usually 0.05) and the row for the degrees of freedom you have calculated. The table entry at the intersection of this column and row is the critical value. If the calculated value is *larger* than the critical value, you can conclude chi-square is significant at the probability level of that column.

Level of significance for one-tailed (directional) test				Level of significance for one-tailed (directional) test		
	0.05	0.025	0.005		0.05	0.025	0.005
Level of significance for two-tailed (nondirectional) test				Level of significance for two-tailed (nondirectional) test		
d.f.	0.10	0.05	0.01	d.f.	0.10	0.05	0.01
1	2.71	3.84	6.64	16	23.54	26.30	32.00
2	4.60	5.99	9.21	17	24.77	27.59	33.41
3	6.25	7.82	11.34	18	25.99	28.87	34.80
4	7.78	9.49	13.28	19	27.20	30.14	36.19
5	9.24	11.07	15.09	20	28.41	31.41	37.57
6	10.64	12.59	16.81	21	29.62	32.67	38.93
7	12.02	14.07	18.48	22	30.81	33.92	40.29
8	13.36	15.51	20.09	23	32.01	35.17	41.64
9	14.68	16.92	21.67	24	33.20	36.42	42.98
10	15.99	18.31	23.21	25	34.38	37.65	44.31
11	17.28	19.68	24.72	26	35.56	38.88	45.64
12	18.55	21.03	26.22	27	36.74	40.11	46.97
13	19.81	22.36	27.69	28	37.92	41.34	48.28
14	21.06	23.68	29.14	29	39.09	42.56	49.59
15	22.31	25.00	30.58	30	40.26	43.77	50.89

TABLE A5. *Critical values for Page's* L *trend test: within subjects designs*

To find the critical value of L, find the column corresponding to the number of conditions (c) and the row corresponding to N. The critical value is shown at the intersection of the column and row. If the calculated value is equal to or *larger* than the critical value, you can conclude that the trend is in the predicted direction at the 0.05 (5%) level.

	c		
N	3	4	5
2	28	58	103
3	41	84	150
4	54	111	197
5	66	137	244
6	79	163	291
7	91	189	338
8	104	214	384
9	116	240	431
10	128	266	477
11	141	292	523
12	153	317	570

TABLE A6. *Critical values for Jonckheere's trend test: between-subjects designs*

To find the critical value of S, find the column corresponding to the number of conditions (c) and the row corresponding to n. The critical value is shown at the intersection of the column and row. If the calculated value is equal to or *larger* than the critical value, you can conclude that the trend is in the predicted direction at the 0.05 (5%) level.

	c			
n	3	4	5	6
2	10	14	20	26
3	17	26	34	44
4	24	38	51	67
5	33	51	71	93
6	42	66	92	121
7	53	82	115	151
8	64	100	140	184
9	76	118	166	219
10	88	138	194	256

TABLE A7. *Critical values for* t

To find the critical value of *t*, check whether you are using a one-tailed (directional) or a two-tailed (nondirectional) test and select the column for the level of significance you are using (usually 0.05). Find the row corresponding to the degrees of freedom (d.f.). The critical value of *t* is shown at the intersection of the column and row. If the absolute (positive) value of *t* you calculated is *larger* than the critical value, you can conclude that the difference between the two means is significant at the probability level of that column.

If the degrees of freedom you have are not shown, use the row for the nearest lower degrees of freedom. For example, if your d.f. = 32, use the row for d.f. = 30.

Level of significance for one-tailed (directional) test

d.f.	0.05	0.025	0.01	0.005	0.0005
	0.10	0.05	0.02	0.01	0.001
1	6.314	12.706	31.821	63.657	636.619
2	2.920	4.303	6.965	9.925	31.598
3	2.353	3.182	4.541	5.841	12.941
4	2.132	2.776	3.747	4.604	8.610
5	2.015	2.571	3.365	4.032	6.859
6	1.943	2.447	3.143	3.707	5.959
7	1.895	2.365	2.998	3.499	5.405
8	1.860	2.306	2.896	3.355	5.041
9	1.833	2.262	2.821	3.250	4.781
10	1.812	2.228	2.764	3.169	4.587
11	1.796	2.201	2.718	3.106	4.437
12	1.782	2.179	2.681	3.055	4.318
13	1.771	2.160	2.650	3.012	4.221
14	1.761	2.145	2.624	2.977	4.140
15	1.753	2.131	2.602	2.947	4.073
16	1.746	2.120	2.583	2.921	4.015
17	1.740	2.110	2.567	2.898	3.965
18	1.734	2.101	2.552	2.878	3.922
19	1.729	2.093	2.539	2.861	3.883
20	1.725	2.086	2.528	2.845	3.850
21	1.721	2.080	2.518	2.831	3.819
22	1.717	2.074	2.508	2.819	3.792
23	1.714	2.069	2.500	2.807	3.767
24	1.711	2.064	2.492	2.797	3.745
25	1.708	2.060	2.485	2.787	3.725
26	1.706	2.056	2.479	2.779	3.707
27	1.703	2.052	2.473	2.771	3.690
28	1.701	2.048	2.467	2.763	3.674
29	1.699	2.045	2.462	2.756	3.659
30	1.697	2.042	2.457	2.750	3.646
40	1.684	2.021	2.423	2.704	3.551
60	1.671	2.000	2.390	2.660	3.460
120	1.658	1.980	2.358	2.617	3.373
∞	1.645	1.960	2.326	2.576	3.291

Level of significance for two-tailed (nondirectional) test

TABLE A8. *Critical values for* F

To find the critical value of F, select the table for the level of significance you are using (0.05 or 0.01). Find the column corresponding to the degrees of freedom (d.f.$_1$) for the numerator and the row corresponding to the degrees of freedom (d.f.$_2$) for the denominator. The critical value of F is shown at the intersection of the column and row. If the calculated value is *larger* than the critical value, you can conclude that the difference between the means is significant at the probability level of that table.

If the degrees of freedom you have are not shown, use the row for the nearest lower degrees of freedom. For example, if your d.f. = 32, use the row for d.f. = 30.

Critical values at the 0.05 (5%) level

d.f.$_2$	1	2	3	4	5	6	7	8	9	10	15	20	30	40
1	161.4	199.5	215.7	224.6	230.2	234.0	236.8	238.9	240.5	241.9	245.9	248.0	250.1	251.18
2	18.51	19.00	19.16	19.20	19.30	19.30	19.40	19.40	19.38	19.40	19.43	19.45	19.46	19.47
3	10.13	9.55	9.28	9.12	9.01	8.94	8.89	8.85	8.81	8.79	8.70	8.66	8.62	8.59
4	7.71	6.94	6.59	6.39	6.26	6.16	6.09	6.04	6.00	5.96	5.86	5.80	5.75	5.72
5	6.61	5.79	5.41	5.19	5.05	4.95	4.88	4.82	4.77	4.74	4.62	4.56	4.50	4.46
6	5.99	5.14	4.76	4.53	4.39	4.28	4.21	4.15	4.10	4.06	3.94	3.87	3.81	3.77
7	5.59	4.74	4.35	4.12	3.97	3.87	3.79	3.73	3.68	3.64	3.51	3.44	3.38	3.34
8	5.32	4.46	4.07	3.84	3.69	3.58	3.50	3.44	3.39	3.35	3.22	3.15	3.08	3.04
9	5.12	4.26	3.86	3.63	3.48	3.37	3.29	3.23	3.18	3.14	3.01	2.94	2.86	2.83
10	4.96	4.10	3.71	3.48	3.33	3.22	3.14	3.07	3.02	2.98	2.85	2.77	2.70	2.66
11	4.84	3.98	3.59	3.36	3.20	3.09	3.01	2.95	2.90	2.85	2.72	2.65	2.57	2.53
12	4.75	3.89	3.49	3.26	3.11	3.00	2.91	2.85	2.80	2.75	2.62	2.54	2.47	2.43
13	4.67	3.81	3.41	3.18	3.03	2.92	2.83	2.77	2.71	2.67	2.53	2.46	2.38	2.34
14	4.60	3.74	3.34	3.11	2.96	2.85	2.76	2.70	2.65	2.60	2.46	2.39	2.31	2.27
15	4.54	3.68	3.29	3.06	2.90	2.79	2.71	2.64	2.59	2.54	2.40	2.33	2.25	2.20
16	4.49	3.63	3.24	3.01	2.85	2.74	2.66	2.59	2.54	2.49	2.35	2.28	2.19	2.15
17	4.45	3.59	3.20	2.96	2.81	2.70	2.61	2.55	2.49	2.45	2.31	2.23	2.15	2.10
18	4.41	3.55	3.16	2.93	2.77	2.66	2.58	2.51	2.46	2.41	2.27	2.19	2.11	2.06
19	4.38	3.52	3.13	2.90	2.74	2.63	2.54	2.48	2.42	2.38	2.23	2.16	2.07	2.03
20	4.35	3.49	3.10	2.87	2.71	2.60	2.51	2.45	2.39	2.35	2.20	2.12	2.04	1.99
21	4.32	3.47	3.07	2.84	2.68	2.57	2.49	2.42	2.37	2.32	2.18	2.10	2.01	1.96
22	4.30	3.44	3.05	2.82	2.66	2.55	2.46	2.40	2.34	2.30	2.15	2.07	1.98	1.94
23	4.28	3.42	3.03	2.80	2.64	2.53	2.44	2.37	2.32	2.27	2.13	2.05	1.96	1.91
24	4.26	3.40	3.01	2.78	2.62	2.51	2.42	2.36	2.30	2.25	2.11	2.03	1.94	1.89
25	4.24	3.39	2.99	2.76	2.60	2.49	2.40	2.34	2.28	2.24	2.09	2.01	1.92	1.87
30	4.17	3.32	2.92	2.69	2.53	2.42	2.33	2.27	2.21	2.16	2.01	1.93	1.84	1.79
40	4.08	3.23	2.84	2.61	2.45	2.34	2.25	2.18	2.12	2.08	1.92	1.84	1.74	1.69
60	4.00	3.15	2.76	2.53	2.37	2.25	2.17	2.10	2.04	1.99	1.84	1.75	1.65	1.59
120	3.92	3.07	2.68	2.45	2.29	2.18	2.09	2.02	1.96	1.91	1.75	1.66	1.55	1.50

Critical values at the 0.01 (1%) level

d.f.$_2$	1	2	3	4	5	6	7	8	9	10	15	20	30	40
1	4052	5000	5403	5625	5764	5859	5928	5982	6022	6056	6157	6209	6261	6287
2	98.50	99.01	99.17	99.25	99.30	99.33	99.36	99.37	99.39	99.40	99.43	99.45	99.47	99.47
3	34.12	30.82	29.46	28.71	28.24	27.91	27.67	27.49	27.34	27.23	26.87	26.69	26.51	26.41
4	21.20	18.00	16.69	15.98	15.52	15.21	14.98	14.80	14.66	14.55	14.20	14.02	13.84	13.75
5	16.26	13.27	12.06	11.39	10.97	10.67	10.46	10.29	10.16	10.05	9.72	9.55	9.38	9.29
6	13.74	10.92	9.78	9.15	8.75	8.47	8.26	8.10	7.98	7.87	7.56	7.40	7.23	7.14
7	12.25	9.55	8.45	7.85	7.46	7.19	6.99	6.84	6.72	6.62	6.31	6.16	5.99	5.91
8	11.26	8.65	7.59	7.01	6.63	6.37	6.18	6.03	5.91	5.81	5.52	5.36	5.20	5.12
9	10.56	8.02	6.99	6.42	6.06	5.80	5.61	5.47	5.35	5.26	4.96	4.81	4.65	4.57
10	10.04	7.56	6.55	5.99	5.64	5.39	5.20	5.06	4.94	4.85	4.56	4.41	4.25	4.17
11	9.65	7.21	6.22	5.67	5.32	5.07	4.89	4.74	4.63	4.54	4.25	4.10	3.94	3.86
12	9.33	6.93	5.95	5.41	5.06	4.82	4.64	4.50	4.39	4.30	4.01	3.86	3.70	3.62
13	9.07	6.70	5.74	5.21	4.86	4.62	4.44	4.30	4.19	4.10	3.82	3.66	3.51	3.43
14	8.86	6.51	5.56	5.04	4.70	4.46	4.28	4.14	4.03	3.94	3.66	3.51	3.35	3.27
15	8.68	6.36	5.42	4.89	4.56	4.32	4.14	4.00	3.89	3.80	3.52	3.37	3.21	3.13
16	8.53	6.23	5.29	4.77	4.44	4.20	4.03	3.89	3.78	3.69	3.41	3.26	3.10	3.02
17	8.40	6.11	5.18	4.67	4.34	4.10	3.93	3.79	3.68	3.59	3.31	3.16	3.00	2.92
18	8.29	6.01	5.09	4.58	4.25	4.01	3.84	3.71	3.60	3.51	3.23	3.08	2.92	2.84
19	8.18	5.93	5.01	4.50	4.17	3.94	3.77	3.63	3.52	3.43	3.15	3.00	2.84	2.76
20	8.10	5.85	4.94	4.43	4.10	3.87	3.70	3.56	3.46	3.37	3.09	2.94	2.78	2.69
21	8.02	5.78	4.87	4.37	4.04	3.81	3.64	3.51	3.40	3.31	3.03	2.88	2.72	2.64
22	7.95	5.72	4.82	4.31	3.99	3.76	3.59	3.45	3.35	3.26	2.98	2.83	2.67	2.58
23	7.88	5.66	4.76	4.26	3.94	3.71	3.54	3.41	3.30	3.21	2.93	2.78	2.62	2.54
24	7.82	5.61	4.72	4.22	3.90	3.67	3.50	3.36	3.26	3.17	2.89	2.74	2.58	2.49
25	7.77	5.57	4.68	4.18	3.86	3.63	3.46	3.32	3.22	3.13	2.85	2.70	2.54	2.45
30	7.56	5.39	4.51	4.02	3.70	3.47	3.30	3.17	3.07	2.98	2.70	2.55	2.39	2.30
40	7.31	5.18	4.31	3.83	3.51	3.29	3.12	2.99	2.89	2.80	2.52	2.37	2.20	2.11
60	7.08	4.98	4.13	3.65	3.34	3.12	2.95	2.82	2.72	2.63	2.35	2.20	2.03	1.94
120	6.85	4.79	3.95	3.48	3.17	2.96	2.79	2.66	2.56	2.47	2.19	2.03	1.86	1.76

d.f.$_1$

Answers to SAQs

SAQ 1.1

An operational definition means that you specify the empirical observations you will use to measure some entity. The definition of short-term memory is not an operational definition, since it does not say how it will be measured. Definition 2 is also not an operational definition, but number 3 is, since it specifies achieving orientation in terms of specified observations (a total score). Definition 4 is not operational, as it includes no specification of how conservatism is measured. Definitions 5 and 6 are both operational definitions, since they define conservatism in terms of empirical observations (scores). Note that although 5 and 6 are both operational definitions, they are defining conservatism in different ways: one uses scores on one questionnaire while the other uses scores on a different questionnaire. This illustrates the fact that one underlying hypothetical construct can be given different operational definitions.

SAQ 1.2

In asserting that McManus *et al.* are wrong when stating her theory and that her theory does not include the misunderstanding which McManus *et al.* alleged, Annett is using the first counterattack strategy, claiming that the critics misunderstood the theory they attacked. She also demonstrates the second type of counterattack, criticizing McManus *et al.*'s research as flawed (because it used small groups of very able people, groups were formed on the basis of an inappropriate pre-test, and left-handers were omitted).

SAQ 3.1

(1) There are two variables – modality of presentation (vision or audition), and length of warning period – so the expression must include two digits. As there are two modalities, this factor has two levels and is represented by a 2. There are four lengths of warning period, so this variable has four levels and is represented by a 4, giving the expression 4×2 (or 2×4).

(2) There are three factors; sex of participant and sex of face shown each has two levels and the other (age of face shown) has three levels. So the experiment

would be represented as: $2 \times 2 \times 3$. (The order is unimportant, so you could have $2 \times 3 \times 2$ or $3 \times 2 \times 2$.)

SAQ 3.2

No. The respondents' confusion was not a confounding variable since it presumably occurred under both conditions, whether familiar or unfamiliar faces were shown. Certainly it is an extraneous variable, which you would wish to eliminate because it is likely to cause participants' scores to vary in an uncontrolled way and lower the sensitivity of the experiment. But it is not a confounding variable.

SAQ 3.3

The experiment described in Box 3.1 used a control group so that the effects of training in memory for faces could be separated out from any other changes in performance between the first and second memory tests. The final sentence in Box 3.1 points out that by using a control group Morris *et al.* were able to argue that the effects found with the experimental group were not just due to practice: the control group had also had the practice, but did not improve as much.

SAQ 3.4

(1) The difference between names and occupations differs only slightly according to the three levels of the 'sharing' variable, being -0.1, +0.6 amd -0.6. This suggests that there was no interaction between the two variables. A graph of the figures will show the two lines for names and occupations are close to each other and close to being parallel. Statistical analysis confirmed that there was no significant interaction in these data.

(2) In the second experiment, the difference between names and occupations varies from -3.4 to -1.2 to +0.5, suggesting that there was an interaction: the effect of the name/occupation variable depended on the level of the 'sharing' variable. Again, a plot of the figures will bring this out. Bruce *et al.* report that when the statistical significance of the interaction was tested using the analysis of variance, it was not significant ($p = 0.069$). This illustrates the need not to rely simply on eyeball inspection in deciding whether there was an interaction.

SAQ 3.5

(1) The information provided does not really allow you to decide whether this was a true experiment, since it does not say how the participants were allocated to the two types of warning condition. If they were allocated by a random procedure, the study was a true experiment, with one independent variable having two levels (the two types of warning).

(2) This was not a true experiment, as the three groups of people observed were not equated beforehand. The study resembles an experiment with two experimental and one control group, but it was a quasi-experiment.

(3) Bednall's study was a true 2×2 experiment, with both variables being within-subjects.

SAQ 4.1

The sampling strategy used by Parker *et al.* was quota sampling. Initially they specified that they wanted 200 respondents from each of four geographical areas, 160 from each of the five age groups, and equal numbers of men and women. This would give 20 of each sex in each age group from each geographical area. (The actual number interviewed was 881, as the specified quota was exceeded in some areas.) Although the respondents were stratified by age, the study did not use stratified sampling as defined in the text since there was no random sampling within the strata.

SAQ 4.2

A problem like this lends itself to a variety of methods of investigation. You might conduct a survey of the awareness of drivers of lorries and buses: do they know how high their vehicles are? Low bridges have warning signs on them, and you might investigate how successful these are using an observational study, or compare different types of warning sign using a field experiment. For example, would flashing lights make the sign more noticeable? Would a flexible bar suspended across the road before the bridge itself reduce accidents? Case studies of these accidents would probably be the starting point of any research programme.

SAQ 5.1

Ethologists observe animal behaviour and try to understand the functions of those behaviours. The term 'ethogenics' was coined to take into account the fact that human beings use language, and all of their behaviour has meaning for them and others. To understand activities ethogenically, we have to get 'inside' the meanings that are important rather than behave as if we were 'neutral' observers.

SAQ 5.2

The 'dramaturgical' metaphor focuses on the ways in which 'acts' are played out by people for others, and the ways in which they are understood as part of the scene. 'Acts' are the result of meaning that is given to 'actions' and simple 'movements' for a real or imaginary audience, and the dramaturgical metaphor sees this meaning as organized 'as if' people were on a stage trying to impress others.

SAQ 5.3

Gilbert and Mulkay (1984) would expect your first, 'objective' account to draw upon the 'empiricist' repertoire, and your second account to draw upon a 'contingent' repertoire. Empiricism is concerned with the ways in which knowledge is obtained only through observation, but Gilbert and Mulkay demonstrated that many scientists draw upon many intuitive ('contingent') factors to explain what they were doing. You may not have been able to screen all of these out in your first account, and discourse analysts would look for contradictions in your account where different ways of speaking find their way into what you say and write.

SAQ 6.1

One answer is to give people a fixed time to read the text and measure their scores on a comprehension test. Performance will be affected by the amount of understanding of the text and by reading speed; fast readers may have read the passage twice in the time allowed, while slower readers may not have read it through once. This is a commonly used procedure but it still leaves you uncertain how far variations in reading speed are influencing the scores. It would be better to have a method of testing reading performance which more clearly reflects both speed of reading and comprehension. Poulton (1969) gave people texts to read which were followed by comprehension items. 'There were 10 open-ended questions on each passage.... The 10 questions were spread evenly over the text, so that a person who had read 80% of the passage would be able to attempt 80% of the questions' (p. 245). So performance on the items would depend on how fast people had read and on how well they had understood the passage. Poulton's technique seems to answer the problem, but has not been widely copied.

SAQ 6.2

There are four main problems. (1) How you score partially correct items. If, for example, the original text said 'The island is 50 miles long' and the person recalled it as 'The island is 40 miles long', does this count as correct, partially correct or wrong? What if the recall was 'The isthmus was 50 miles wide'? (2) What do you do if the person 'recalls' information that was not present in the original message (importations)? Should you subtract points when this happens? (3) Should different parts of the original count for more points because they are more important? (4) How can you check on the reliability of the scoring, so that you know that two different scorers give the same score to one recall protocol? The answer here is to have different markers scoring the responses and then compare their marks. To deal with these problems you need a list of the points that were contained in the original text and an explicit set of rules about what counts as right, wrong, and partially right, plus explicit conventions about how many marks each is to be awarded. As you mark a set of protocols, keep a record of those which have been given full and part marks so that future cases are marked to the same standard.

An example of this approach is provided by Furnham *et al.* (1990, experiment 1), who compared people's ability to recall the content of a science programme which was presented as a five-minute film, as a sound broadcast only, or as a transcript to be read. Afterwards, respondents were given six minutes to write down all they could remember (free recall), and they were also given a set of 24 questions to answer (cued recall). The answers to each of the questions was scored 2 for completely correct and 1 for partially correct. 'The free recall section was scored using the same basic points from the cued recall section' (p. 206).

SAQ 6.3

Although many students think psychophysics is dull and irrelevant to real life, we are continually making judgements about the relative magnitude of different things (and different people) and these often involve some type of magnitude estimation. Here are a few examples. (1) Attractiveness of people: if Marilyn Munroe is 100, on the same scale how many points do you or your partner score? (2) Prestige of occupations: if the job of being a nurse has a prestige of 10, what on the same scale is the prestige of a Member of Parliament? (3) Subjective value of prizes: suppose you won a lottery prize of £100 which gave you a certain amount of happiness. How much would you need to win to double your happiness? Most people do not say £200; the subjective value of money depends on how much you have, so that an increase from zero to £100 is worth much more than an increase from £100 to £200. Stevens' comments on the seriousness of theft being related to the amount stolen by an exponent of 0.17 makes the same point in a different way.

SAQ 7.1

Ms Brown is a technical supervisor in a public sector organization, and so the relevant norms are those from sample X in the table. For sample X, a raw score of 13 corresponds to a percentile of 20, so Ms Brown has scored at the 20th percentile compared with her peers. Observe that if you used the wrong sample to compare her with, and had incorrectly referred to the column for sample W, you would have given Ms Brown a percentile score of 5. This emphasizes the need to be absolutely accurate when using test manuals.

SAQ 7.2

Basically reliability and validity are concerned with two quite separate aspects of a test. A test might show stability when people take it on a number of occasions, have clear marking criteria so that different markers give the same score to a particular set of responses, be structured so that all items correlate together, and yet not measure what it claims. For example, graphology tests claim to assess personality by examining people's handwriting. It is possible that people have a consistent handwriting style, so that their responses are consistent over time, and it is possible that different graphologists agree on how the features of handwriting should be scored. Similarly, it is possible that the various items, the scoring of the way the various letters are written, correlate. But to establish validity you would need to demonstrate that the graphological scores relate to some true index of personality. If they fail to do so, you would conclude that the graphological tests is a reliable test of something, but you do not know what: you would then have to discover what it was that the scores did correlate with. In fact, the evidence suggests that while handwriting characteristics are stable, inter-marker reliability is questionable (Klimoski and Rafaeli, 1983). When graphological analyses are correlated with personality test scores, the data are equivocal according to Klimoski and Rafaeli (1983), although there is evidence that university teachers, who are presumably untrained in the techniques of graphology, can tell the sex of the writer from handwriting (Eames and Loewenthal, 1990).

SAQ 8.1

As was explained in Chapter 7, there are different types of validity. The aim of an attitude scale is to distinguish between those who are for and against the topic, so that concurrent validity is needed. To establish concurrent validity you correlate the responses on the scale with some 'true' measure of the person's attitude to the topic, known as the criterion.

You might ask people for a simple 'global' judgement: are they generally in favour of the scale topic or not? Give the final set of items to a fresh set of respondents, and also ask them to indicate whether they are generally in favour or opposed to the topic of the scale. Calculate the scores of each respondent, and compare those who said they were in favour with those who said they were against. You expect a statistically significant difference between the two sets of scores. (How to do the statistical testing is explained in Chapter 11. Attitude scale scores are usually treated as interval scores and parametric tests such as the *t*-test are used.) This may seem rather fruitless: why develop the scale at all if self-assignment is the basis for validation? The answer is that the scale will allow you to obtain more precise measures of the strength of people's attitude and let you differentiate between those who all describe themselves as 'for' or 'against'.

SAQ 8.2

You will almost certainly find that even though you tried to follow the advice given in Box 8.1 your respondents can point out some difficulties in understanding exactly what you meant. If you are using questionnaires in a research project, you should go through at least one pilot stage like this, and often need to do it twice.

SAQ 8.3

A record of one's slips and lapses can be a useful source of information, but of course you then need to have some method of categorizing the data. The list of events may itself suggest a category system which helps you organize the events into types. You could use the diary record to see whether you make more slips and lapses at certain times of the day, or whether there seems to be some consistent pattern of 'trigger' events. If you keep a diary you will amost certainly find that slips and lapses are more common than you anticipated!

SAQ 8.4

When you are planning to use any technique, you should always try it out on yourself first if at all possible. You will then be able to appreciate any difficulties that arise. In this case, you may appreciate how hard it is for people to verbalize as they think, and why they may claim that it prevents them thinking in their normal way. When you have obtained protocols from one or two respondents, you will have to apply some method of analysing them by creating a coding scheme which lets you sort parts of the protocol into categories in a consistent and useful way. The scheme will develop from the protocols themselves, but the process of creating it will give you an insight into the problems of ensuring that it is comprehensive and reliable.

SAQ 9.1

An experience of conducting an observational study will demonstrate that it is by no means as simple a technique as one might imagine. Deciding what to record and what to ignore is always difficult, and you may find at the end that you made a wrong decision and left out an aspect of behaviour that now seems important or that it proved impossible to record all that you had planned. This emphasizes the value of conducting a pilot study on one or two cases before you make a final decision on how to proceed for the main study. If you are able to calculate the reliability of two observers, their disagreements can be instructive: what were the causes of disagreement? How could they be avoided in future?

SAQ 11.1

Group A: noise		Group B: music		Group C: silence	
S1	8	S9	14	S17	22
S2	9	S10	9	S18	21
S3	10	S11	3	S19	15
S4	13	S12	25	S20	20
S5	15	S13	8	S21	26
S6	18	S14	16	S22	28
S7	22	S15	18	S23	17
S8	25	S16	27	S24	19

Median: 14   Median: 15   Median: 20.5

Σx: 120 Σx: 120 Σx: 168
$\bar{x}$: 15.00 $\bar{x}$: 15.00 $\bar{x}$: 21.00

SAQ 11.2

Group B: music	x	$(x-\bar{x})$	$(x-\bar{x})^2$
S9	14	-1	1
S10	9	-6	36
S11	3	-12	144
S12	25	10	100
S13	8	-7	49
S14	16	1	1
S15	18	3	9
S16	27	12	144

Σx: 120 $\Sigma(x-\bar{x})$: 0 $\Sigma(x-\bar{x})^2$: 484
$\bar{x}$: 15 $\Sigma(x-\bar{x})^2/n$: 60.5
$\Sigma(x-\bar{x})^2/(n-1)$: 69.14

SAQ 11.3

Using formula (c), the standard deviation for the data for group C in Table 11.2 is 4.34. It is calculated like this: $\Sigma x^2 = 3660$, $(\Sigma x)^2 = 168^2 = 28224$, $(\Sigma x)^2/n = 28224/8 = 3528$.

$\Sigma x^2 - (\Sigma x)^2/n = 132$. $(n - 1) = 7$ so $(\Sigma x^2 - (\Sigma x)^2/n) / (n-1) = 132/7 = 18.86$. The square root of $18.86 = 4.34$.

SAQ 11.4

(1) Hand breadth of 80 mm is 1 s.d. below the mean. The proportion falling below this, the smaller portion of the distribution according to the table of z, is 15.87%.

(2) An IQ of 85 is 1 s.d. below the mean. The proportion of the curve between the mean and 1 s.d. below is 34.13%. An IQ of 115 is 1 s.d. above the mean, and the proportion of the curve between the mean and +1 s.d. is also 34.13%. So the proportion between 85 and 115 is 34.13 + 34.13 = 68.26%.

SAQ 11.5

(1) As Jones predicted that the group would behave more aggressively after viewing the film, this is a directional hypothesis.

(2) Since Klein predicted that the conditions would yield different scores, but not which one would score higher, this is a non-directional hypothesis.

(3) Dobbs predicted the direction of attitude change, that it would increase, so this is a directional hypothesis.

SAQ 11.6

(1) Franks was testing for a difference between scores, using a parametric test. There were two sets of scores, and the respondents were the same people in both conditions. So a related t-test is appropriate.

(2) Larkins is testing for a difference. As the set of data is skewed, a non-parametric test is needed. There are three groups of different respondents, so a Kruskal–Wallis test is appropriate.

(3) Myers is testing for a difference, and decided to use a parametric test. There are two sets of data, from different respondents. So an independent t-test is appropriate.

(4) Oliver was testing for a difference, and using a non-parametric test. There were three conditions and so three sets of scores. The same people appeared in each condition, as it was a within-subjects experiment. So the Friedman test is appropriate.

(5) This is a less straightforward situation. You might think that Ross is looking for a difference between the groups with and without alcohol. But imagine what the results table looks like. The participants are divided into an alcohol group and a no-alcohol group, and the number of people scoring eight or more errors and the number scoring less than eight errors are reported. So we have a frequency table like this:

Condition	Number of errors in 15 minutes	
	More than 8	*Less than 8*
Alcohol	20	5
No alcohol	7	18

Tabulated like this, you can see that Ross has frequency data, has categorized respondents into two sets, and is looking for an association between the alcohol/ no-alcohol variable and number of errors. As the data consist of frequencies, a nonparametric measure of association is needed. The data are frequencies, and there is more than one set. So the chi-square is appropriate here.

(6) Evans was looking for a relationship using a parametric measure. There were two sets of ratings, so a Pearson correlation is appropriate.

(7) Young is looking for a difference in the two sets of ratings, and uses a parametric test. As the same observers were used to rate the group of children on both occasions, a related t-test is appropriate.

Questions (6) and (7) show that different types of test are appropriate even when the procedure of the studies are similar. In (6), Evans was looking at a possible relationship – did those who were rated as aggressive before also get high aggressiveness ratings afterwards? So a correlation is needed. But in (7), Young wanted to know whether there was a difference between the scores on the two occasions, so a t-test (with a directional hypothesis) is the one to use.

SAQ 11.7

	n_1	n_2	t	$d.f.$	p
a Between-subjects design	8	8	2.86	14	<0.05
b Between-subjects design	50	52	1.15	100	>0.05 (NS)
c Between-subjects design	17	8	4.09	23	<0.05
d Within-subjects design	9	9	1.51	8	>0.05 (NS)
e Within-subjects design	11	11	2.51	10	<0.05

Remember that $p>0.05$ means the result was not significant.

SAQ 12.1

Unlike many questions and answers in quantitative psychology, there is no one right answer to this task. It would be helpful, though, to look at your list of reasons, and to see how many of these concern the rights or feelings of the interviewee. There would be something wrong, and you should think again, if all you are doing is a result of idle curiosity, or even if it is only that you are fascinated by the topic. A useful further exercise at this point is to identify points in your list that are to do with (1) the benefits to the interviewee, (2) the benefits to someone who reads your report, and (3) the benefits to someone who tries to change things as a result of reading your report.

SAQ 12.2

A 'semi-structured' interview format would be most useful because it would be focused enough to ensure that the topics were covered in the interview and flexible enough for the interviewee's own thoughts on the topic to be picked up. A 'structured' interview schedule would force the interviewee to fit responses into your assumptions (and you may as well give a questionnaire), and an 'unstructured' interview is a misnomer for a free-flowing conversation in which not only is the purpose of the investigation forgotten but which also obscures the way an agenda is always structured by the person with power (which in this case is likely to be you, in your position as researcher).

References

ALAM, S., LUCCIO, R. and VARDABASSO, F. (1986) Regularity, exposure time and perception of numerosity. *Perceptual and Motor Skills, 63,* 883–888.

ALLPORT, G. (1962) The general and the unique in psychological science. *Journal of Personality, 30,* 405–422.

ANNETT, M. (1993) Rejoinder to 'Annett's theory' by McManus, Shergill and Bryden (1993). *British Journal of Psychology, 84,* 539–544.

ARMISTEAD, N. (Ed.) (1974) *Reconstructing Social Psychology.* Harmondsworth: Penguin.

ARONSON, E., ELLSWORTH, P.C., CARLSMITH J.M. and GONZALES, M.H. (1990) *Methods of Research in Social Psychology,* 2nd ed. New York: McGraw Hill.

ATKINSON, J. M. and HERITAGE, J. C. (Eds) (1984) *Structures of Social Action: Studies in Conversation Analysis.* Cambridge: Cambridge University Press.

BADDELEY, A. (1976) *The Psychology of Memory.* London: Harper and Row.

BADDELEY, A. (1990) *Human Memory: Theory and Practice.* Hove: Erlbaum.

BADDELEY, A., LEWIS, V. and VALLAR, G. (1984) Exploring the articulatory loop. *Quarterly Journal of Experimental Psychology, 36(A),* 233–252.

BADDELEY, A. and WOODHEAD, M. (1982) Depth of processing, context, and face recognition. *Canadian Journal of Psychology, 36,* 148–164.

BALES, R. F. (1950) A set of categories for analysis of small group interaction. *American Sociological Review, 15,* 257–263.

BANISTER, P., BURMAN, E., PARKER, I., TAYLOR, M. and TINDALL, C. (1994) *Qualitative Methods in Psychology: A Research Guide.* Milton Keynes: Open University Press.

BANNISTER, D. and FRANSELLA, F. (1989) *Inquiring Man,* 3rd ed. London: Croom Helm.

BEDNALL, E. S. (1992) The effect of screen format on visual list search. Ergonomics, 35, 369–383.

BELOFF, J. (1993) *Parapsychology: A Concise History.* London: Athlone Press.

BETTELHEIM, B. (1986) *Freud and Man's Soul.* Harmondsworth: Peregrine.

BHAVNANI, K.-K. (1990) What's power got to do with it? Empowerment and social research. In I. Parker and J. Shotter (Eds) *Deconstructing Social Psychology.* London: Routledge.

BILLIG, M. (1987) *Arguing and Thinking: A Rhetorical Approach to Social Psychology.* Cambridge: Cambridge University Press.

BOWER, G. H. and Clapper, J. P. (1990) Experimental methods in cognitive science. In M. Posner (Ed.) *Foundations of Cognitive Science.* Cambridge, Mass.: MIT Press.

BRUCE, V., BURTON, A.M. and WALKER, S. (1994) Testing the models? New data and commentary on Stanhope & Cohen. *British Journal of Psychology, 85,* 335–349.

BULL, R. (1982) Can experimental psychology be applied psychology? In S. Canter and D. Canter (Eds) *Psychology in Practice: Perspectives on Professional Psychology.* Chichester: Wiley.

BURMAN, E. (Ed.) (1990) *Feminists and Psychological Practice.* London: Sage.

CARDWELL, M. (1992) Gender differences in the aggressive behaviour of schoolchildren. In R. McIlveen, L. Higgins, A. Wadeley and P. Humphreys (Eds) *BPS Manual of Psychology Practicals: Experiment, Observation and Correlation.* Leicester: BPS Books.

CARLSON, N. R. (1994) *Physiology of Behaviour,* 5th ed. London: Allyn and Bacon.

CHADWICK, P. D. J., LOWE, C. F., HORNE, P. J. and HIGSON, P. J. (1994) Modifying delusions: the role of empirical testing. *Behavior Therapy, 25,* 35–49.

CLARKE, S.G. and HAWORTH, J. (1994) 'Flow' experience in the daily lives of sixth-form college students. *British Journal of Psychology, 85,* 511–523.

CLAXTON, G. (1980) Cognitive psychology: a suitable case for what sort of treatment? In G. Claxton (Ed.) *Cognitive Psychology: New Directions*. London: Routledge and Kegan Paul.

COHEN, G. (1989) *Memory in the Real World*. Hove: Erlbaum.

CURT, B. (1994) *Textuality and Tectonics: Troubling Social and Psychological Science*. Milton Keynes: Open University Press.

DIMATTEO, M.R., SHUGARS, D.A. and HAYS, R.D. (1993) Occupational stress: life stress and mental health among dentists. *Journal of Occupational and Organizational Psychology*, *66*, 153–162.

EAMES, K. and LOEWENTHAL, K. (1990) Effects of handwriting and examiner's expertise on assessment of essays. *Journal of Social Psychology*, *130*, 831–833.

ELLIS, H.D., ELLIS, D.M. and HOSIE, J.A. (1993) Priming effects in children's face recognition. *British Journal of Psychology*, *84*, 101–110.

ENTWISTLE, N. and MARTON, F. (1994) Knowledge objects: understandings constituted through intensive academic study. *British Journal of Educational Psychology*, *64*, 161–178.

ENTWISTLE, N.J., NISBET, J., ENTWISTLE, D. and COWELL, M.D. (1971) The academic performance of students: predictions from scales of motivation and study methods. *British Journal of Educational Psychology*, *41*, 258–267.

ERICSSON, K.A. and SIMON, H.A. (1993) *Protocol Analysis: Verbal Reports as Data*, revised ed. Cambridge, Mass.: MIT Press.

EVANS, J.S.B.T., NEWSTEAD, S.E. and BYRNE, R.M.J. (1993) *Human Reasoning: The Psychology of Deduction*. Hove: Erlbaum.

EYSENCK, H.J. and WILSON, G.C. (1973) *The Experimental Study of Freudian Theories*. London: Methuen.

EYSENCK, M.W. and KEANE, M.T. (1990) *Cognitive Psychology: A Student's Handbook*. Hove: Erlbaum

FAZIO, R.H. (1990) A practical guide to the use of response latency in social psychological research. In C. Hendrick and M.S. Clark (Eds) *Research Methods in Personality and Social Psychology*. Newbury Park, California: Sage.

FEYERABEND, P. (1975) *Against Method: Outline of an Anarchistic Theory of Knowledge*. London: Verso.

FINCH, J. (1984). 'It's great to have someone to talk to': ethics and politics of interviewing women. In C. Bell and H. Roberts (Eds) *Social Researching: Politics, Problems, Practice*. London: Routledge.

FISHER, S. and HOOD, B. (1987) The stress of transition to university: a longitudinal study of psychological disturbance, absent-mindedness and vulnerability to homesickness. *British Journal of Psychology*, *78*, 425–441.

FLIN, R., BOON, J., KNOX, A and BULL, R. (1992) The effect of a five-month delay on children's and adults' eyewitness memory. *British Journal of Psychology*, *83*, 323–336.

FOSTER, J.J. (1993) *Starting SPSS/PC+ and SPSS for Windows*. Wilmslow: Sigma Press.

FRANSELLA, F. (1984a) Personal construct therapy. In W. Dryden (Ed.) *Individual Therapy in Britain*. London: Harper & Row.

FRANSELLA, F. (1984b) The relationship between Kelly's constructs and Durkheim's representations. In R.M. Farr and S. Moscovici (Eds) *Social Representations*. Cambridge: Cambridge University Press.

FUCCI, D., HARRIS, D., PETROSINO, L. and BANKS, M. (1993) The effect of preference for rock music on magnitude-estimation scaling behavior in young adults. *Perceptual and Motor Skills*, *76*, 1171–1176.

FUENTES, L.F. and ORTELLS, J.J. (1993) Facilitation and interference effects in a Stroop-like task: Evidence in favour of semantic processing of parafoveally-presented stimuli. *Acta Psychologica*, *84*, 213–229.

FURNHAM, A., GUNTER, B. and GREEN, A. (1990) Remembering science: the recall of factual information as a function of presentation mode. *Applied Cognitive Psychology*, *4*, 203–212.

GASKELL, G., WRIGHT, D. and O'MUIRCHEARTAIGH, C. (1993) Reliability of surveys. *The Psychologist*, *6*, 500–503.

GILBERT, G. N. and MULKAY, M. (1984) *Opening Pandora's Box: A Sociological Analysis of Scientists' Discourse.* Cambridge: Cambridge University Press.

GILLIGAN, C. (1982) *In a Different Voice: Psychological Theory and Women's Development.* Cambridge, Mass.: Harvard University Press.

GLASER, B. and STRAUSS, A. (1967) *The Discovery of Grounded Theory.* Chicago: Aldine.

GOFFMAN, E. (1959) *The Presentation of Self in Everyday Life.* New York: Doubleday.

GOFFMAN, E. (1961) *Asylums: Essays on the Social Situation of Mental Patients and Other Inmates.* Harmondsworth: Penguin.

GOODRICH, S., HENDERSON, L., ALLCHIN, N. and JEEVARATNAM, A. (1990) On the peculiarity of the simple reaction time. *Quarterly Journal of Experimental Psychology, 42(A),* 763–775.

GROSS, R.D. (1992) *Psychology: The Science of Mind and Behaviour,* 2nd ed. London: Hodder and Stoughton.

GUBRIUM, J. and SILVERMAN, D. (1989) *The Politics of Field Research.* London: Sage.

HANSEL, C.E.M. (1966) *ESP: A Scientific Evaluation.* New York: Scribner.

HARRE, R. (1979) *Social Being: A Theory for Social Psychology.* Oxford: Blackwell.

HARRE, R. (1982) Ethogenic methods: an empirical psychology of action. In G.M. Breakwell, H. Foot and R. Gilmour (Eds) *Social Psychology: A Practical Manual.* Leicester and London: British Psychological Society and Macmillan.

HARRE, R. and SECORD, P.F. (1972) *The Explanation of Social Behaviour.* Oxford: Blackwell.

HARRIS, P. (1986) *Designing and Reporting Experiments.* Milton Keynes: Open University Press.

HARTLEY, J., TRUEMAN, M. and RODGERS, A. (1984) The effects of verbal and numerical quantifiers on questionnaire responses. *Applied Ergonomics, 15,* 149–155.

HENWOOD, K.L. and PIDGEON, N. (1992) Qualitative research and psychological theorizing. *British Journal of Psychology, 83,* 97–111.

HOLLWAY, W. (1989) *Subjectivity and Method in Psychology: Gender, Meaning and Science.* London: Sage.

HOTOPF, W.H.N. and BROWN, S.A. (1988) Constant errors in judgements of collinearity due to the presence of neighbouring objects. *Perception, 17,* 523–534.

HOUSTON, V. and BULL, R. (1994) Do people avoid sitting next to someone who is facially disfigured? *European Journal of Social Psychology, 24,* 279–284.

HOWELL, D.C. (1992) *Statistical Methods for Psychology,* 3rd ed. Belmont.: Duxbury Press

HUNTER, J.E., SCHMIDT, F.L. and JACKSON, G.B. (1982) *Meta-analysis.* Beverley Hills: Sage.

IRVINE, J., MILES, I. and EVANS, J. (1979) *Demystifying Social Statistics.* London: Pluto Press.

JOYNSON, R.B. (1973) *Psychology and Common Sense.* London: Routledge and Kegan Paul.

KALAT, J.W. (1992) *Biological Psychology,* 4th ed. Belmont, California: Wadsworth.

KELLY, G.A. (1955) *The Psychology of Personal Constructs,* vols I and II. New York: Norton and Co.

KERLINGER, F.N. (1986) *Foundations of Behavioral Research,* 3rd ed. Fort Worth: Harcourt Brace Jovanovich.

KINNEAR, P.R. and GRAY, C.D. (1994) *SPSS for Windows Made Simple.* Hove: Erlbaum.

KITZINGER, C. (1987) *The Social Construction of Lesbianism.* London: Sage.

KITZINGER, C. (1990) The rhetoric of pseudoscience. In I. Parker and J. Shotter (Eds) *Deconstructing Social Psychology.* London: Routledge.

KLIMOSKI, R.J. and RAFAELI, A. (1983) Inferring personal qualities through handwriting analysis. *Journal of Occupational Psychology, 56,* 191–202.

KLINE, P. (1993) *Handbook of Psychological Testing.* London: Routledge.

KUHN, T.S. (1970) *The Structure of Scientific Revolutions,* 2nd ed. Chicago: University of Chicago Press.

LATOUR, B. and WOOLGAR, S. (1979) *Laboratory Life: The Construction of Scientific Facts.* Princeton: Princeton University Press.

LE BON, G. (1947) *The Crowd: A Study of the Popular Mind.* London: Ernest Benn.

LOVIE, P. and LOVIE, A.D. (1991) *New Developments in Statistics for Psychology and the Social Sciences,* vol. 2. London: British Psychological Society and Routledge.

MACKINNON, D.P., O'REILLY K.E. and GEISELMAN, R.E. (1990) Improving eye witness recall for licence plates. *Applied Cognitive Psychology, 4,* 129–140.

MACRAE, S. (1994) *Drawing Inferences from Statistical Data.* Leicester: BPS Books.

MANSTEAD, A.S.R. and McCULLOCH, C. (1981) Sex-role stereotyping in British television advertisements. *British Journal of Social Psychology, 20,* 171–180.

MANSTEAD, A.S.R. and SEMIN, G.R. (1988) Methodology in social psychology: Turning ideas into action. In M. Hewstone, W. Stroebe, J-P. Codol and G. Stephenson (Eds) *Introduction to Social Psychology: A European Perspective.* Oxford: Blackwell.

MARSH, P., ROSSER, E. and HARRE, R. (1974) *The Rules of Disorder.* London: Routledge and Kegan Paul.

McILVEEN, R., HIGGINS, L., WADELEY, A. and HUMPHREYS, P. (Eds) (1992) *BPS Manual of Psychology Practicals: Experiment, Observation and Correlation.* Leicester: BPS Books.

McMANUS, I.C., SHERGILL, S. and BRYDEN, M.P. (1993) Annett's theory that individuals heterozygous for the right shift gene are intellectually disadvantaged: Theoretical and empirical problems. *British Journal of Psychology, 84,* 517–537.

MIDDLETON, D. and EDWARDS, D. (Eds) (1992) *Collective Remembering.* London: Sage.

MILGRAM, S. (1963) Behavioral study of obedience. *Journal of Abnormal and Social Psychology, 67,* 371-378.

MILGRAM, S. (1974) *Obedience to Authority: An Experimental View.* New York: Harper and Row.

MONK, A. (1991) *Exploring Statistics with Minitab: A Workbook for the Behavioural Sciences.* Chichester: Wiley.

MORRIS, P.E., JONES, S. and HAMPSON, P. (1978) An imagery mnemonic for the learning of people's names. *British Journal of Psychology, 69,* 335–336.

NEALE, J.M. and LIEBERT, R.M. (1986) *Science and Behavior,* 3rd ed. Englewood Cliffs: Prentice Hall.

NEISSER, U. (1976) *Cognition and Reality.* San Francisco: Freeman.

NISBETT, R.E. and WILSON, T.D. (1977) Telling more than we can know: verbal reports on mental processes. *Psychological Review, 84,* 231–259.

OPPENHEIM, A.N. (1992) *Questionnaire Design, Interviewing and Attitude Measurement,* new ed. London: Pinter Publishers.

ORNE, M. (1962) On the social psychology of the psychology experiment: with particular reference to demand characteristics and their implications. *American Psychologist, 17,* 776–783.

PARKER, D., MANSTEAD, A.S.R., STRADLING, S.G., REASON, J.T. and BAXTER, J.S. (1992) Intention to commit driving violations: An application of the theory of planned behavior. *Journal of Applied Psychology, 77,* 94–101.

PARKER, I. (1989) *The Crisis in Modern Social Psychology, and How to End It.* London: Routledge.

PARKER, I. (1992) *Discourse Dynamics: Critical Analysis for Social and Individual Psychology.* London: Routledge.

PARKER, I. (1994) Reflexive research and the grounding of analysis: social psychology and the psy-complex. *Journal of Community and Applied Social Psychology, 4,* 239–252.

PARKER, I. (1995) Discursive complexes in material culture. In J. Haworth (Ed.) *Psychological Research: Innovative Methods and Strategies.* London: Routledge.

PARLIAMENTARY OFFICE OF SCIENCE AND TECHNOLOGY (1993) Screen violence. *The Psychologist, 6,* 353–356.

PETERSON, L.R. and PETERSON, M. (1959) Short-term retention of individual verbal items. *Journal of Experimental Psychology, 58,* 193–198.

PHEASANT, S. (1986) *Bodyspace: Anthropometry, Ergonomics and Design.* London: Taylor and Francis.

POPPER, K.R. (1972) *The Logic of Scientific Discovery*, 3rd ed. London: Hutchinson.

POTTER, J., STRINGER, P. and WETHERELL, M. (1984) *Social Texts and Context: Literature and Social Psychology*. London: Routledge and Kegan Paul.

POTTER, J. and WETHERELL, M. (1987) *Discourse and Social Psychology: Beyond Attitudes and Behaviour*. London: Sage.

POULTON, E.C. (1969) Asymmetrical transfer in reading texts produced by teleprinter and by typewriter. *Journal of Applied Psychology, 53*, 244–249.

POULTON, E.C. (1982) Influential companions: Effects of one strategy on another in the within subjects designs of cognitive psychology. *Psychological Bulletin, 91*, 673–690.

POULTON E.C. (1989) *Bias in Quantifying Judgements*. Hove: Erlbaum.

RAYNER, K. and POLLATSEK, A. (1989) *The Psychology of Reading*. Englewood Cliffs: Prentice Hall.

REASON, J. (1990) *Human Error*. Cambridge: Cambridge University Press.

REASON, J.T. and LUCAS, D.A. (1984) Using cognitive diaries to investigate naturally-occurring memory blocks. In J. Harris and P. Morris (Eds) *Everyday Memory, Actions and Absent-Mindedness*. London: Academic Press.

REASON, P. (1981) Issues of validity in new paradigm research. In P. Reason and J. Rowan (Eds) *Human Inquiry: A Sourcebook of New Paradigm Research*. Chichester: Wiley.

REASON, P. and ROWAN, J. (1981a) Issues of validity in new paradigm research. In P. Reason and J. Rowan (Eds) *Human Inquiry: A Sourcebook of New Paradigm Research*. Chichester: Wiley.

REASON, P. and ROWAN, J. (Eds) (1981b) *Human Inquiry: A Sourcebook of New Paradigm Research*. Chichester: Wiley.

REAVES, C.C. (1992) *Quantitative Research for the Behavioral Sciences*. New York: Wiley.

REICHER, S.D. (1984) The St. Pauls' riot: an explanation of the limits of crowd action in terms of a social identity model. *European Journal of Social Psychology, 14*, 1–21.

REICHER, S.D. and POTTER, J. (1985) Psychological theory as intergroup perspective: A comparative analysis of 'scientific' and 'lay' accounts of crowd events. *Human Relations, 38*, 167–189.

RICHARDS, B. (1989) *Images of Freud: Cultural Responses to Psychoanalysis*. London: Dent.

ROBSON, C. (1993) *Real World Research*. Oxford: Blackwell.

ROISER, M. (1974) Asking silly questions. In N. Armistead (Ed.) *Reconstructing Social Psychology*. Harmondsworth: Penguin.

ROSENBERG, M.J. and HOVLAND, C.I. (1960) Cognitive, affective and behavioral components of attitudes. In C.I. Hovland and M.J. Rosenberg (Eds) *Attitude Organization and Change*. New Haven: Yale University Press.

ROSENTHAL, R. (1965) The volunteer subject. *Human Relations, 18*, 389–406.

ROSENTHAL, R. (1966) *Experimenter Effects in Behavioral Research*. New York: Appleton Century Crofts.

SCHWARZ, N. (1990) Assessing frequency reports of mundane behaviors: contributions of cognitive psychology to questionnaire construction. In C. Hendrick C and M.S. Clark (Eds) *Research Methods in Personality and Social Psychology*. Newbury Park: Sage.

SEARS, D.O. (1986) College sophomores in the laboratory: Influences of a narrow data base on social psychology's view of human nature. *Journal of Personality and Social Psychology, 51*, 515–530.

SHALLICE, T. and WARRINGTON, E. K. (1970) Independent functioning of verbal memory stores: A neuropsychological study. *Quarterly Journal of Experimental Psychology, 22*, 261–273.

SHOTTER, J. (1975) *Images of Man in Psychological Research*. London: Methuen.

SIEGEL, S. and CASTELLAN, N.J. (1988) *Nonparametric Statistics for the Behavioral Sciences*, 2nd ed. New York: McGraw Hill.

SILVERMAN, D. (1993) *Interpreting Qualitative Data: Methods for Analysing Talk, Text and Interaction*. London: Sage.

SPRADLEY, J. (1979) *The Ethnographic Interview*. New York: Holt, Rinehart & Winston.

SQUIRE, C. (1990) Crisis what crisis? Discourses and narratives of the 'social' in social psychology. In I. Parker and J. Shotter (Eds) *Deconstructing Social Psychology*. London: Routledge.

STANHOPE, N. and COHEN, G. (1993) Retrieval of proper names: Testing the models. *British Journal of Psychology, 84*, 51–65.

STEPHENSON, W. (1953) *The Study of Behaviour: Q-technique and its Methodology*. Chicago: University of Chicago Press.

STERNBERG, R.J. (1993) *The Psychologist's Companion,* 3rd ed. Cambridge: Cambridge University Press.

STERNBERG, S. (1967) Two operations in character recognition: Some evidence from reaction-time measurements. *Perception and Psychophysics, 2*, 43–53.

STEVENS, S.S. (1975) *Psychophysics: Introduction to its Perceptual, Neural and Social Prospects*. New York: Wiley.

STRAUSS, J. and CORBIN, A. (1990) *Basics of Qualitative Research: Grounded Theory Procedures and Techniques*. London: Sage.

STROOP, J.R. (1935) Studies of interference in serial verbal reactions. *Journal of Experimental Psychology, 18*, 643–662.

TEASDALE, J.D. and BARNARD, P.J. (1993) *Affect, Cognition, and Change*. Hove: Erlbaum.

WALKERDINE, V. (1991) *Schoolgirl Fictions*. London: Verso.

WANN, T.W. (1964) *Behaviorism and Phenomenology: Contrasting Bases for Modern Psychology*. Chicago: Chicago University Press.

WEISNER, W.H. and CRONSHAW, S.F. (1989) A meta-analytic investigation of the impact of interview format and degree of structure on the validity of the employment interviews. *Journal of Occupational Psychology, 61*, 275–290.

WILKINSON, S. (1988) The role of reflexivity in feminist psychology. *Women's Studies International Forum, 11*, 493–502.

WOGALTER, M.S., GODFREY, S.S., FONTANELLE, G.A., DESAULNIERS, D.R., ROTHSTEIN, P.R. and LAUGHERY, K.R. (1987) Effectiveness of warnings. *Human Factors, 29*, 599–612.

Index